LESSONS MY CLIENTS HAVE TAUGHT ME AND OTHER STORIES

FRANK D. YOUNG

PH.D., R. PSYCH.

Lessons My Clients Have Taught Me and Other Stories
Copyright © 2019

Second printing: 2019

Published by Solution Oriented Counselling
www.solutionorientedcounselling.ca

Author Dr. Frank D. Young, Ph.D.

Design and production Electra Design Group, Vancouver, BC

Colour and prepress Coast Imaging Arts, Comox, BC

Printing and binding Island Blue Book Printing, Victoria, BC

ISBN 978-1-9990755-0-7

Printed in Canada

To all my clients and teachers that have
taught me lessons for living.

Contents

ACKNOWLEDGEMENTS

As you will come to see, my clients were the main inspiration for this book, and I heartily thank them for their insights and lessons to inform my practice of applied psychology over the years.

I would like to thank my friend and former associate Dr. Arnie Slive for volunteering to edit this book. Arnie continues to edit collaboration books and is still on the editorial board of the *Journal of Systemic Therapies*. His comments have been quite helpful in shaping our work together as we have developed as professionals. I would also like to thank Don Efron M.S.W., the original founder and editor-in-chief of the pioneer *Journal of Strategic and Systemic Therapies*, where many of our founding editorial board members published some of our first original journal articles. In publishing I would like to thank my consultant Ernst Vegt of Coast Imaging Arts, and page layout and cover design by Lisa Eng-Lodge of Electra Design Group for their technical support in making this book a reality.

I also appreciate the support of my wife, Donna, and family and friends in steadily encouraging me to publish this book about my professional journey. Thanks also to all of you readers who keep me going forward with enthusiasm and passion.

FOREWORD

As a student of psychology and as a psychotherapist, I have been informed by many lessons my clients have taught me over the years of my career. Through the collaboration of therapeutic relationships, I have learned about life, relationships, meaning, and interventions that provide patterns of possibility for solutions that uniquely fit life dilemmas.

This book began very long ago, in 1981. In the early days of the *Journal of Systemic Therapies*, one of my first articles as a Founding Editorial Board member was the first chapter of a proposed quarterly column "Lessons My Clients Have Taught Me." The first one was called "Teach Me Your Symptom." This was a great deal of fun to write and was received very well by our readership. Then life became increasingly busy for all of the editorial board as we reviewed and edited the many submissions of articles for publication in the Journal. Somehow, I never got back to writing stories about my cases, although I would occasionally talk about them in workshops and lectures that I gave. Perhaps I was intimidated by the formal requirements of publishing in a professionally-refereed journal.

After moving to Calgary, Alberta, in the early 1980s, I was invited to write a column on Mental Fitness for *Impact Magazine*, a western Canadian fitness publication with a circulation of over 35,000. The writing requirements were quite different, being very succinct, topical, and for a general audience. Now I could write in an informal manner similar to how I talk, engaging the audience or readership as if we were in a private conversation. Still, life seemed too busy in career, family life, judo, music, and other projects.

Now, as I settle in to semi-retirement, I have more time to focus on a more generative agenda, that of writing short stories and essays, assembling enough chapters and coherence to begin a few short books that are easy reading for the public.

This book is aimed towards those who are interested in coaching, counselling, and psychotherapy, and those outside these professions that are merely interested in human nature, and how therapy can work in transforming lives. It provides an inside view of what can happen in the therapy room, turning points in therapeutic conversations, and the brilliance and creativity of clients as they respond to the therapeutic alliance and collaborate for a successful and enduring outcome. It also at times reveals the strategies and structures involved in designing and delivering interventions, and the mind of the therapist in focusing on pivotal points. Some chapters outline metaphors and stories that are not provided by clients but are useful in reframing life dilemmas so that they become more solvable.

This book is supposed to be fun and easy to read, so I have largely dispensed with literary references giving proper credit for the origin of the idea. So, in an academic sense, I confess to the offense of plagiarism. There are so many ideas that have been repeated and quoted so many times that I have largely forgotten their origin. Like many Native cultures, most of these stories are passed on by the oral wisdom of the elders. My stories are best understood as merely historical fiction, although you may see yourself in them. I sincerely hope that you, the reader, have as much fun with these "Lessons" as we have had in developing them for your pleasure.

Preface

Squirrels In The Attic

Sometimes I wonder why I am writing this book. Perhaps my main hope is that the reader will be entertained, fascinated, and maybe even enlightened by these stories. Others may get a better understanding of the elements of a solution-oriented model of psychotherapy, counselling, and coaching. Some may use the lessons as an approach for self-help and discovery of inner resources liberated by different ways of perceiving and describing a problem, thus making it more solvable. Some consultants and life coaches might be intrigued by the novelty of some interventions. So I guess a major motivation for writing is attempting to be altruistic in helping others.

But mostly, this book is written in homage to the many clients who have informed my professional practice as a counsellor over the last three decades. Their creativity has inspired me to use my own ingenuity in collaboration with them in the therapeutic alliance.

However, perhaps the most selfish reason for writing is to get these stories out of my memory banks and out on disk or in print somewhere so that I don't have to keep them locked inside my mind. That reminds me of a story...

Around the time of my early professional psychology career, I lived in the upper level of a rented house in London, Ontario. Directly below us lived two prostitutes, but that's another story. Above us lived a family of grey squirrels in the attic. Despite our repeated requests, the landlord took no action to evict them, neither the prostitutes nor the squirrels, but it certainly made for rather noisy and distracting evenings. There seemed to be minimal sound insulation, especially between our ceiling and the wooden attic floor above us.

Each night, as we tried to sleep, the squirrels would carry on their evening ritual. There were many large oak trees around our house, so there was an abundance of acorns to be collected and stored. That's the official version. But I have it by good authority that there was something else going on. This squirrel family was running a bowling alley. Each night they would invite in the neighborhood squirrels for games where they would roll acorns from one end of the floor to strike the other nuts at the other end. You could hear the scratching of their toes, the rolling of the acorn, the scatter at the other end, accompanied by chattering that could only be interpreted as cheering and scoring by the teams gathered there. This would go on for about a half-hour, then would mercifully tail off. We would have a chuckle or two, then fall off to sleep ourselves. While we were mildly anxious about the remote possibility of an electrical fire caused by squirrels gnawing wires, we came to regard their antics as comical, rather than annoying. Still, their evening ritual somewhat disturbed our drowsy thoughts as we prepared for sleep. Staying up late to outlast them was not productive, nor was banging on the ceiling, which merely prolonged their games. Eventually, we solved the problem after a few months by buying and moving into our first home, and you can bet I sealed the attic in our new house thoroughly.

So, as you can now see, I write to get the story squirrels and their rolling thoughts out of my head so that I can be free and open to new ideas and inspirations. I hope in reading these chapters that you will find some of their acorns worthy of enjoyment and utilization.

Part One:

PATTERN DISRUPTION INTERVENTIONS

Perhaps at this point you were expecting the next chapters would be about hypnosis. And if that is all you want, you can skip this section and go directly to the chapters on hypnotically-based interventions. In the meantime, I invite you to read the stories in this section to examine how a certain hypnotic principle can work to invite new patterns of possibility.

In a solution-oriented approach (see www.solutionoriented counselling.ca) one of the best ways to intervene in a problem situation is to disrupt the sequence of events in which the problem is imbedded or disturb the usual consequences of the symptomatic behavior. Sometimes that is all that is required. New patterns can arise spontaneously in client repertoires that emerge as solutions to the presenting problem. Here are some examples.

CHAPTER 1

Teach Me Your Symptom

OCCASIONALLY PEOPLE ASK ME "Whatever got you interested in hypnosis in the first place?" I invariably break out in a wry smile and reflect back on how it all happened. The story reminds me that our client-teachers are often neither random nor passive as they collaborate in the therapeutic process to catapult our thinking to new levels of consciousness.

The prototype client-teacher in my mind is a young woman who propelled me into strategic hypnotherapy long before I heard of the utilization approaches of Milton Erickson or the problem-solving concepts that were later to evolve into a field known as strategic and systemic therapies.

Sue Doenimm[1] was a virtuoso in the lifescript role of failure. The scapegoat sib of a rather large German-Canadian family, this 17-year-old had learned an unusual way of coping with the binds and disqualifications that prevailed in her perfectionistic family communication. When exposed to untenable situations she would become quiet and rigid, unable to move or talk for hours and sometimes days. At those times she would seem to conform to the image of being a useless person, the total failure scripted by family and others in a loop of self-fulfilling prophecy.

---

[1] In case you have not figured this out already, Sue Doenimm is a pseudonym for her real-life name. In keeping with the tradition of writing case vignettes, the real names of all clients have been changed to protect their confidentiality.

What made Sue Doenimm outstanding, however, was her consummate hypnotic skills in unconsciously drawing others into her self-image of hopelessness. She contaminated all those who came in contact with her, including friends, family, former therapists, with her dread disease of failure. Even her boyfriend, a ballet dancer, could not escape this aura, and on one occasion lost his balance and fell down a staircase, breaking his leg in the process. Beyond her ability to distract and dissociate, Sue's autonomic control (and simultaneous denial of it) was impressive, almost like a fakir, the way she could raise welts and nearly blister her skin during anxious moments in her sessions. Most dramatic, however, was her ability to go into a rigid and almost catatonic trance for several hours to several days depending on her stress level and the severity of the conflicts and binds she was facing. This symptom was her presenting problem, which had been unresponsive to several previous attempts at psychodynamic therapy and psychotropic medication. Her psychiatrist, in desperation, referred her to me. At that time I was an enthusiastic, if perhaps unseasoned, cognitive behavior therapist.

In the first several sessions I tried to use progressive relaxation training and everything else I could think of at the time in an effort to build her abilities and skills in coping with stress and distress. After ten sessions it was clear that her prophecy was about to come true: she would try hard and I would try hard and the result would, of course, be complete failure. After all, the symptom had been going on for years, and was completely involuntary, so how could it be otherwise? Finally, in exasperation I told her, "In this session I want you to teach me how to paralyze myself. I want you to paralyze me."

She said, "I can't do that! I don't know how! I told you I have no control over it!" The fear and frustration were evident in her tone of voice at this sudden switch.

I said, in my best answer to her formidable rationalization, "Never mind. Do it anyway. I have to learn how you do this so I can figure out a way to help you, because right now I am incompetent to help you."

The anxiety generated by this declaration and demand already had begun the process of her "freezing," but she obediently began coaching me on how to hyperventilate and autosuggest as she went further into her paralysis. I became aware of stiffness in my entire body, including my face, so that I could barely talk. As I became more rigid and immobile she became slightly more relaxed and somewhat curious about the zombie-therapist she had produced over the last twenty minutes. I could just barely move my lips to tell her that her hour was nearly over. I implored her to get me out of my paralysis because another client was due to arrive in a few minutes.

Again she panicked, saying, "But I can't! I can't! I don't know how to get you out!"

Now I too began to worry about my dilemma, as I tried unsuccessfully to move my limbs or talk. Through clenched teeth I could barely whisper, "Use some of the techniques I taught you to get me out of here!" So she did, and gradually with her coaching and feedback I was able to regain movement and bodily control. I then thanked her gratefully for returning me to my normal condition and providing me with a rather unique experience, and rapidly ended the session.

After Sue left the office in a somewhat confused but pleasant daze I began to come out of my dissociative fog. A new feeling of excitement swept over me, with the realization that I had just had my first experience of deep trance and hypnotic catalepsy. Now I really knew what it was like for her to be imprisoned in her own body. Of greater importance, I was also deeply confident that now the crucial corner had been turned in her therapy. After all, how could she really accept that such paralysis was involuntary and uncontrollable when somebody could be trained to both go into it and come out of it in less than an hour? And how could she continue to protest incompetence after successfully paralyzing and rescuing her therapist who had placed his trust in her abilities?

In subsequent sessions my client had no difficulty in voluntarily inducing and removing paralysis both in me and herself. She also began learning and using other coping mechanisms and assertive communication skills to deal with family and social situations and overcome her failure script with a tentative but positive self-image. Throughout her improvement I kept on cautioning her, "Remember, don't lose this power to hypnotize yourself. You may want to use it some day, and there are people who would go out of their way to have unusual experiences and altered states like you brought me through." However, she did not want any part of it, and was glad to see this pattern totally disappear from her responses to stress and distress. Her family and friends were quite amazed, but pleased and relieved that she was now progressing in school and other aspects of life.

About seven years later I met her again in a restaurant where she was working as a waitress and assistant manager. She told me that life was going well for her now. As for me, this lesson began the intense fascination and respect I have for hypnosis, utilization, and unusual strategies for dealing with perplexing cases as both a therapist and consultant.

One day I went back to the restaurant and asked if she still had the ability to paralyze herself. She told me that, although she had not done so since her therapy, she felt confident that she could if she had to. I asked her why she felt so sure about it. She calmly replied with a knowing smile, "Well, I taught you how to, didn't I?"

CHAPTER 2

Taming A Squirrel

THIS IS A SHORT STORY, but it is a relatively easy and adaptable intervention. The exact details are scant, as I remember peering through the mists of time, but the most important details stand out. Once again, this happened when I was travelling throughout southwestern Ontario doing outreach mental health clinics as part of an interdisciplinary team. We were quite effective given our limited resources in a team of four who visited small communities once a week. As the saying goes, a good highway generates its own traffic, so soon our reputation exceeded our capacity, so we had to institute a waiting list. Sadly, we had to triage cases in terms of urgency, such that easier cases were sidelined by severe and acute cases. As all of you know, this becomes a crisis-generating system, where easy cases become difficult through chronic neglect. It is not a good way to deliver mental health from both the receiver and provider perspective. Nevertheless, it was all we could do given our limited time and clinical resources.

As part of the triage assessment procedure, we would interview prospective clients for ten minutes, assess their urgency, and place them on waiting lists. One woman I assessed was a 50-ish spinster who talked quickly, sharply, and incessantly, and moved her limbs and body frequently in almost sudden movements. She said that she found herself unable to relax and that her mind never stood still. I did a quick mental status exam and found out that she had no history of bi-polar or ADHD symptomology; it's just that she was chronically a very frantic and nervous type of person, with no particular reason to be agitated, and relatively mild current stresses.

I told her that I likely would not be able to counsel her in the near future, but I could give her a homework assignment that might be helpful for her disorder. Given some motivational interviewing preparation, she became receptive and agreed to carry out the assignment. She was tasked to tame a squirrel while talking to it in soft and slow tones, rather than her rapid staccato usual way of talking. Taming would be indicated when a wild squirrel would willingly eat from her hand. Now, we all know that any loud noise or sudden movement of any sort would spook most animals, so I thought this discipline would constitute an ideal meditative focus activity for my client. She would have to be still, talk slowly, and access her internal sense of peace and quiet confidence in order for a wild animal to trust her.

During our ten-minute follow up interview a month later, she proudly proclaimed that she had tamed her first squirrel. As we mutually celebrated, I noticed that her breathing was slower and deeper and more confident, and her tone of voice was softer and friendlier. She also reported that she could now walk around her neighbourhood with less fear of dogs in back yards that used to bark at her. I commended her for her diligence in following through with the assignment and for her level of mastery in overcoming her fear of novel situations where the outcome is uncertain. I asked her to repeat the same homework for the following month to make sure the results were not merely a fluke, but rather evidence of a steady way to overcome her "nervousness and lack of confidence."

As you likely anticipated, she reported in our next monthly ten-minute interview that all was going well. She had tamed two squirrels now, and she had made friends with almost all of the neighbourhood dogs, so that they barely barked beyond a greeting "Woof!" She reported many other ways in which her life and relationships had improved, so I happily discharged her from my waiting list with mutual congratulations on our therapeutic alliance in helping her face and resolve her problems.

Taming a wild or frightened animal is a task that requires calmness, soft voicing, slow and rounded movement, rhythmic breathing, attention to your animal, and calm responsiveness to its non-verbal behavior, empathy, compassion, acceptance, and vast patience. In short, it is one simple pathway to a Zen sense of living in the Now.

CHAPTER 3

Favourite Dress

UPON MOVING in 1982 to Calgary, Alberta, I continued my beginning interest in treating eating disorders. Dr. Arnie Slive and I had begun to consult with each other about treating these cases in London, Ontario, in previous years, but we were continuing our fascination with the complexities of treating anorexia and bulimia nervosa. I was interested in them as an aberration of the search for excellence and over-control resulting, paradoxically, in the disorders controlling them.

In addition to some severe anorexic cases seen as inpatients in our mental health clinic in a general hospital, an increasing incidence of bulimia nervosa began appearing in our outpatient referrals. I seemed to be their therapist of choice, as I had an accident of competency in successfully treating several cases. They told their network of friends, and soon a flood of referrals emerged.

One such case involved a woman in her early twenties. She fit all the classical signs of an eating disorder, such as perfectionism, obsession around physical beauty and body image, dyscontrol of eating followed by purging in almost daily episodes, black-white thinking, almost incessant food-and-figure obsessions, etc. Nevertheless, she was otherwise quite functional in her career and social life, and had an absence of family or personal history trauma or communication pathology. The habit component had ascended to become the primary reason why she was unable to stop her compulsive ritual of overeating followed by purging through induced vomiting.

During our two assessment sessions, I asked her if she had a favourite dress. She responded that she did, a red cocktail dress in which she felt especially attractive. I asked her that, in the interest of her recovery, would she be willing to pack this dress in a gym equipment bag next to her workout clothes. She was curious about this question, wondering where it was leading.

After another session of motivational interviewing, we both came to the conclusion that she was ready to take direct action to end enslavement to her eating disorder. She just needed a compelling ritual to break free from it. I was by this time quite well-versed in pattern-disruption interventions during the several previous years where they had yielded good results in intractable cases. So, by the time my client was ready to do almost anything to break free from her disorder, she agreed to the following intervention:

My client could from now on indulge in purging as often as she wanted to, with one limiting condition: she would agree to vomit only while wearing her favourite dress. She was shocked but intrigued with this arrangement. It would imply a great deal of inconvenience and limited opportunity to practice her habit, especially at work and in social situations, which were some of her primary trigger contexts. Moreover, the idea of contaminating her favourite dress in the privacy of her apartment was also distasteful. Nevertheless, she had agreed to this intervention, and left the session perplexed as to how this would play out in the subsequent week.

Several times during that week she was triggered to purge, but was overwhelmed with the burden of difficulty and thought of contamination, so she did not complete her changing into her favourite dress. Predictably, as the urge passed, each time the compulsion became weaker. Within a week, no purging had occurred. The urges became less frequent and intense. Because purging was eliminated, overeating episodes also subsided. My client reverted to regular well-balanced eating patterns with minimal coaching and encouragement from me in the ensuing weeks. Thus, by five sessions the bulimia patterns had vanished, and we closed the case successfully. There had been no relapses at her six-month follow-up. However, by that time she had referred her friends and fellow-sufferers to me, which created a new problem for my practice in a public clinic. Client demand was now surpassing my capacity to treat. Perhaps the lesson was: watch out for success; it could trap you in a ghetto of restricted practice with a narrow population and an unwitting specialty.

CHAPTER 4

THE REPLACEMENT RULE

AS MOST OF YOU KNOW, bulimia nervosa is a complex disorder involving self-imposed food deprivation, followed by chronic intermittent episodes of disordered food intake, called binging, followed by some type of purging or attempted undoing of the caloric intake. Purging behaviours can involve self-induced vomiting, laxative abuse, and several other patterns. Therapy for these disorders is often multidimensional, as is the disorder. We intervene at the biological, nutritional, psychological, familial, and social and cultural levels to address the many factors that drive this problem pattern. Among these, food intake requires moderation and structure; we cannot stop eating. On the other hand, purging can stop "cold turkey" with virtually no complications. So, you could stop purging totally while learning a moderation strategy for eating, if only there were an adequate intervention to accomplish this result. Thus, I developed this idea called the replacement rule.

This idea will not work unless the therapist has prepared the client with motivational interviewing. That is, the client must be fully motivated and ready to do whatever is required to end the misery of bulimia. The whole literature about Milton H. Erickson M.D. (Haley, 1976) is full of examples of how to conduct motivational interviews with restraints, scepticism, future pacing of scenarios of change versus non-change, and many other strategies to help the client come to a commitment to change no matter what. These devices are too elaborate to outline here. If you are a therapist, you likely know how to prepare the client for such an intervention.

The prescription goes like this: from now on you can purge just as much as you want to, provided you agree to end each purging episode by replacing the food you vomited in the episode. For example, if you ate 6 donuts before vomiting, you would have to end the incident by eating and digesting another 6 donuts. In other words, a bulimic episode would thus end with food being maintained rather than expelled.

This prescription worked exceptionally well with more than 40 clients over a period of four years. However, at least 10 clients wiped out when, despite their best intentions, they were so overwhelmed with anxiety and guilt and fear of weight gain that they could not follow through with the agreement. In several of these cases, the issue was to revisit readiness and bolster anxiety management strategies and peer support for persistence.

Overall, the replacement rule worked quite well when used in conjunction with a comprehensive therapy plan. Encouraged by success with pattern-disruption interventions in eating disorders, such as bulimia nervosa, I began to think in greater depth about why they were so powerful. Essentially, many pattern disruptions derive their effectiveness by stopping or reversing the usual reward or payoff that typically maintains the habit or disordered sequence of behaviour. That is, the client is encouraged or ordered to continue the symptom, but with some unusual twist of timing, place, order, sequence, or context that disrupts the integrity and symbolic payoff of the ritual itself. The replacement rule nullifies the reason for purging itself, so motivation for the behaviour unravels each time the rule is invoked. It is also powerful in that relapse prevention is built into the design of the intervention. That is, whenever a relapse occurs, your client now has a way of undoing the undoing of the relapse, by reaffirming the overall context of therapy.

There is also the added advantage that pattern interventions such as the replacement rule usually involve a symptom prescription. The client is often perplexed by the paradox that the therapist is demanding that the client do a variant of the very behaviour they wish to eliminate. Often such interventions invoke a spirit of rebellion against the symptom itself.

However, it is likely the main reason why these prescriptions work is that the very integrity of the symptom complex is shattered or unravelled. When the core of integrity is removed, the parts of the pattern begin to fall apart, and the symptom problem dissolves almost by itself. The replacement rule has proven to be effective in eliminating the purging habit, thus disrupting a major component of the bulimic cycle.

CHAPTER 5

Quit Smoking With Chain-8

ANOTHER EXAMPLE of the Replacement Rule is a method for ending cigarette smoking, called Chain-8. Once again, this rule can apply when proper motivation and other supports are in place. The procedure is to chain-smoke eight cigarettes in a row non-stop as your last experience with smoking. When you have finished the last cigarette, you rip up the remaining cigarettes and flush them down the toilet. You resolve that, from now on, every time you even have a drag or puff from someone else's cigarette, or have a cigarette or even a partial cigarette, the next thing you do is you buy a pack of cigarettes, chain-smoke eight of them, and destroy the rest. This commitment ensures that if you slip up on your record of being several hours, days or weeks being smoke-free, you have an instant ritual that will ensure the slip will be unlikely to happen again. How does it work?

When you first learned to smoke, you were overwhelmed with the bitter taste, the urge to cough, the dizziness and almost nausea as the poison of nicotine and the irritation of the smoke choked your throat. As your eyes watered, you wondered why anyone could ever feel this as a pleasant experience. Gradually, after many repeated exposures, you habituated to the drug, numbed your body's reaction to the poison, and became addicted. In the Chain-8 ritual, you override your body's adaptation to poison by overdosing on the substance. Your body now returns to the revulsion and disgust you had initially when you started smoking. Thus, in each instance, your last experience of smoking was a very negative one.

This happens every time you have a slip backwards in your recovery. Usually, all it takes is one or two instances of relapse and chain-8, and you will never want to smoke again. Furthermore, the last negative experiences imprint so strongly, that positive memories and images of smoking are virtually erased. You are now smoke free, and never have to feel deprived of smoking again. Recovery from smoking also requires learning other behaviours and techniques for dealing with trigger situations, stressful events, and strong emotions. These need to be well-rehearsed prior to quitting smoking as part of your relapse prevention strategy. With the added structure of the Chain-8 commitment, you and your clients can break free from addiction to cigarette smoking.

Again, a pattern intervention based on prescribing the symptom can break up a highly compulsive addictive ritual.

CHAPTER 6

Compulsive Hand Washing

IN MY THERAPEUTIC WORK, I have often used the ideas of Strategic Therapy. These are structural interventions based largely on Jay Haley's documentations of the pattern disruption strategies utilized by Milton H. Erickson, M.D., the most famous hypnotherapist of the 20th century (Haley, 1976).

One example earlier in my career was a woman in her early 30s who had a severe case of compulsive hand washing. She had been treated psychiatrically with a series of ineffective medications, some brief insight-oriented psychotherapy and brief hospitalizations in psychiatric wards in two general hospitals in our medium sized city of London, Ontario. Finally, she was admitted as an in-patient in a provincial psychiatric hospital, with a repeat of previous interventions, now augmented with group therapy on the ward over the past two months. Nothing worked. Her hands were raw, and she was actually losing patches of skin on her hands that were by now bandaged. She was agitated and distressed that nothing could stop her painful compulsion. She was going through several laundry hampers a day in washcloths and towels. In desperation, the staff referred her to me.

In our initial interview, she revealed that she had a severe dread that arose gradually in her early adulthood that her germs would infect others such that they would die. I asked her for her data that this was a reasonable fear. She said that no one had died or even got sick because of her diligent efforts to shower and wash her hands. Of course, she knew that this logic was flawed, but that did not diminish her feelings of the certainty of doom if she were less than diligent. I told her that pattern reminded me of the story of another client.

This man came in rubbing his left temple continually every minute of two. I asked him why he did that. He replied, "to keep the tigers away!" I said, "but there are no tigers in our city." He continued rubbing his head, saying "pretty effective, eh?" My current client was hardly amused by this story, and that made me somewhat concerned, because a client who has lost her sense of humour often has lost the perspective to meta-observe and describe her predicament. The ability to create a space between you and your problem situation is a first step toward examining patterns of possibility for its resolution. However, my client did not have access to this resource.

She did, nevertheless, have one important factor that pointed towards solution: she was what I call "**suitably desperate**." In motivational interviewing, we set the stage by exploring the extent of influence the problem has in our client's life, previous attempts to solve it, and explore with the client the risks and benefits of a proposed therapeutic change. We then assess with them the stage of readiness they are at before beginning treatment (Weeks and L'Abate, 1996). As my client was ready to do almost anything to resolve her situation, I had her make a "pact with the devil." That is, she agreed to enact an intervention without full knowledge of its technical details, provided that it was legal, ethical, and did not require any more than her current level of physical pain. Upon securing her agreement, I outlined the treatment plan.

I told her that, beginning this minute, she could now wash her hands and body as much as she wanted, with the requirement that she would terminate every washing occasion with one simple behaviour: she would touch the tips of her fingers of each hand to her nostrils. At that moment, she had a brief look of horror in her eyes, but she had agreed to the pact, so she swallowed hard and began to contemplate the dire consequences that she believed would happen. I assured her that I would teach her affective regulation strategies to deal with her anxiety, and would be on hand to help refer the victims of her contamination for further medical treatment as necessary. She was relieved that I was willing to unburden her responsibilities for the catastrophes that would ensue.

Within two days the bandages were off her hands. She had washed her hands several times at appropriate intervals. She had followed through with her closure assignment each time, had touched doorknobs and other common items on the ward. No one got sick or died (thank God!). In our second session I made a custom audiotape of the session and loaned her a tape player so that she could practice these relaxation strategies as often as necessary, but certainly once a day. Within a week, her compulsions had vanished, her obsessions were reduced to occasional thoughts totalling less than 20 minutes a day and steadily diminishing. She had no other problems or complications. Her level of confidence was boosted by her own self-efficacy and mastery of this problem pattern. At the end of the week she was discharged from the hospital, her hands fully healed, although still somewhat reddish from residual irritation.

I saw her weekly for three more sessions to ensure that the results were enduring. She had now returned to work productively. She still used her tape daily, and enjoyed the profound sense of relaxed trance it induced. Back in those days, hypnosis was not permitted in public hospitals, so I referred to our work as "guided imagery" and "relaxation training" which it basically was. She asked if I had used these relaxation techniques with other patients and clients, and of course I routinely did. She suggested that I make a commercial version of our tape, as she felt it would help many people beyond my caseload. As I frequently respect the advice of my clients,

I eventually worked in a sound studio and wrote and produced the audiotape "Wave-Pattern Breathing: Meditations for stress management" which became a best-seller in the Mind State Management Audiotape and CD productions series. These products are now available as MP3 Downloads (www.solutionorientedcounselling.ca). I guess no program is complete without a commercial, so there you have it.

As an interesting epilogue to this case, I heard from my former client approximately 10 years later. She had many years symptom free, but now some of her obsessive thinking was returning in other forms such as checking stoves and locks several times. She did not want her symptoms to regain their former control over her thinking and behaviour, so would I please make another tape as she had long since worn the old one out. I was pleased to reply that, although I now lived in Calgary, Alberta, several thousand miles away, that I had followed her earlier advice, so that she could order her own copy of Wave-Pattern Breathing. She did so and resumed her daily practice to a level of five times a week. The obsessive symptoms reduced in severity and frequency almost immediately. Within three weeks they were virtually gone. She thanked me for this follow-up telephone contact. That was over 20 years ago. Pattern interventions can work dramatically well. Both the therapist and the client must be fully aligned for them to do their magic, and so it was in this case.

Part Two:

Paradoxical Interventions

At times it is not sufficient to merely disrupt the symptom context or pattern. Sometimes it is best to prescribe the symptom itself, even without the modifying rules for how and where and when the symptom should occur. The basic premise still applies: you are asking the client to perform the symptomatic behavior, which is by definition not at the client's conscious control, again at the therapist's demand, supposedly at the therapist's control. Thus, once again the symptom becomes an integral part of the therapy, a beneficent paradox.

In these stories there is an added element of risk. The symptom must be prescribed with an acceptable rationale for the client. But more importantly, the therapist does so without the assured knowledge of how this might turn out. Intuition and previous experience might guide the therapist, and a sincere wish for no negative or harmful outcomes for the client. Still, as you will see, many of these prescriptions are counterintuitive. My experience with judo leads me to believe that one of the safest places is what we call "the eye of the tiger" or "the eye of the hurricane." This place is momentarily totally safe, but you need to jump into it with total commitment to be effective. As such it takes courage on the part of the prescribing therapist, and great motivational preparation for the client. You will see what I mean.

CHAPTER 7

THE OLD MAN

THIS IS ONE OF MY FAVOURITE STORIES. As you can imagine, in my career as a psychotherapist, I get a chance to see human nature at its worst, but more often, at its best. In this marriage therapy case, although I found the husband to be charming and loveable, it was the wife who was truly an inspiration about the essence of loving.

This story dates back to an era before cell phones. Around the late 1970s, there was a fad among long-haul truckers known as the CB (Citizen's Band) craze. There was even a popular culture of songs and movies around the ideas of truckers getting together by CB communication to inform each other and outwit speed traps and other roadside hazards, as well as rather mundane chatter, today's equivalent of Twitter and blogs. Back then, it was a relative novelty of remote communication. Part of the culture was to have a nickname, and one of these was "The Old Man." Now, for reasons of confidentiality, I have changed his handle for the purposes of our story, but it was something like that.

The Old Man drove an 18-wheeler semi through various cities and towns hauling freight on a long-distance highway. He was in his late-forties, with thinning black hair, a disarming boyish grin, and a pleasant way of instant engagement. As it turned out, he used these skills in flirting with truck stop waitresses, and had developed a reputation that had leaked back to his wife. She was in her late forties, rather attractive, and like her husband, mildly overweight. Now that the kids were grown and almost launched, she had resumed her career as an executive assistant in a small company in their hometown.

She had put up with her husband's shenanigans, and reputation as a flirt, as a necessary evil and an extension of his flamboyant personality. She didn't take it seriously, nor did the trucker friends on his main routes, until more persistent rumours circulated that he had special favourites that he almost bragged about without being specific in his CB blurbs. After her nagging suspicions, which he cavalierly denied as malicious rumours, he finally admitted he had been sexually intimate with Lark, a 28-year-old waitress. Perhaps, and who knows, there might have been other affairs in terms of one-night-stands, but The Old Man swore this was the only infidelity. His wife, who I will call The Old Lady in the vernacular of the day, guardedly accepted this version of reality. However, she needed a verdict about his commitment to his marriage to her. Did he really love her? She said in the initial marital interview she needed to know if the marriage was going forward. Other than facilitator, I was not guiding this interview. It merely unfolded before my eyes and ears.

The Old Lady stated boldly that she was the best woman for him, and that it was about time he knew it. Then she made a daring and unpredictable move: she challenged The Old Man to move out and live with his new fling! She said that there would be no animosity. She loved him with all her heart, but if he could find greater happiness with this younger woman, she would not stand in the way of his happiness. That would be the signature of her love for him. However, she also said that she was the best lover he could ever want, and she would await the verdict without judgment, and would accept him back if he returned from this experiment. She also said if the experiment went on for years, she could not guarantee that she would still be available.

I was awestruck as a therapist witnessing this interaction of love and permission. Mind you, I was relatively young in my career at that point. I had never encountered this form of love before. It was a combination of being fed up with nonsense and the genuine acceptance of the inner child within her 48-year-old spouse. I noted that here was no condemnation or criticism, just nurturance for an adult pup gone astray with chasing his own tail, in both meanings. And so it was that I was almost merely a witness to their new arrangement. At first The Old Man could not believe his ears. Did she really mean it? She said she was serious: both he and she needed to know that others could not match her genuine love for him, and that he could make a final and enduring commitment of monogamy with her. The now- liberated Old Man was free to pursue his new romance, but the stakes were also high. She also made the stipulation of no unprotected sex, so that the health of all would be safe during and after this experiment.

In the next several weeks by mutual agreement he moved in with this young waitress in a nearby city. As predicted, the sex was great in terms of novelty, as the Old Man was also in love with the state of being-in-love with Lark. Perhaps he fooled himself that he was in love with her, perhaps as an unconscious way to justify the affair. However, fairly soon this illusion was unravelling with each day they spent together, hanging out with her friends and activities. Her friends were into their own almost teenage way of talking, taste in music, shallow values, uninformed opinions, and casual involvement with alcohol and street drugs, almost daily. Her friends were also amused with Lark's relationship with a man old enough to be her father. However, they were respectful, if somewhat awkward, with the Old Man as he tagged along with them to nightclubs. The more he and Lark talked, the wider the generation gap became, both finding out they had almost nothing in common. Furthermore, the Old Man began missing the comfortable and caring conversations with his wife. Most of all, he missed her gentle and kind sense of humour, as compared to the edgy and cutting jibes that Lark and her friends thought to be funny. After three weeks, the Old Man decided that he wanted to end the affair and return home. Lark also agreed that this decision would be the best for everyone. The novelty had worn off, and she was feeling increasingly uncomfortable in his presence. They knew that they did not fit in each other's lives. The breakup was not in any way an angry one. Lark still held some affection for him but was relieved that their awkward affair was over. It was just a fling, and Lark went on with her life without missing a beat. For the Old Man, the breakup had more impact. He was shocked at Lark's casual detached attitude and lack of grief. He became aware of how much he had projected his hopes and dreams into this fantasy, and how quickly it had dissolved into a cloud of smoke within weeks. He also felt ashamed of being so foolish in risking a great marriage in chasing this illusion in his own mind.

About a week after his return home, the couple came in for their next session. They had been having many heart-to-heart talks that week. The Old Lady was cheerful and felt validated that in many ways her husband was a changed man. He was far more humble and sincere, and appreciated her qualities more than he had in years. In our conjoint session, he repeated for me and his wife the life lessons of the last month, especially what he had learned about himself, the value of his marriage, and the profound respect and admiration he had for his wife. In this session they both displayed their care, affection, and love for each other. There even were a few comments about greater mutual passion in their sexual relations, a nice side benefit of their greater emotional closeness. There was surprisingly little processing to do, as all was by now forgiven and restored.

By a month later the couple had recalibrated their relationship to a new normal. Among his trucker friends, he was still The Old Man, but he had lost a lot of his swagger. He was no longer a big braggart. Those who did know about his escapade accepted it with a shrug and a smile, calling it an AFGO, code for Another F...ing Growth Opportunity. To them, he had merely embarrassed himself, as in the saying "There's no fool like an old fool." They still accepted him. He still occasionally flirted with waitresses at truck stops, but now it was more light banter, no longer loaded with innuendo. He never again wanted to have any of these women calling his bluff.

The marriage continued to solidify over the coming months, with the couple going on more trips and sharing activities together. In my follow-up call about a year later, they reported continuing marital happiness, and a warm relationship with their grown-up children.

As I look back on this case, I had virtually no work to do in our sessions. I merely had a privileged window into the inspirational workings of true love. Later in my career, I also saw other variations of sending your spouse away to find him-or-herself with an outside lover, or a dramatically different lifestyle and trial separation. In each case the gamble paid off; the marriage was reaffirmed. However, in all of these stories, none impressed me as much as the love of The Old Lady for her Old Man.

CHAPTER 8

I Just Came Back To Say Goodbye

JUDY WAS AN attractive and intelligent 28-year-old executive assistant who had been living for more than a year with Giles, a 30-year-old used car salesman. All of Judy's friends warned her not to date Giles. Although he was charming and handsome, there was something about his glib manner and superficial values and attitudes that warned them that Judy would get hurt, but she was hopelessly in love with her man. They just didn't understand him, that's all. While Giles was somewhat successful as a salesman, in his spare time he enjoyed going to bars, drinking, and smoking marijuana occasionally. Judy had met him at one of those bars, and quickly liked the sensual way he danced and made her laugh with his goofy antics and juvenile humour.

In the year they lived together, their fit was becoming more ragged, as the very features of her original attraction were becoming tiresome. He resented her taking night courses towards her B. Comm. Degree, while he still hit the bars. On more than one occasion her friends had seen him flirt and dance with other women. He claimed it was all just innocent fun, but she began to be more suspicious as he stayed out later, made alibis about being out with his male friends, and became generally more defensive. Several times she had caught him out in lies, but in the face of his repeated denials she often forgave him, and allowed him a chance to build back trust, while he coped with her seemingly oversensitive undue jealousy and unfounded suspicions. After these arguments about his escapades the couple would settle into a honeymoon phase and another new start. There were other signs that Giles did not fit with Judy's goals and social circle of her student and faculty friends at university. He could not keep up with their conversations, and he would withdraw into alcohol and generally behave rather boorishly in her intellectual crowd. As the months went on, Giles would deny having affairs, but would finally be confronted with inconsistencies in his cover stories, erotic emails, and other telltale signs. When cornered Giles would try to lie, distract, counterattack by accusing Judy, but would finally admit he had an affair. At that point he would cry and say he truly loved only her, that these other dalliances were meaningless, and that he would reform. There were at least three of these discovered affairs in their year together. Each time, against the advice of her friends, Judy would take him back.

One night Giles came home more drunk than usual. He said he could not stand their relationship any longer. He was going to leave by the next day. Judy was shocked, but level headed enough to ask him where he was going to live. Giles then disclosed that he was going to move in to live with his mistress of the last month. At that point Judy lost it, screaming at Giles in her rage at yet another betrayal. All through the night she helped him pack all his belongings, apart from some shared furniture and larger items, and pushed him out the door that morning.

All of this story came from Judy in her first interview with me. She felt lonely and was grieving the breakup that occurred three weeks before her first session. Although I tried to reserve judgment about Giles, given that this was just one side of a story about relationship breakdown, it seemed to me he was a manipulating philanderer, in plain terms, a jerk. However, what was even more remarkable was Judy's huge attachment to this man. There was a strong element of co-dependency in her insistence that, given enough support, Giles would prove to be a diamond in the rough, a great guy. Coming as she did from a family where her father was an alcoholic and divorced her mother after many affairs, it was easy to see how transference was clouding her judgement in her dedication and loyalty to a losing cause. Her personal history also explained why she had always been attracted to carefree and charming men and was bored by more stable and goal-oriented men. Furthermore, her teenage rebellious nature accounted for her former party lifestyle around alcohol and pot, previously dropping out of university to get a job to support her lifestyle. She also was continuing to rebel against her strict and controlling mother. Her younger sister had dealt with the struggles of life in this single-parent family by being passive and obedient towards her mother, quietly focusing on her studies. Now that Judy was more mature in the last year, she had graduated beyond the shallowness of her party lifestyle, focusing instead on her night school courses, while continuing to work dutifully during the day. Only two aspects remained of her delayed adolescence: attraction to charming goal-less men and refusing the sage advice of her friends. She had this "I'll show you" or "I'll live my life my way" insistence about her that was fiercely independent, and quite like the gender script of her father.

Given the strong transference issues in an adult child of an alcoholic family, our first sessions were devoted to healing the "Inner Child." We worked through on an emotional level the mystique about pursuing the absent father with the hopes of reforming him, a theme replicated in her relationship with Giles. They say that "love at first sight" is likely an instance of transference. And so it was with Judy and Giles. She instantly felt a sense of familiar comfort and kinship in this passionate and tumultuous relationship with this wild but wonderful man. Regardless of this insight, her longing for Giles persisted, and only he could unlock her heart, or so she felt. Lately she had heard that he had moved out from his new girlfriend's place and was living on his own in an apartment. She desperately wanted to reconnect with him. She asked my professional opinion on what to do. I kept throwing the decision back in her lap, going over potential scenarios of what could happen if she took him back, versus what could happen if she just pursued her studies, and left herself open for potential other relationships in the future. I think Judy must have detected my bias toward the latter path. Even though we worked on integrating parts of herself with empty chair techniques, she still had the resolve to get Giles back, no matter how irrational that path seemed.

Once more she asked for my professional opinion. I was in somewhat of a therapeutic quandary. To refuse to answer would be a breach of authenticity and our therapeutic relationship of support. So I told her that, as a registered psychologist, it might be unethical of me to recommend that she return to a psychologically abusive relationship. All reasonable signs indicated that to follow such a path would lead to further suffering and harm. On the other hand, I knew in my core consciousness that Judy was determined to return to Giles regardless of my cautions, as she had rejected her friends' and family counsel as well. I told her jokingly that "maturity is being able to follow your parents' advice, even if they are right." She pressed me further for a definitive opinion, so I told her, "I know, regardless of what I or others say, that you are going to return to Giles. All I ask is that you take full responsibility for your decisions and its consequences, keep your eyes open, and that you learn from your experience, no matter how it turns out." Judy thought this was sound advice. Within a month she had convinced Giles to move back in and give their relationship another try.

What followed was really an enlightening experience for me as an observer in their life. Judy was never a member of Al-Anon, although in retrospect I could have recommended it to her. She never went to a meeting of ACOA (Adult Children of Alcoholics), even though it might have been helpful. Judy was one of those people who are caught in the Groucho Marx Paradox, namely, "I would never join a club who would accept me as a member." She was staunchly independent. However, almost miraculously, she had internalized some key principles of these organizations. In contrast to her mother's stance of over-controlling co-dependency, Judy no longer criticized Giles' drinking and partying. She made no excuses for his behaviour in front of others when he made a fool of himself. She made his attendance at her social gatherings optional, and he gradually excluded himself. I don't know exactly what their arrangement was regarding his potential infidelity, but I think the writing was on the wall: one more strike and you're out. Giles seemed to accept those terms, and gradually his drinking and partying curtailed as he settled down.

I met Giles on three occasions. Twice in their early relationship of living back together, Judy dragged Giles in for a session or two to talk about their relationship. He was suitably distant and defensive, given that I had been Judy's individual therapist in their time apart. However, he went beyond that stance into belligerent ridicule and derision of "shrinks," most of them screw-ups anyway, and couples should be able to sort out their own stuff anyway, without anyone else snooping in.

Despite my best attempts to engage him, he was not interested in couple therapy. He struck me as not very intelligent, but also arrogantly self-opinionated. I regret not being objective, but that was my impression of him.

Over their months together in this new arrangement, the couple was gradually and peacefully drifting apart, on separate paths. I only saw Judy now on a monthly basis, as she felt satisfied that all was going in the direction she wanted. She had by now realized that the spell was broken: she was no longer in love with Giles. She still had a soft spot for him, but it was now like a distant smile for a rascal dog that she once knew. Of course, she eventually moved on to graduate with her B.Comm., moved up the career ladder to a much better executive position, met a great guy and got married.

The last time I saw Judy and Giles together was in the latter phase of their relationship. They were on the grass at a Folk Festival and called me over to talk with them. They still shared their original love of music, and liked being together for that purpose, but they told me that they had both outgrown each other. They were no longer in love, but still cherished memories of some of the good times they had together. It was bittersweet, but now they acknowledged the time to separate had come. They were making arrangements to live separately within that month. Judy assured me that she would be fine. Giles looked resigned but calm that Judy had grown beyond him, and the gap could never be filled. They were different people, and that was that. Judy contacted me by phone message two months later, saying she felt fine, and was moving on with her life as a single woman. I have not had any further contact with Giles, so I don't know what he learned from the whole experience of their relationship, but I suspect he will conclude, "We weren't meant for each other." But my guess is that he will wistfully remember her as "the one that got away," with a sense of remorse about how he misplayed that relationship. That is looking hopefully, that he learned from experience. Many like him grow old, but don't grow up. I hope he has a better fate.

As for Judy, well, I think her reason for returning to Giles was based less on love and compassion, and perhaps more on ego. Perhaps she could not stand the narcissistic insult that this creep dumped her. As the song goes, "I just came back to say goodbye" might sum up her involvement to resume this hopeless relationship for the final triumph of rejecting him. Actually, it was not a real victory of rejection for either of them, just the realistic conclusion that their relationship was unworkable. Perhaps more charitably, we could say, she just needed more time with Giles to break the spell of her transference projections upon him, so that she could release her heart and mind for more suitable life partners.

CHAPTER 9

THE BLUSHING CONTEST

IN TORONTO A WHILE BACK I conducted an all-day workshop for about 30 realtors, called "The Psychology of Sales." At the end there was some time left over for questions and concerns. One middle-aged woman rather tentatively held up her hand for a question. She said that she had a problem sometimes in sales presentations, especially in larger groups. As she talked and her colleagues watched, her face and neck glowed a crimson red in a noticeable blush. She asked if I could help with this problem, as it was quite embarrassing. I replied that solving this perhaps lifelong problem might require more than a half-hour of intensive group therapy. However, in a bold move I asked the audience if anyone else present had this problem. About ten heads turned toward another woman, who immediately flushed in embarrassment. I asked her if she would volunteer to help her colleague and herself to overcome this problem. She agreed, and I asked her to join her flush-faced client at the front of the room.

What happened next was a gamble on my part as a health coach. I asked the spectators to place side bets, not to exceed two dollars each, on which realtor could remain the reddest after I announced the start of the race. My women clients at the front of the room looked in astonishment as their fellow-realtors eagerly placed their bets in the service of light-hearted fun. When all bets were placed, I announced to my two blushing clients: "When I say, 'Go!' I want you to try to blush as darkly as you can. Got it? Okay, 1-2-3 Go!" At this moment they both turned as white as sheets!

Actually, this is an exaggeration. The point is, both of my clients lost their blushes and returned to their normal flesh tones in their complexions. The audience was aghast and had a hard time in declaring the winner of the bet. Both of my contestants were dumbfounded at the disappearance of their mutual symptom of blushing. I asked them, the next time they felt warmth in their faces, to remember The Blushing Contest, and how they had both assisted each other in eliminating this shared individual problem by trying to make it worse, and in public, no less! This demonstration had a great impact on all concerned, and, in a six-month follow-up by their district sales manager, both the realtors no longer had problems of blushing in presentations.

My quick insight into an idea for a blushing contest was not a total leap of faith. I already knew that in many anxiety symptoms, as the saying goes, "you have nothing to fear but the fear itself." In other words, if you go with the flow, rather than resisting it, the force dissolves itself when you abandon the struggle against it. This prescription is certainly counter-intuitive to people with anxiety symptoms, but from a mindfulness perspective, yielding to a symptom and allowing it to take charge beyond our control often turns out to be an excellent strategy. The key is to allow surrender of control to be supplanted by an attitude of peace and acceptance, allowing the symptom pattern to overtake and flow through you without your resistance and attempted control. I have used this strategy of paradoxical surrender and acceptance in helping many clients overcome their anxiety and panic disorders over the years of my practice. Although surrender seems counter-intuitive to the anxiety-combatant client, it can be helpful tool to overcome anxiety dilemmas.

CHAPTER 10

FAINTING IN CHURCH

MANY YEARS AGO, I worked in rural mental health clinics in Southwestern Ontario. Each day of the week would serve a different community, so sometimes our team would not visit the same town more than once every two weeks. Accordingly, often there were wait lists, and our team would have to triage the cases according to urgency of care needed. Unfortunately, that kind of patient care often generates a crisis generating system, but it was the best we could do with limited public health care resources. Thus, as noted in Chapter 2, part of our mandate in these roving clinics was to do a brief 10-minute assessment of a case for triage purposes. This requirement meant that we clinicians would often need to assess situations astutely based on limited information and clinical intuition. Most of the time, this process worked rather well.

In one case a woman in her late thirties presented with the problem of being very frightened of "fainting in church." Actually, I am familiar with this problem. In my childhood I served as an altar boy on the sanctuary of our Roman Catholic Church. In some of the longer formal masses and ceremonies, for some undiagnosed reason I would become sick and dizzy, and either have to leave the altar area or faint on the spot, needing to be revived so that I could make my exit and other people would have to carry on in my place. Fortunately, these were rare incidents, but they certainly were embarrassing, and I sometimes had anticipatory anxiety that such incidents might reoccur at any given time in church.

As a cognitive behaviour therapist, I wanted to know the triggers, frequency, severity, and duration of this woman's fainting episodes. She told me rather embarrassedly that she could not tell me this information, as she had never quite fainted in church. She coped with a feared episode by merely staying in church, struggling through the service, and leaving greatly relieved, but still fearful that the dreaded event might happen next time. You might think that the fear would extinguish after so many repeated exposures without incident, but sometimes these anxiety problems seem to have a life of their own. A cognitive intervention of reframing her experience perhaps might have been enough, but in a mere 10 minutes I did not have a strong enough therapeutic alliance to attempt an intervention that could be seen as superficial or dismissive, given how strongly fearful she felt about the issue. She was not very afraid of physical harm, just the intense embarrassment of seeming weak and frail in her church community.

I told her that I had some potentially effective ideas about how she could be cured of this condition, but that I currently had no appointments available to treat her. Meanwhile she could do something to prepare for treatment: she could begin to collect data on the problem. She was highly motivated to cooperate, so I asked her in the next month to go to as many church observances as possible with two of her friends, one on each side, to catch her whenever she faints, so that no damage would happen to her head or teeth. She agreed to do her homework assignment.

A month later she faithfully attended her five-minute reassessment interview. She told me she was not able to collect any concrete data, as she had been unsuccessful in generating a fainting spell in church. I told her in a spirit of mild consternation that I would be unable to treat her if she was not able to collect any baseline data. She would need to renew her efforts, trying as hard as she could to faint in church so that we could examine the problem she was dealing with. She agreed, with the modification that perhaps only one friend in attendance would be enough to safely catch her as needed. I agreed to this variance on the original assignment.

A month later this woman returned to announce that she still had no data to present about fainting in church; however, she had a new insight. She discovered that sometimes she **did not want** to go to church. This revelation was tantamount to blasphemy in this bible-belt community. Nevertheless, she now wondered if she didn't have to go to church if she didn't want to, and therefore could end her homework assignment. I replied that this would be unwise, as a phobia could return with even greater force if she started to avoid church to avoid the fear itself. No, she would have to face the fear directly by continuing to try to faint in church so that we could gather enough data so that we could treat her disorder. She bravely soldiered on with the assignment.

A month later she returned to announce that she was now **convinced that she could not faint in church!** I asked her if she was totally sure, and she repeated that she was. I said that I guess she didn't need to continue her homework any further. She was triumphantly relieved. I shrugged my shoulders and apologized for being unable to treat her. We shook hands and exchanged a knowing smile.

CHAPTER 11

THE NEAR PERFECT LOANS OFFICER

DORIS WAS A MIDDLE-AGED loans officer in a bank. She was proficient, competent, knowledgeable, and had good customer relations skills. Nevertheless, she had been referred to me by her human resources department, as she was about to be fired if she did not change her pattern of persistent minor errors that were increasingly annoying to her new supervisor, a male assistant manager that had been transferred to her branch six months ago. The situation between them had become progressively worse over the months. As the case was a referral through her employee assistance program, I would have no mandate for organizational development intervention. I would not be able to interview the supervisor. All our sessions would be strictly confidential, with no reporting or contact with the bank other than a billing number. Whether her employment could be saved would be strictly up to her work performance.

In her first session with me, Doris presented as highly anxious, suspicious, somewhat irritable and annoyed that the situation had come to this critical point. She described her supervisor as old-school, somewhat sexist and disrespectful of her and other female employees in the branch. While she prided her work, he was unusually picky about small details, and increasingly critical of the loans applications she submitted to him for his approval. What was really maddening for Doris was not only that her errors were becoming more frequent, but they were more serious. Sometimes, she would even do a sloppy credit check that would come back negative, in this industry a huge error of neglect and due diligence. She was so angry that these mistakes would give her smug boss the satisfaction of chastising her. You can see from reading this that on some subconscious level she was transferring some sadomasochistic drama from her past, perhaps with her father or a demanding teacher. However, a history probe revealed no previous enactment of this dynamic. Nevertheless, it represented a classic case of passive aggression, covert rebellion against arbitrary authority. What made it more impressive was that this mild but hyper-efficient woman had always followed the requirements of detailed precision in her job until now. Something in the imperious attitude of her boss was triggering this unconscious but self-destructive rebellion accompanied by self-embarrassment. It was so maddening for her to play directly into the hands of her adversary. Given these obvious psychodynamics, we explored them in her personal history, with negative results. Then it occurred to me: maybe she had never encountered in her sheltered and blessed history a genuine a..hole. Just to be sure, we did empty chairs and other role-play enactments with other bosses and authority figures in her life. Despite our best efforts, nothing seemed to be working. Her unconscious errors persisted. Then I had an inspiration from my work with self-handicapping athletes (see Chapter 33): I told her a story about Japanese pottery. It goes like this:

It is said that in many places in Japan there are centres of pottery where many artisans produce beautiful vases and other art pieces upon pottery wheels, shaping them with their fingers and other hand tools. At the end of their creation, the artisan typically looks at this wonder of symmetry and perfection that the artist has created, but just before firing in the kiln, the artist does a crucial but spiritual act.

The artist deliberately puts a tiny indentation or nick in the work. This act is to deconstruct hubris, the attempt at man's ego to assume god-like proportions. To state a rule of discipline: every human act should be made into a state of close to absolute beauty, but one step short of perfection, as an acknowledgment of humble reality and the human condition in this changing and capricious world.

Based on this story, I gave my client a piece of homework that I have used with virtually all my perfectionist clients: you can do any act you feel you need to do, as long as you do it leaving one tiny element unfinished. This means that you can clean an entire carpet, but you need to leave one dust bunny by the corner unswept. You dust an entire plant but leave an entire leaf undusted. In other words, a perfectionist pattern cure prescription is to require your client to do everything they do to a standard that is imperfect, but not-catastrophic. In other words: your client is to perform every action in a minor but deliberately imperfect way. To give you an example, supposing you have to submit a report written in MSWord format, and you deliberately insert a space between the end of a word , and a comma as I did just did here. The green prompt tells you that you have made some formal, but likely not critical, violation of best English grammar.

So, as you might guess, I prescribed that my client should deliberately make a minor and not-crucial mistake on every document she made, especially loans applications and their investigation documentation. As you can imagine, she resisted this idea, but her job was on the line, so she resolved to make deliberate but annoyingly minor errors, such as writing the loans applicant's address entirely on one line rather than three, which was dictated by the form of the loans application document.

After her initial resistance to this intervention, she took surprising delight in vexing her supervisor with minor but non-crucial edits to her "typos." She stopped making unconscious errors, because her therapist demanded that she make conscious mistakes in a deliberate way in every report. After a while, she delighted in this assignment. It not only delivered from her state of paranoia and performance anxiety about evaluation, but also allowed her a sense of showing off to evaluative observers just how valuable she was to her bank. As an afterthought, her assistant branch manager moved on, and the problem resolved itself. Perhaps in his future promotion he met his fate. About him there are such clichés as: "all cream rises till it sours." My mother had an expression for this as well: "time wounds all heels." As often happens in organisations, by the time a terrible manager is found out, many key employees have left the business to go elsewhere. In this case, my client outlasted this manager's transfer rotation and she got to keep her position.

What is most important in this story for me is that my client preserved her career by deliberate rather than unconscious errors. She made the covert obvious and thereby temporarily defused the attacks of her boss, who after awhile came to see her mistakes as silly but minor and moved on to other concerns. I know she never challenged and channelled her unconscious anger towards this officious male supervisor. That is an inequity that exists in office politics. I was not mandated to reverse office power structures, nor was Doris. The main thing was that she finally found a way of taking charge of her unconscious impulses, and hereby saved her career.

CHAPTER 12

Validating The Decision To Not Change

MIKE AND KAREN were a middle-aged couple with two young children. They originally presented with marital problems, and there were concerns about their children as well as family-of-origin issues. They were both likeable, and readily engaged in the process of couple therapy. Karen was very anxious and easily threatened. She had suffered lifelong psycho-physiological disorders, aggravated by stress and sensitivity to perceived criticism. She coped with obsessive-compulsive and perfectionistic defenses to lower her worries and insecurities. Difficulties and conflicts tended to loom larger for her, and at the time of referral she felt depleted and exhausted by the complexities of raising young children at home.

Mike played the complement of Karen's amplifier position by being a conflict-avoidant stimulus reducer. His role was that of family provider and protector, trying to put out fires as fast as they ignited, and becoming quite agitated whenever Karen became upset, taking on her position in dealing with conflicts with teachers and other parents and children in the exclusive private school in which their children were enrolled. Mike also took on the role of family protector when Karen's parents would try to spoil the children with treats instead of the strict diet of healthy foods that Karen prepared. It was as if her parents were passive aggressive in undermining Mike and Karen's way of raising children. However, Karen was also critical at times when she thought that Mike overplayed his role, and he felt caught in between Karen and the perceived threats of the outside world. Mike was the eager Rescuer trying to soothe Karen whenever she became upset, but Karen often felt dismissed and invalidated when Mike would try to take an external position, himself trying not to worsen the distress of the couple. It was a classic dance of gender issues contaminating the couple's mutual wish for domestic peace and emotional security, the systemic loop of a problem-amplifying solution. Predictably, the more Mike tried to play the role of over adequate protector, the more Karen would become the worrying damsel in distress. This loop had become worse, such that the escalations of her helplessness trumped his inadequate attempts to rescue. Both felt frustrated and powerless, while each of them had an unconscious investment in their respective roles. Despite these conflicts, Mike and Karen were a loving couple, eager to help each other and "do the right thing" in balancing the demands of modern family living.

The approach I employed to deal with this core issue was essentially couples emotion-focused therapy. I guided them through several enactments of their core struggles, addressing their attachment styles and their underlying wishes and dreams of how they could function beyond this negative spiral. I also used EMDR in helping Karen break out of the conflict arising from her identity fusion and enmeshment with her mother. After about ten sessions the couple were doing much better, and strife around schooling issues settled down with their calm but firm teamwork.

Nevertheless, there was one deep scar in their couple history that they could not heal. About four years earlier, at the time of birth of their second son William, Karen had a prolonged labour. The couple had poor sleep the night before as some contractions began increasing in frequency and then subsiding. Mike had worked in his computer consulting job during the day, taking Karen to the hospital in the early evening and remaining there with until about two o'clock in the morning. The waters had not yet broken, and Karen by this point was feeling something was very wrong. She felt pain and nausea, and was highly anxious. The doctors examined her but could not detect any abnormalities. Karen could not be consoled and wanted Mike to stay in her hospital room. Both were exhausted, and Mike was intensely drowsy from being awake for almost two days. The hospital staff told him that there was nothing he could do, so he should go home and get some rest. Mike took their advice and went home. Karen eventually fell asleep.

The next day William was delivered, and within two days Karen was discharged from hospital with their new son. Still, Karen did not feel well, but the medical staff thought she was just feeling discomfort recovering from the delivery. However, after a week of progressively worsening symptoms including excessive and severe abdominal bleeding, she was readmitted to hospital. It turns out she had an undiagnosed hematoma and had to have transfusions of blood and emergency surgery to correct her condition. She was then able to make a fairly rapid recovery, at least from a physical standpoint.

However, she found the whole sequence was very traumatic. She felt invalidated, abandoned, and betrayed by Mike for not staying by her side and not insisting that the doctors look harder and further for the cause of her distress. At that moment in the middle of the night she felt like she was dying and that nobody would listen, and her husband had abandoned the situation, perhaps leaving her to die. Bearing in mind that she had a history of high anxiety and hypochondriasis, it is understandable that this was a very important and terrifying moment in her life. She felt that, from that moment on, she could never again trust Mike to be there for her, regardless of their previous or subsequent history together. Although Mike continued to be the try-hard husband, and they were getting along much better than before, Karen felt she could not forgive Mike for that incident of betrayal, and nothing could assuage her distrust and ultimate fears of abandonment. She would become upset, angry, and tearful at any mention of that night or related themes. Then something rather amazing happened.

Since Karen had already had a positive experience with EMDR in resolving feelings and issues with her relationship with her mother, I proposed that, if she wanted to get beyond the PTSD around the birth of William, we could use EMDR to process those emotions and thoughts. Suddenly at that point she dug in her heels and firmly but not angrily refused to work on resolving the issue. It was as if she was declaring a boundary, even though at some level she knew that her decision might perpetuate their underlying conflict and keep Mike in the role of perpetual offender. Both Mike and I were puzzled by her stance but admiring her courage and honesty in holding her position.

My response was also surprising, in that I felt okay about her decision. It certainly is a client's right as a consumer to refuse treatment, and I fully respected her calm but firm refusal to deal with the issue. Also, it was not a matter of dislike for the process of EMDR, nor even doubting its effectiveness. Karen merely wanted to stand firm and be validated for doing so. So I did.

Then I praised the couple for progressing as far as they had, and perhaps this was good enough, and they could leave therapy with the satisfaction of what they had achieved over our months together. At that point Mike said, "Wait a minute! How about we do EMDR with me? I was pretty upset about the whole thing, too. I want to work on resolving some of my feelings about it." Karen was surprised and curious, but we all thought it was a good idea. So there we were, me doing

EMDR with Mike, with Karen silently observing in the corner seat of the office.

For those of you not familiar with Eye Movement Desensitization and Reprocessing (EMDR), you can go to www.emdr.com or any number of books and articles available from the Internet. Over the years I have found it to be a remarkably useful technique to assist people with post traumatic stress disorder (PTSD) and other cases of strong but unwanted emotional reactions to remnants of past situations and their echoes in current life.

In reviewing the key scenes of that night at the hospital, Mike's negative cognition or caption was "Whatever I do, it's never good enough." We worked together to come up with a positive cognition statement or caption of the scenes: "I am a loving person within the limits of my stamina and my understanding." Going back to the hospital scene, no one but Karen sensed that something was terribly wrong. As the doctor and nurses examined her and said that everything was normal, she became increasingly invalidated and agitated. She considered it a betrayal that Mike did not back her up and insist on a second medical opinion. (This was at 2 a.m. in the morning). Karen thought it a further betrayal and abandonment that Mike took the advice of the medical staff without much protest and went home to sleep.

Recalling this scene, Mike was now agitated to the level of 9 out of 10, feeling tension in his jaw, stomach, and right shoulder, thinking "I should do something!" but feeling powerless and defeated, unable to help his distressed wife. As we went through several passes of bilateral stimulation in the EMDR protocol, he thought "Next time this happens, I will stop the nurse and refuse to leave Karen in this state and fall asleep with her in her hospital room." This was his relearning of what he could have done. His subjective units of distress (his SUDs level) then dropped to 5, as tension began to drain from his body. In subsequent EMDR passes his SUDs level dropped to 1, or neutral, whereupon we infused the attribution "I forgive myself for being tired, confused, and helpless." I think this affirmation was more powerful than the previous phase, where he was still trying to perfect the role of superhero. Now he was acknowledging defeat of his superhero status, coming to terms with his own impotence and the futility of his ego role. This was a huge shift away from personal hubris toward humility and acceptance. More important still, it was a unilateral declaration of the end of his role of codependency, a role that Karen appreciated but resented because she unconsciously knew was unsustainable. We ended the session with Mike exhausted but relieved. Karen, observing this process, felt a little unsteady while strangely relieved. We agreed to meet for a follow-up session two months later.

Needless to say, I was intensely interested in what might happen with this couple. Would Mike's EMDR session shift their dynamics as a couple? Would his abandonment of superhero status lead Karen to her greater emergence as an emotionally stable person? It turned out that Mike continued with his changes from the day of our session. He announced to workmates that he would no longer be the Rescuer of the corporation; he would merely do his reasonable job, but others had to step up to fill the gaps of his long hours. He closed his office door more often, and let others find solutions to their problems. As he explained it, "I have less on my plate. It's only a saucer now, but I'm eating well." This assertive shift at work pleased Karen immensely, as Mike was far more emotionally present and attentive in family life and their relationship. Furthermore, he was far more likely now to push back when Karen tried to put the burden of problem-solving on his shoulders, tending to active listen rather than go into action mode on her behalf. Initially, this stance activated her abandonment issues, but increasingly she sensed the rise in her own power of self-efficacy in dealing with life issues as they arose, consulting with Mike as she needed, but often willing to carry the ball herself.

Well, with all these positive developments, I again congratulated the couple on their progress and resolution of key partnership issues. I was about to close their case as significantly improved, even in the first half-hour of our last session, when Karen made a surprise announcement. She had continued to be amazed at the steadfastness of Mike's abandonment of his superhero stance after the EMDR treatment, so now she wanted to complete her own work to put the hospital saga behind her. At this point, I was even more in admiration of this couple as Karen reached out for her need for closure.

In this EMDR session, all three of us were braced for a reactivation of all the emotions that happened many years ago at her horrible moment of abandonment and terror. However, I suppose that over the previous two months she had done a great deal of her own work in emotionally processing and cognitively reframing the scenes of that night. The EMDR passes worked smoothly and effectively to reduce the SUDS to a level of 1, with Karen's affirmation, "Even though Mike isn't perfect or hugely powerful, I can trust that he loves me." With this completion, we virtually ended their therapy, although once or twice a year we do follow-ups to consolidate their gains.

Looking back, I thought the most pivotal point in the therapy of this couple was our mutual decision to affirm Karen's refusal to change, despite the potentially limiting implications of this choice. What made it especially beautiful is that Karen displayed the choice actively and responsibly, rather than the more passive-aggressive way of her persuading Mike to terminate couples therapy. Many couples avoid recalibrating their relationship by withdrawing from therapy at the threshold of potential realignment. To those couples the dictum is: better the devil you know, than the devil you don't know, the uncertainty of change. I applaud this couple for their courage and honesty, and the abiding love they continue to share.

So, there you have it: a superhero gratefully dethroned, and his damsel in distress arising to the call of her own personal power. Life is good.

CHAPTER 13

"Unethical" Therapy?

WELL, IT'S ABOUT TIME I wrote this chapter, actually, quite late in my career. It has to do with an earlier point in time, about four years ago. The story encapsulates several "pseudo-dilemmas." That is, upon reflection, every decision in this case seems so clear and obvious. But back to the story:

I was referred by Veterans Affairs Canada to treat a 74-year-old former soldier who was diagnosed by his social worker as "Major Depressive Disorder, with Suicidal Ideation."

When I first met Joe, he was formal and dignified in demeanor, but amazingly direct and open about his anguish about his situation. Joe wanted to know about the options available to eventually kill himself. While I admired his candor and directness, I wanted to know about the nature of his current distress.

Well, it turned out that no one in his personal circle wanted to talk about his anticipated death. His wife and family and friends were horrified at his obsession with death, although he was a war veteran suffering from pain syndromes and PTSD resulting from his many military deployments over the years of his army career. Even though his death was not immanent, he did not want to remain alive in a future time when he was no longer able to feed or toilet himself. He did not want to depend on others to deal with his indignities, especially if he became demented. He was already noticing some cognitive decline in recent memory and in the naming of objects. Of course, in that era there was no provision for medically assisted dying in Canada.

In fact, there were only a few countries in the world where you could engage that service.

What disturbed Joe worst was that no one was willing to talk about suicide. He felt alone, isolated, and invalidated in his concerns. Other than the distress over this issue, Joe seemed to be coping rather well with his physical pain and progressive disabilities resulting from his military career.

Now that we had established the main presenting problem, I informed him that I had a professional ethical dilemma to ponder. As a registered clinical psychologist, I was not supposed to counsel clients about how to plan their suicide. To do so was outside our ethical code of conduct. However, I asked Joe if he would be willing to engage in **"unethical" therapy** with me. He quickly answered that he would like to explore that option. Encouraged by his assent, we spent the rest of the session talking about several jurisdictions in the world where he might travel to have a death with dignity when he felt the time was right. His mood brightened with relief and even enthusiasm as the session went on. We even rehearsed how he would deal with other people who would try to shut down discussion about his plans, how he would calmly but assertively tell his family that this was a key issue for him.

Close to the end of the first session I told Joe that I had concerns about his diagnosis to address, so we went through the 21 questions in the Beck Depression Inventory. As expected, his answers confirmed that he was not depressed at all, just mildly unhappy with his life and frustrated with his family's stance on his key issue. I told Joe that perhaps I was just lucky to catch him on a good bounce when he was thinking clearly and lucidly. He agreed to arrange a follow-up interview in one month to reassess how he was doing.

Not surprisingly, the validation and relief that Joe felt in our initial interview had spread to give him greater confidence and efficacy during the ensuing weeks. His family and friends shifted their stance to listen to his concerns and even validate his potential future plans. Armed with the confidence that he would have some control over his life and even death, his feelings of urgency greatly diminished. His disposition was cheerful and thankful that our first session was a turning point for him. We both celebrated his successful outcome. However, I told him about one final dilemma.

During that month between sessions I pondered about how I would write the final report about his therapy for the Department of Veteran Affairs. While accurately reporting Joe's progress in counselling, I wanted to avoid invalidating the social worker that had rendered such a severe diagnosis just two months previously. I sensed that Joe was not depressed in the first 15 minutes of that first session, and it turns out that my intuition was accurate. While It was true that he did indeed have suicidal ideation and was in fact wanting to discuss a suicidal plan, that didn't seem like a problem for either of us as we worked together. Still there remained the difficulty about the diagnosis. Then the answer occurred to me a few days before our follow-up session.

For a person with cancer, after treatment when the symptoms are gone and the X-ray pictures are clear, we don't say that the cancer is cured, only that it is "in remission." The diagnosis remains in effect, but with the qualifier that it seems to be inactive at the current time. Joe laughed out loud at this solution and heartedly endorsed it.

In the treatment report we concluded with the diagnosis: **Major Depressive Disorder with Suicidal Ideation, in Remission.**

Part Three:

Systemic Interventions

This group of chapters has its own intrigue, because often problems dissolve when we change the interpersonal context in which they are embedded. The metaphor I think about is repairing a car engine or a plumbing repair situation. Often you need to take the whole assembly out of its container, get leverage on the specific element that needs replacing or updating, then reassembling the entire package and putting it back carefully in its container, making all the necessary reattachments necessary for the whole unit to function properly. Doctors also use this principle in complex surgeries.

The stories in this section also change the interaction patterns of the people involved such that symptomatic patterns are not as necessary to maintain relationships in a satisfactory and improved way.

CHAPTER 14

THE TOXIC MARRIAGE

CONVENTIONAL WISDOM dictates that the most effective and efficient way to help a couple deal with marital breakdown is to have them in for marriage therapy, featuring conjoint sessions where both attend therapy together, perhaps augmented by some individual sessions as well. There are, of course, variations on this theme.

A female client can come in for personal help and soon it becomes remarkably clear that 90% of her stress comes from marital conflict. Naturally, we do whatever we can to engage her often-reluctant spouse to come in for at least one session, so that we can better assist our work with her.

At this point, she is still the identified client, i.e., the one who has the problem. Her husband is merely there to provide his guidance as to how best to help her, and to tell us his side of the story as to why she is unhappy. Of course, this scenario is less than optimal, as the husband is typically building a case for his blameless and/or bewildered stance. However, his input and involvement in a supportive way is often an indirect way of getting him involved and invested in a positive outcome where he can play a vital contributing role as individual therapy progresses. These situations can also happen with the genders reversed, although that is relatively rare.

In other presenting scenarios, the marriage is definitely the problem, but she seeks help first, vetting the credentials and supportiveness of the therapist before inviting her husband into the Dragon's Den of marital therapy. At this point the therapist needs to do some elaborate and special manoeuvres to ensure the partners have an equal footing in conjoint therapy, rather than the perceived imbalance of prior alliance between the therapist and the first-in wife. Usually, the therapist sees the husband in one or more individual sessions to match the lead of his contact with the wife. Then conjoint sessions can begin. Often, however, despite the therapist's invitations, husband refuses to take part in therapy whatsoever. In these cases, therapy for the marriage using individual sessions for one spouse can still succeed. It is just that the work may be longer and more difficult to turn the marriage around. Let me tell you a story to illustrate this point.

Once there was a woman in her late forties, let's call her Joyce. Joyce was a senior nurse in a smaller community hospital near her rural community near the metropolis of Calgary, Alberta. Joyce was married to Brian, who was a V.P. Exploration of a junior oil company that was doing very well in what is called Calgary's Oil Patch, the downtown hub of Calgary's oil and gas industry. Brian was also a very entrepreneurial person, so he had also established a landscape and plant nursery business in this satellite community where there were many acreages and need for vegetation, crops, bushes, trees, and flowers. Still, this enterprise was mostly a hobby farm operation, catering to boutique farmers working their acreages like gentleman farmers as a sidelight to their main careers in the city. Therefore, a mainstay of the plant nursery business were local people, especially stay-at-home wives and homemakers on these rather vast but unwieldy properties that featured lots of unused or underused space. For convenience, we'll call this sideline business The Nursery.

Joyce for many years filled the role of Superwoman in this family. Despite holding down her job as part-time nurse in their rural community hospital, she had raised their two children, taking them to school, athletic, and community team functions, long before Brian would return from his twelve-hour days in the city. It felt to her as if she were a single parent. The couple had almost no intimate time alone. Worse still, Brian's evenings and weekends were consumed by scheduling and business operations planning for their very successful garden nursery business. They had enormous financial success, but time poverty. Nevertheless, Brian refused to hire a full-time manager for The Nursery, preferring to do it all by himself to cut inventory and staffing expenses. As you might imagine, the brunt of the shortfall fell on Joyce's shoulders, especially on early weekend mornings. Finding the Nursery office vacant, they would politely ask on the family's back door. Joyce would dutifully oblige their needs, rake in the profits, but collapse at the end of the day where Brian would assist in making sure all were well-supplied. Joyce kept on protesting that Brian needed to hire on a full-time manager for the Nursery, at least in the key peak seasons of spring and summer. Brian kept refusing, thinking that all demands could be met within the family business, now that Vanessa, aged 16 was still living at home, and Kevin aged 14 was there as well to handle peak volume. The kids were truly gifted at handling sales and customer relations, but over the years the tensions in this family business were brewing. In particular, the teenagers were objecting to the demands placed upon them by their mother, who seemed to be often demanding in her standards and controlling their lives. While Brian backed up his wife in her bossing the children around, he left almost all the power and discipline to Joyce, so that she was seen by them to be an over controlling tyrant.

Joyce came to me alone in her first interview. She described her marriage as "toxic," appropriate enough for a nurse depicting her marriage as polluted with negative toxins from which she seemingly could not escape. In fact, she felt she was "trapped" in this union. She was consumed with bitterness and anger that she had no choices in life except to follow this miserable script. My first intervention with her, after establishing trust and rapport, was to ask her to invite the entire family in for our next session so that I could better help her assess her options. She was sceptical that they would cooperate. Her husband and children had repeatedly labelled her as the crazy one who needed help, and they had refused to get involved with "her problem." I said I would call her husband directly and invite the family in on a one-time basis to get their opinions on how I could best help Joyce in her individual therapy. I explained to Joyce that I would go along with the family definition of their dilemma in order to get their cooperation to at least participate in one session. When I talked with Brian on the phone for the first time he was cooperative but adamant that there would only be one family session, as the rest of the family was too busy and scheduled to participate any further. I agreed to see the parents and the teenagers in one family session the following week. This session merely confirmed the coalition of father and the teenagers against Joyce. Although they all were stressed with their busy lives, schedules, work and school demands, and the strain of running the family gardening centre business, they still managed to maintain their balance and sanity, and there was a bond of caring among all of them. Still, everyone's anger at Joyce's over control was unmistakable. Furthermore, when we talked about the possibility of others shouldering some of Joyce's responsibilities, they all claimed to be too busy in their own lives to do anything more to help the mother of this busy family. It seemed there was no wiggle room for solutions to the family stuckness, defined as mother being bossy, demanding, and angry.

In her next individual session, Joyce felt vindicated that the family session had validated her sense of being hopelessly trapped in a toxic marriage. While offering empathy and emotional support, I said I could not completely agree that she was hopelessly trapped. I pointed out the resources available to women in abusive relationships. There are many shelters for women and children for temporary housing while they work out arrangements to separate from their marriages. Of course, although Joyce was very unhappy and frustrated, her marriage could not really be called abusive. Nevertheless, she could muster many community resources if she wanted to end the relationship. After considering her options carefully, her cloud of anger and resentment lifted. Joyce reframed her situation. She was no longer trapped or imprisoned by the marriage. She chose to remain in her relationship until her son turned 15 years old, about a year from now. Establishing this plan for delayed action gave her a greater sense of security and empowerment. Now we were free to consider the preliminary steps of preparation for her exit path.

Changing an entire family system using individual therapy is not an easy task. Usually the best place to begin is one small change. It needs to be focused at a point of minimal resistance, and have enough impact that it can become a "difference that makes a difference," shifting the goalposts of the system. The change must be more than a random fluctuation that merely slides back to its former level after a few weeks.

Continuing this theme of minimal but significant change, Joyce decided that it was time for everyone in the family to do their own washing and ironing. The teenagers were old enough that they should learn how to master these skills, and Brian could resume the self-maintenance he was doing before they got married. She wrote an email each to Brian, Vanessa, and Kevin telling them that, effective that

Wednesday forward, she would be handling laundry only for the family towels and bed-sheets and her own personal clothes, no exceptions. The emails and their time signatures would later come in handy, as in the coming weeks Brian and the children began to wear stale and wrinkled clothes. They assumed they would exhaust mother's patience until she could stand it no more and would revert to doing all the family laundry. Joyce stood by her resolve, and within weeks Brian and the kids picked up the slack and did their own laundry. Whenever they would protest or plead with her to press a shirt before an important event, Joyce would patiently show them a copy of her email, then go peacefully to a different part of the house to start or resume another activity.

Over the coming weeks and months, Joyce attended bi-weekly sessions, as she gradually but firmly and unilaterally relinquished other household duties and responsibilities, in each case giving advance notice. While she was "going on strike" by refusing to handle all the household chores, she was more than willing to do one quarter of the work involved in any common area, provided Brian and the children upheld their end. If they slacked off, Joyce would go totally on strike until Brian and the children restored the family schedules to normal, with Brian in charge of discipline of the teenagers to make it happen. There were several showdown situations in which a minor family crisis occurred, such as no family dinner one night because someone neglected to shop for groceries that week. The family came to understand that mother was going to hold firm on her responsibilities but was relinquishing control over the executive functions of the family.

These steady changes shifted the family dynamics considerably. Brian was no longer seen by all as the gentle, soft, and kind figure he had been. He now had to make schedules and assure they were adhered to. Vanessa and Kevin no longer liked their father as they had before, but they respected him because he was fair and firm. Brian was more burdened, but actually liked this new role in the family, where he could exercise organization and respect in a manner similar to his effectiveness at work. Joyce also enjoyed this shift. In place of her former anger and resentment, she took secret delight in her husband and children's discomfort and accountability. As she abandoned each area of sole responsibility, she ceased nagging and shrugged her shoulders instead, letting the consequences fall where they may. All family members displayed far more mutual respect and cooperation. They still were a time-stressed family, but the dynamics of anger, resentment, and coalitions were now greatly diminished, and at times, notably absent. Vanessa and Kevin came to develop more respect and affection for their mother. While Brian was installed in the role of chief executive of the family, he listened carefully to the input of his wife in making decisions, allocations, and fair consequences. Brian and Joyce had a greater feeling of presence, communication, and teamwork than they had experienced for many years. In her monthly sessions, Joyce announced that her marriage was no longer "toxic" but merely "sterile."

Still there remained the issue of how to deal with the greenhouse, plant nursery, and garden equipment business. By now, six months had elapsed since Joyce's first therapy session. In January, two months earlier, Joyce had written the edict to all family members that, effective March 1, she would no longer have anything to do with business. She would no longer do administration or sales or even answer the door or calls of customers and suppliers. As she had in previous years, she strongly advised Brian to hire a manager to ensure that key executive decisions would be made and operationalized in a timely manner. By now it was March 15, and still Brian was procrastinating and not dealing with hiring decisions.

Then one night it happened. It was a cold night in late March, below freezing. All the spring inventory was in the greenhouse awaiting displays, merchandising, and pricing. Joyce momentarily wondered, "Did Brian check to make sure the greenhouse heating system was on and fully functional?" That question, and the prompt and warnings and scoldings that usually followed, were the duty and script of the old Joyce. For a moment she was tempted to revert to form; then she just let that impulse go. She said nothing and went to sleep. The predicted outcome happened. The next morning, a panic-struck Brian came screaming into the family kitchen to announce that almost all of their inventory was frozen. Lost. Ruined. He looked at the rest of the family eating breakfast. They exchanged looks of shock and bewilderment, all fumbling to give father consolation at his moment of dismay. Everyone had the courtesy of not telling father "I told you so." They all supported him in calling the insurance broker. Later that day, they found out that the insurance would only partially reclaim the loss, as human error and neglect was at least partly to blame. They would subsidize a partial payment, but the net loss to the business would be approximately $14,000 after expenses. Still, in order to salvage the business year, Brian would have to pay out-of-pocket to restore the inventory. He would also need to hire a manager ASAP to supervise these purchases, merchandising, and staffing in the coming months. Within two weeks he hired a manager, a local person with considerable business experience. After a great deal of hard work and anguish, he managed to finish the peak season with only a minor operating loss to the business. Vanessa and Kevin occasionally worked retail shifts at peak volume, as did Joyce, whenever it suited her schedule. She was still working shifts as a nurse in the community hospital and enjoying her vital professional life. As well she was returning to an active social and fitness lifestyle while still driving her children to most of their activities, car-pooling with other parents. While the family remained very busy and almost frantic with time stresses that spring, they had a little more time and energy for each other as the greenhouse manager and his staff took over that business. They even went on a family vacation in August, the first in many years. It would likely be their last vacation together for a while as the teenagers were increasingly branching out in their lives with their friends. It was a lovely two weeks together. That autumn, Brian began a strange practice of courting Joyce, taking her out on dinner and dancing dates in Calgary and the surrounding communities. Date night became installed as a weekly ritual that remained intact as of our six-month follow-up session. Joyce now described her marriage as "fertile in the romantic sense." In our follow-up phone conversation a year later, the family had decided to fold the greenhouse-nursery business, selling most assets at a modest profit to another community family. In all, every member of the family was thriving, and they all were happier than they had been in years.

When I look back on this case, it changed my outlook. Even now, I am not daunted when a family member or significant members refuse to take part. I am confident that significant and enduring change can happen in a family by working in individual therapy with a motivated key member of that family system. What a pleasant story that has replicated many times in my career, and I am sure for many other therapists and families as well.

CHAPTER 15

A Terrible Session

AS I LOOK BACK on a career in psychotherapy, I suppose there have been quite a few marital sessions that were terrible for me and the couple involved. These were primarily where couples were verbally abusive and either one party or both were more interested in character assassination than saving the marriage or finding a graceful exit from it. In those sessions, even when I tried to retrieve the prospect that these warring partners could learn and use guidelines that could save their children from collateral damage, their amygdales were so thoroughly engaged that a circus lion tamer with a whip could not disentangle their death spiral. These couples were essentially using me and their lawyers as pall-bearers of a funeral they dare not attend. "Yes, we tried marital therapy, but it didn't work." Sometimes it is more important to be right than to be happy.

Another failure scenario was again marital. In a last desperate attempt to save the marriage, wife drags emotionally avoidant husband into therapy hoping that he will engage. Despite my best attempts to join him, he will have none of it. Therapy is icky, and therapists are emotional saps that want men to be more like women and talk about feelings, worse still, in front of a man. What a scenario for dishonour to machismo. Any man with adequate testosterone would never fall into that trap. And so the couple leaves, and my office is left with the energy debris of failure. Thankfully these sessions are rare, but they sure have an effect on the therapist, shocked and temporarily wondering, how could I have salvaged this situation? Yes, some marital sessions are doomed to failure despite what the therapist does, but let me tell you a story about a really terrible session.

This was the third session of a family who had a 15-year-old daughter who was under the influence of bulimia nervosa. Carrie had all the usual symptoms and had been impervious to three other therapies. This was her first attempt at family therapy. She was rather aloof and uncommunicative, as some 15-year-old females are wont to do. Her parents were eager to help in whatever way they could. However, they were at a loss as to how they could support their daughter's recovery without inadvertently enabling the bulimia by ignoring it or trying to overcontrol it. These are standard dilemmas for eating-disordered families.

What made this session different was the behaviour of their 9-year-old hyperactive son. From the start of the session, Jason was disruptive. He was fidgeting, moving around the office, lifting and moving and threatening to destroy some delicate native art objects that decorate my office. I asked his parents to intervene to call Jason to order, as his racing around the room was disrupting any communication patterns we were trying to develop to help his family deal with his sister's affliction. They tried their usual patterns, scolding, advising, threatening, and then begging Jason to PLEASE SETTLE DOWN! Nothing worked. Jason became more hyperactive, claiming he was bored with this silly family session, and wanted to go home to his computer games. In the interest of our family therapy session, I asked the parents to take charge to remove Jason or time him out in a supervised restraint of his out-of-control behaviour. It turns out they had never restrained Jason in this way. Their body language showed that they were physically frightened to restrain this relatively small child from threatening their family equilibrium.

After asking them to intervene, and seeing their nervous eyes, I made a bold move. I asked them if I could have their permission to deal with Jason's behaviour by enforcing a time-out myself. They were at first bewildered but gave in to my plan to enforce a time-out on their son.

I excused the family into the waiting room while I escorted Jason back into the therapy room. I told him he would be in time-out for nine minutes plus a half-minute for every attempt to escape time-out. I pointed out a large upholstered chair where he could sit. He immediately bolted for the door. Anticipating this move, I caught him by the arm and directed him firmly back down in the chair. This time he tried more strongly to escape. I caught both his arms and wrapped them crossed in front of his chest, with me holding each wrist. I sat down in the chair, holding Jason so that he was sitting on my lap, all 80 lbs of him. He was thrashing wildly, but I locked my legs around his ankles, preventing him from kicking me. He could not bite me because my hands were holding his wrists under his armpits. Jason went on thrashing and yelling obscenities beyond his years for about ten minutes. After cursing me out with every expletive he could think of, he then proceeded to tell me I was the worst therapist in the world and that his sister would never get better with this f(***)ing therapy. After several minutes of his struggling and thrashing in this manner, I could tell he was starting to tire. All the while I remained quiet and calm, using only enough muscle to prevent him from escaping. He tried to bargain with me, apologizing for his behaviour and promising to not disrupt the therapy session if only I would let go of him immediately. I remained quiet. Jason broke into loud sobs of despair. I matched his broken breathing, gradually slowing our pace as he fatigued and remained still.

As I was holding him, I just felt a sense of sadness and compassion for this poor kid under the influence of this tantrum.

To me it felt like a neurological storm which neither he nor his family could control. We just needed to contain it and ride it out. The whole episode took probably 20 minutes, but it seemed like an eternity. Meanwhile I could hear the rest of the family talking calmly in the waiting room, as if they had forgotten about us and our drama. Breaking my silence, I asked Jason if he was ready to cooperate with family therapy rather than disrupting it. He quietly nodded. I released my grip and let him resume his usual seat across the room. I invited the family back in to debrief our experience and theirs. At first, when Jason had been screaming and struggling, they had the urge to break in and rescue their son from his imprisonment, but they decided to let it play out. His sister was also concerned but settled down when she heard Jason's protests fading. The family then began talking about mundane topics like school, work, and weekend activities. They asked Jason what it was like to be forcibly restrained during a tantrum. He said, "At first I was up against this mean jerk, but he held firm; after a while I could not overpower or outsmart him, so I gave up. I was very tired, so I had to relax and settle down."

I apologized for my being so distracted that I could not deal with the family's presenting problem. Correspondingly, the family apologized for the disruptive behaviour of Jason, now perhaps an even greater undeclared problem than their bulimic daughter. We ended in one of those awkward apologizes that is a therapist's dread, the moment of respectful disconnection. The clients came without resolution of their presenting problem and feeling ambivalent about proceeding further. The parents said they had a lot to think about, and they would get back to me in a few weeks to tell me what they would decide to do going forward; their bulimic daughter did not render an opinion either way about should happen, nor did Jason. Several weeks elapsed with no contact. Then came the rush and distraction of Christmas holidays.

By this time I had assumed the worst: that no change had happened and the family was still disinterested in engaging in therapy after their experience of this terrible session. Finally, in early February, the father of the family called me to announce that no further therapy was necessary. After our session, he reported, everything suddenly changed in the family. Jason had learned the valuable lesson of the need to time himself out when he was overwhelmed with the urge to disrupt others. He regularly took time-outs from family activities, but with their permission, and not getting into mischief or other attention-seeking behaviours. Given their success at home, his parents and Jason approached his teachers about making a similar arrangement in his classroom. Given that Jason had a history of class disruptions and defiant behaviours, it was easy to convince his teachers to give it a try. After a month of this success, the parents decided that prescribing Ritalin was not needed. Meanwhile his sister Carrie had decided on her own that she would stop bingeing and purging. She was apparently impressed that Jason could turn a corner with his problem, so she was not about to be upstaged by her little brother. Nobody fully knew why, but Carrie stopped her bulimia about a week after our session, shortly after she saw Jason time himself out for the third time, and realized he was serious about getting better. On behalf of the family, father thanked me for showing them a way out of their exasperation of dealing with their children's problems.

At this point I can only guess what allowed this terrible session to be turning point for the family. Sometimes in families, it seems that as soon as one problem is solved, another pops up. It is as if the family system needs to organize around problems to keep them together. However, there are many situations in seemingly chaotic cases where the family settles down after the resolution of a major stressing problem. It then becomes easier to untangle the remaining dysfunctional knots. The therapist has a strong role to play in modelling how to instill hope, establish order, and demonstrate efficacy through an effective intervention. Luckily, these factors played out well in this interview.

I think one other key element worth noting was that when order was established, other more human emotions emerged in the temporary bond between Jason and me. I felt genuine empathy and caring. He felt the safety and compassion I extended. He felt that someone finally understood that basically he was a good kid who sometimes got under the influence of a storm of bad behaviour. I'm sure his parents had felt that way as well, but in moments that seemed chaotic and unsafe, they sometimes felt helpless to render the support that Jason needed at those crucial times. Finally, I share their admiration for a child who figured out how to generate his own safety net at those times, so that no one in future had to restrain him forcibly. What a family! What a case! What a terrible session! What a lesson.

CHAPTER 16

LOSING HER TEETH

JENNIFER, A 28-YEAR-OLD married homemaker and mother of a 2-year-old son, was currently being fitted for dentures. Her chronic and severe bulimia had progressed to the extent that stomach acids from purging had rotted her teeth. It was amazing and disheartening to interview this physically beautiful but mentally tormented woman. She had most of the symptomatic patterns associated with bulimia: weight and beauty preoccupation, perfectionist striving, black-white thinking, anxiety, and unstoppable daily bingeing and purging episodes whenever she had any time relief from caring for her son. Although she was motivated and cooperative, nothing seemed to be effective in diminishing her bulimia.

In conjoint sessions, I also enlisted the support of her husband, Brad, and her parents that lived nearby. After some preliminary reduction of her purging, nothing seemed to last very long. Her husband was patient but becoming increasingly frustrated. He knew she had an eating disorder during their year-long dating, but hoped that it would gradually improve during the course of their five-year marriage. In fact, it had become more severe and chronic, apart from some reduction during the course of her pregnancy and immediately after her son's birth. In our conjoint sessions, I noticed that Jennifer was cheery and deferential toward her husband Brad, although at one point she said that she was repeatedly annoyed that Brad typically left things around the house for her to clean up. Worse still, their son Adam was now doing the same. Brad sheepishly admitted that messiness had always been his problem, but that he just repeatedly forgets to put clothes and other household objects in their proper place. Despite her objections and reminders, nothing had shifted in this problem pattern throughout their marriage. The few arguments they did have seemed to center around his exasperation with her bulimia and her resentment of having to clean up after Brad. Could there be a connection between these two unsolvable problems? Would Brad be willing to solve his problem as an inspiration for Jennifer to solve hers? He agreed that he certainly would cooperate with a plan to get him to be more neat and organized.

Parents of toddlers usually have an ample supply of disposable diapers, unless they are more environmentally conscious and use cloth diapers. This family was the former, so of course they would often have a large cardboard box, called the Pampers Box (after a brand name of disposable they used) around somewhere in the household. Also, in their three-bedroom duplex was a back deck. I asked them to put out the empty Pampers Box on the deck, exposed to winter weather.

Any household article that was out of place for more than a half-hour after it was last used was to be put in the Box on the deck. Either parent could put it there. If stuff was missing in their duplex, they could go out in the snow on the back deck and retrieve the missing item. Although the thought of this idea seemed mildly inconvenient, the couple hardly knew how profound the result would be when the program was enacted. In the first week, Brad left his suit jacket on the chesterfield. During a commercial break from his NFL game, when Brad was away from the TV, Jen quietly removed the jacket and put it in the Box. During the next evening, the couple had bowls of spaghetti. Jen removed her bowl and put it in the dishwasher. Brad left his bowl, cutlery, and glass on the dining room table. About an hour later, Jennifer quietly took his dirty dishes and casually overturned the bowl on to his suit in the Box. She did this quietly and covertly, taking sadistic delight in the mischief she was perpetrating. During the next week Brad was searching for the jacket for his blue suit, asking Jen to help him find it. She asked him to check the Pampers Box; perhaps it was there. Brad rummaged around under several layers of clothes and articles, finding the suit jacket stained with spaghetti sauce. Seriously annoyed and caught out, Brad wore a different suit that day and took his blue suit jacket to the cleaners. These kinds of encounters occurred occasionally that week, with Brad unable to complain because, after all, it was he who set up his own demise by being sloppy and neglectful.

In their next session at the beginning of the following week, Jen reported being more cheerful than she had been for months. Moreover, curiously enough, her urge to binge and purge had mysteriously vanished! The couple were quite puzzled but somewhat pleased that both these problem patterns were reducing. Now they decided in the coming two weeks they would try a smaller cardboard box, as Brad hardly ever left items out of place. Our follow-up session three weeks later revealed that Jen had continued to be free of her bulimia. There were very few items needing retrieval from the back deck box. However, there was one incident where Brad was almost late for work because he couldn't find his car keys anywhere. Finally, in desperation, he checked the Box under some clothes there, muttered something incoherent, and went off to work in a huff. By dinner that day all was well. In monthly follow-ups there were no further incidents of bulimia or misplaced items. Even their son Adam was now in the habit of putting his toys back in his toy box area after using them. It is quite predictable that children in a family will follow the modelling of their parents' behavior, so I was not surprised but shared their pleasure in this unexpected bonus.

Was this simultaneous resolution of their problem patterns merely coincidental? Was repressed and displaced anger at the core of Jen's bulimia? I don't know. Jen and Brad said they didn't know, nor did they care. They were just happy to put that phase behind them and resume a happier life together as a couple and family. It still remains a mystery, but a pleasant one.

CHAPTER 17

A Fast Way to Build A Support Network

IF YOU NEED TO MAKE a fairly radical change in your compulsions or build new habits, it really helps to have a social support network to contact at times of temptation to overcome trigger situations. That is, you negotiate with family and friends to help you overcome your problem or condition. We know from research that in trigger situations, you can likely overcome the peak of an impulse by doing something else for at least twenty minutes. The substitute activity can be phoning and/or texting the people on your list. Most of them will not be available to answer at that very moment you call, but some will. Talking with them and hearing their encouragement helps you stay focused on your recovery and going beyond that momentary impulse to relapse. Even the act of leaving a voice message to ask them to return your call reaffirms your mutual commitment to accountability in your recovery. You are less likely to cave in when you know you will soon be dealing with your friend's return call. A support network is especially vital in overcoming compulsions, impulse control disorders, and even more so, with addictions. You can overcome these disorders without a support network, but the job is much harder, and for some, impossible.

Many people are somewhat reluctant to set up a support network for several reasons. The first one is the myth of independence. This barrier is much more prevalent in men than women, and in addictions more than other compulsions. They say to themselves, "I'm fine, my life is fine, I just have this little problem that I have to solve. It's nothing, really." Such people believe that they should be able to overcome their problems without leaning on the help of others. They don't need a "crutch." They fancy themselves as independent people and resist any potential evidence to the contrary. A second related factor is the element of shame. They do not want others to know they have a problem or "weakness." They fear embarrassment and potential loss of social status, ridicule, or even possible rejection. Of course, most of these catastrophic outcomes never happen; they are merely projections of our clients' worst horrors. We often have to help them through these barriers by a process of de-catastrophizing them, walking them through facing their worst scenarios with our support.

The third barrier to establishing a support network is the crucial step of commitment and accountability. It is one thing to privately stop smoking cigarettes or drinking alcohol. It is another thing to have a stop-smoking day, or a stop-drug day, and commit to friends and family that this is the day you intend to be smoke-free. If you have a support net and you fail, where can you hide? Your relapse is their front-page news, and you are deeply ashamed with their misplaced hope for your cure. No wonder people wither at the prospect of committing to engage a support system network. They are often still ambivalent about whether they want to end the problem compulsion. At this point, the therapist needs to reset with motivational interviewing, preparing the groundwork for change.

But let's come back to the forth element of resistance to generating a support network. That is, our client does not want to be "a burden" on her friends. This position is a minor variant of the issue of shame, but it also is often associated with low self-esteem. Our client may feel that she is not worthy of the caring consideration of her friends. Perhaps she does not want to take the risk of alienating her friends by making claims on their time and support. In fact, seldom will friends or family refuse to help a person who is trying hard to overcome a problem, especially if the help needed only involves a few phone calls and brief conversations. In fact, most friends would be honoured to help.

Now that we have established the value of a support network, what about a situation in which our client has no friends in an entirely new community? This problem arose several times in treating eating-disordered clients who relocated from other cities and even provinces to Calgary to engage in psychotherapy with me. There were about ten such cases over the course of several years. They would take a leave of absence from their careers for three to six months. Upon arrival in Calgary, they would often find temporary work to support themselves while coming for outpatient sessions in the Bulimia and Anorexia Program here. Given the often-secretive nature of these disorders, sometimes it made sense for them to move away from their home communities, especially if these smaller centres lacked specialized programs and therapies geared specifically to treat eating disorders. So when these clients arrived, they knew no one that could form the base of a support network quickly. Fortunately, we had a contact sheet of volunteers who themselves were recovered eating-disordered former clients, so that was a start. Still our clientele needed to expand their circle of support, often enlisting people they had only recently met. Often they would solicit support from workmates in their new temporary jobs. Some of these clients were quite clever and bold in how they generated a support net within weeks of arrival in Calgary.

One such case was an assistant manager for a McDonald's restaurant who had transferred into a Calgary branch to receive treatment here. A standard feature of treatment is the use of a food log, sheets of paper on which you document everything you eat, time of day, place, any emotional trigger situations, etc. My client Cathy used her food logs in a highly unusual and creative way: she "accidentally" left them on top of the company copier machine. Of course, when other employees came into the copy room, they would ask around the branch "Who left these on the copier?" She would then say these sheets of paper were hers. Next would come the inevitable question, "Why are you writing down everything you eat?" She would tell that person that she is in treatment to overcome an eating disorder, and could they please help her recovery? She never had a refusal. Within her first week she had the names and numbers of twelve people she could count on to help her. Within three weeks Cathy was now virtually symptom-free. By the end of the summer, she was recovered from her case of bulimia nervosa. She returned to her regular position in a smaller Alberta city, and commuted from her hometown to Calgary for two follow-up appointments that autumn. She was still doing fine, so we mutually agreed to end her therapy.

A central curative element for Cathy was the pilgrimage she made to another city to get better. In another case, a university student from Vancouver came to Calgary for four months specifically to focus on overcoming anorexia nervosa. She also rapidly overcame her disorder. Their dedication and commitment became even more focused when they had to generate and use their support network. The public disclosure of commitment to a goal greatly amplifies the prospects for success.

CHAPTER 18

THE PARENT DE-BUGGING PROGRAM: A POSITIVE CHILD MANAGEMENT SYSTEM

OVER SEVERAL YEARS I have seen families where yelling and coercion have been overused as methods to try to get people to do what other family members believe they should do. This pattern applies between parents and their pre-teen and teenage children, but also can have as its precursor the way both parents try to manage each other's behavior.

Onset of referral to a family therapist often happens in the teenage years, with one or more children rebelling against the exasperated overcontol of one parent, often the father, with the unwitting covert support of the other parent, in a classic too tough – too lenient parental split. By the time of referral, there may have been family control struggles in which police were called to quell the domestic disturbance, but no charges were laid. A less extreme and more common example is a nag-withdraw cycle in which one or both parents nag the child into doing household chores, and the child passively avoids carrying out the assignment or misses deadlines repeatedly, sabotaging family structure and order. The child himself becomes a victim of the habit of procrastination and passive rebellion.

Many interventions have been aimed at resolving this pattern. The program suggested here is merely a variant, proposed because it often is strongly supported by the teenagers, with some curious reactions by the parents.

A. THE PARENTS MAKE A WRITTEN DOCUMENT WHICH THEY BOTH WILL PRESENT TO THE TEENAGER.

B. THIS DOCUMENT WILL STATE IN CLEAR BEHAVIORAL TERMS WHAT THEIR WEEKLY REQUIREMENTS ARE ABOUT THE TEENAGER'S DUTIES IN THE HOUSEHOLD. This would include minimum standards for the task.

C. FOR EACH DUTY SPECIFY A WEEKLY DEADLINE.

D. FOR EACH DUTY STATE A REWARD.

E. IF THE DEADLINE IS MISSED, THE CHILD IS IMMEDIATELY GROUNDED AND SUSPENDED UNTIL THAT TASK IS COMPLETED. This means that apart from school attendance and attendance at organized activities such as lessons or team practices and games, the child is denied TV, radio, telephone, cellphone, and computer games, until the task is done to minimum standards. Furthermore, the child receives NO PAYMENT for doing the task that week.

F. IF THE DEADLINE IS MET, THE CHILD RECEIVES PAYMENT CREDIT FOR THAT TASK AND FULL HOUSEHOLD PRIVILEGES.

G. IF EITHER PARENT NAGS, PROMPTS, OR "REMINDS" THE CHILD THAT THE TASK NEEDS TO BE DONE (for example, a day before deadline) THE TEENAGER IS ALLOWED TO CHALLENGE THE PARENT "Why are you bugging me?" The parent must then provide a plausible RATIONALE (e.g., "The deadline is tomorrow, but you have hockey practice so you won't get home in time to clean your room."

If the rationale is reasonable, it is allowed. IF THE RATIONALE IS DEEMED BY PARENTS AND TEENAGER TO BE UNNECESSARY, THE PARENT MUST DO THE TASK AND FULLY PAY THE TEENAGER THE CREDIT FOR THAT TASK THAT WEEK.

Typically, what happens is the parent forgets and habitually bugs the teenager. The teenager challenges successfully, the parent has to do the task without pay while the teenager gloats, the parent fumes, and resolves to not get caught again in the nagging trap. Within 2-3 weeks the new system runs smoothly. The family therapist monitors and fine-tunes the program with the family and is brought in as an external arbiter, if necessary, on whether a parent rationale for bugging was warranted and legitimate.

In my experience, this has worked well in all families. Sometimes, in cases of ADD or ADHD, the teenager has requested one "free prompt' by the parent, and that has worked out well to everyone's satisfaction.

So that's the program! I hope you enjoy it. Your teenager will.

CHAPTER 19

HER MIDLIFE CRISIS

THE TERM "MIDLIFE CRISIS" has been used by many therapists and commentators over the last half-century. It used to be a label of a phase primarily describing men. The archetype would be a man in his late 40s or early 50s, fairly affluent, who is perhaps beginning to have doubts about his fading virility and attractiveness to women. Often he is married but dare not act out his fantasies of being with a younger woman, so he sublimates it by driving a flashy sports car. A single man might date many women that he finds attractive or wind up with a flashy "trophy wife." There are the well-worn typical stereotypes that we think of when the term "midlife crisis" is used.

However, increasingly women are the middle-aged explorers considering leaving their marriages. Sometimes the theme may involve infidelity or sexual freedom, but often the motivation may have more to do with autonomy and self-discovery. Many women are dissatisfied with their marriages and the multiple demanding roles that parenthood demands. They often have ambivalent feelings about their striving for an identity independent of their family, especially in marriages where the wife left her family of origin directly into engagement and marriage, with relatively little time living on her own. This configuration is not universal, but is frequently seen in cases where independence is the main issue. This pattern is so stereotypic that it is well-described in Michele Weiner Davis' (2001) second best-seller "The Divorce Remedy." Her Chapter Twelve is entitled "Surviving His Mid-Life Crisis," but the language is gender-neutral, such that either partner might be afflicted with a desire to leave the marriage.

Usually the leaving member of the couple is experiencing a general dissatisfaction with life in general, including home, work, spouse, and kids. Usually, when this occurs, the other spouse redoubles their efforts to soothe and reassure their partner. However, the leaving spouse's needs seem to be a moving target, and no repair effort is good enough to dispel the notion that the remaining spouse is the source of almost all of life's problems. Thankfully, Michele outlines a guide for surviving and patiently waiting through this phase in your partner, with minimal damage to your own self-esteem and living patterns. The chapter helps you realign your expectations about yourself and your partner, to secure self-help rituals and emotional support from friends and family, and to calmly but firmly assert your own needs and boundaries. Meanwhile your partner comes to terms with issues of identity, independence, attractiveness, sexuality, freedom, unfulfilled life ambitions, failure, limitations, and even, the first signs of mortality. I urge all therapists to read this book, especially if you assist couples in reassessing the viability of their marriages.

Now to my story. Tom and Marsha were in their late 40s. He was a successful geophysicist with an entrepreneurial flair, becoming the vice president of exploration in a second junior oil company after making a tidy profit selling his former company. Marsha was their homemaker in the child-rearing years, also leveraging her managerial and executive assistant skills in keeping the books for Tom's enterprises. As often happens when the teenage children are leaving home for university out-of-town, or pursuing careers elsewhere, the parenting couple might question where their lives are going, especially if they had been drifting apart in parallel lives for several previous years. Furthermore, Marsha and Tom had been finding that affection and intimacy had been increasingly displaced by bitter bickering over many topics, often trivial. Their marital communications featured defensiveness, disrespect, and dismissal of the other's needs and opinions. They often contradicted their partner's versions of who said what and how in their bitter but not explosive but corrosive arguments, frequently interrupting each other in mid-sentence. Sometimes it seemed they would rather be right than be happy, as they competed for whose reality would prevail.

Both were highly competitive in life, and especially with each other. Marsha had been a nationally ranked tennis player, leaving the sport after the birth of Janice, her younger daughter, by then aged 21. Janice was now in Halifax in her third year of university in a marine biology program. Working in co-op placements during her summers, she was now an infrequent visitor to the family, although Marsha and especially Tom missed her intensely. Carrie, age 18, was finishing grade 12 and already accepted into university. She was looking forward to living in residence in another city to escape the bickering of her parents. The house was becoming empty and the family glue was now becoming dry and brittle.

In several of our initial marital sessions, I worked first on settling down the intensity of the arguments and disrespect. I used various communication approaches, including those advocated by John Gottman (1999), such as the soft start-up, rescue attempts, and the other active listening practices. Then we shifted to more emotionally focused sessions, dreams, wishes, and passions. Marsha's great unmet ambition was to become a tennis pro at a community racquet club and run her own programs and pro shop. Tom wanted to support her with venture capital, but she flatly refused his offer. She wanted to say she made it on her own, did it her own way, and owed him nothing to claim credit for her achievements. Since she blamed him for virtually every dissatisfaction that she encountered, she wanted to be fully independent of the person that was dragging her down with his cautions about business life.

Tom really wanted her to stay in the marriage and protested that she did not have to separate to be independent; but Marsha was adamant. She wanted her own condo where she could come and go as she pleased. It did not seem that there was any ongoing affair or prospect of one. The couple had at least one extramarital fling early in their married years, but it seemed as if sex was not a hot issue for either of them in the last few years. Still it seemed at least to me that Marsha wanted to be free to date other men, or more likely, be free of all romantic relationships and commitments for at least the near future. And so the couple decided to separate, Tom reluctantly, Marsha eagerly.

Within a month after that session Marsha had secured a lease on a condo, and she agreed to accept Tom's help in terms of short-term rent and moving arrangements. The tension between them had dropped noticeably since they had agreed on this new life course. They were able to negotiate a legal separation and division of marital assets. Tom bought Marsha out of the marital home, providing her with a healthy nest-egg. Carrie remained mostly in the marital home for the remainder of finishing high school and in preparation for university. She seemed happy and relieved that the constant bickering was now over so that she could resume the life of a busy teenager. Janice was more distant but also relieved to hear that her parents were both getting on with their independent lives. About a month after moving out, Marsha was now employed as the assistant tennis pro in another racquet and fitness club closer to her new home. She was busy and happier than she had been for a long time. The couple now felt that they had no further need for separation counselling, so they stopped their work with me.

From time to time months later I would run into Tom in our community. He would tell me that he was doing okay but feeling somewhat lost and lonely. He would occasionally talk with Marsha on the telephone and hear snippets about her through their daughter's overnight visits with Marsha. I also would sometimes talk briefly with Marsha in the following year. After the initial thrill of freedom and a single life, many aspects of living were not as wonderful as she had hoped. She found that the complexity of managing her career and her personal life were also a source of tension and strain, but now she had no one to blame for her misfortunes, and no one to share her successes. As she was no longer my client, I did not probe for details in our brief conversations. Nevertheless, I got the impression that many of the men she had met and briefly dated were temporarily interesting but proved to be lacking many of Tom's somewhat boring but steady understated qualities: warmth, humor, and support. Although not a couple, they still remained friends, and Tom continued to offer chances for them to get together. They even combined occasionally for hikes in nature and the mountains, something they both enjoyed that did not involve too much talking or personal disclosure.

And so, as the years went by, Tom's quiet and steady persistence and friendliness seemed to be turning a corner for both of them. They got together for hiking and other shared interests and occasional family activities and rituals with their adult children. Marsha had by now become tired of the tedium of teaching tennis, and the emptiness of single life now became more prominent than the long-past thrill of freedom.

Some more years passed and I lost touch with each of them. I no longer even heard about what had become of Marsha after she quit her job as assistant tennis pro. I even heard some rumours that she and Tom were back together, but that was mere hearsay. As life would have it, I told a friend I was going out for a holiday to Kelowna, British Columbia. He mentioned that Tom and Marsha had remarried and were now retired and living there. I got some contact information, called them up, and arranged to meet them for lunch. In that nice visit, I learned the missing chapters in their story. They rekindled their friendship after Marsha had lost her edge of bitterness and blame, and mellowed with the realities that a shared life was more fun and more deeply satisfying than she had ever imagined in years. Gradually their relationship deepened and became more affectionate and loving. They discovered that their mutual care for each other had always been there, even when obscured by the storms of their bickering, the roaring tides of menopause, and the loneliness during their years apart.

This story is by no means unique. There are many other couples who go through the tumultuous years of a mid-life crisis. One partner or sometimes both partners want to explore other life possibilities and even other partners only to discover that the grass always was greener at home. And so, after several years, they return to each other. However, their original marriage had died. They grieved it separately, came to new growth and understandings about themselves and life, and rediscovered their newly transformed selves and their partners. In these stories, and I have witnessed quite a few, the couple forms a new, warmer, wiser, and more respectful relationship. Knowing that there are many more frequent possible outcomes to separation and divorce, including those in which the participants move on to find new and separate lives, these stories of transformed reunion are also warming to remember. It is a privilege of our profession to observe and facilitate these transitions and transformations.

CHAPTER 20

SHE WAS DEPRESSED, AND HE DRANK WAY TOO MUCH

MIKE AND DEBBIE were a couple in their late thirties with two school age children. Mike drank way too much alcohol and Debbie was depressed with Mike's drinking. Mike drank to escape from Debbie's depression. That was their formulation in their first session of name-calling and mutual blame. By now they had built up years of resentment and disrespect for each other. It was a wonder they were still functional in raising their children, which they both loved. They kept on their best behaviour and coordination in looking after the children, but it was hard for them to maintain their emotional discipline and not break out into mutual blame arguments in front of the kids. They did okay, but both retreated into their silent realms of loneliness and resentment after the children were put to bed.

Mike was highly functional in his career as an engineer in an oil company in downtown Calgary, Alberta. Although he worked long and hard, Mike prided himself as a provider for the family. If you do not know Calgary culture, it can often feature traditional roles and family values typical of 1950s America. Accordingly, Debbie was your archetype stay-at-home mom, dedicated to her kids and her household but drowning in the anonymity of her support role and lack of social significance. She had accepted her sealed fate passively since the birth of her youngest, now five. She was unhappy and unfulfilled in her role as homemaker. Mike had long since suggested she resume her administrative assistant career, to give her social and career stimulation now that the kids were in school. Instead, Debbie collapsed into inactivity and self-neglect, barely able to look after her own hygiene and basic maintenance of the household and daily childcare.

A typical day would involve Mike commuting away at 6:00 am from their beautiful over-leveraged acreage in the rural suburbs, Debbie getting the children ready for bussing to their school. Debbie tried to get motivated to work out with neighbourhood mothers but just could not muster the energy. Dinnertime would arrive, with Debbie throwing together a hastily contrived meal to satisfy her children's taste for junk food. Mike would then arrive home at 6:00 pm. Mike would start drinking lightly for the evening meal. The children might watch TV and procrastinate about their light homework before finally getting down to it. Then came the bedtime rituals and stories for the kids. Mike would reload on alcohol and catch up on his emails and Debbie would watch TV, and another day would go by, loneliness and resentment quietly but poisonously building. Weekends were mildly better with family activities and contact with neighbours and other parent friends and sleepovers. This banal script had repeated itself over and over again, over the years and the couple was now weary of it. It might have been tolerable except for Mike's distain for his wife's "laziness and neglect of herself and the household." Debbie retaliated that Mike only cared about his work and his booze and that their marriage was in ruins. What a mess! It has been estimated, I forget the reference, that the average couple does not seek marital counselling until six years after the trouble in their relationship began. This marriage was indeed in trouble. Furthermore, Debbie refused to seek any medication help for her considerable depression, nor did Mike acknowledge a willingness to consider his addiction to alcohol a focus of therapy.

In addition to the usual guidelines that marital therapists provide about physical and emotional safety, and rules for conduct during the therapy so that crises are pre-empted, the first job of a marital therapist is to somehow instill hope for the outcome of what could be an arduous process for all.

Continuance of the marriage is not assured, but at least the couple can be assured they will find greater clarity in their search for the ultimate answer: is this marriage viable? My approach to this couple was simple and small. Could I find one or two simple interventions that might start their movement toward each other? I was looking for anchors of security in a sea of chaos. I knew that they were workable, at least as co-parents of their lovely children, so I started to tell a story. It is not my own, and I do not know from where it arose, but I told them:

"Imagine that there has been a terrible flood, such that all land has been inundated with sea water. As the lone survivor, all you have left are your lifeboat and enough water and basic provisions to last several weeks. Day after day, all you can see is the ocean, stretching relentlessly towards every horizon, no land in sight. After almost two weeks of this bleak existence, suddenly you awaken to see an island in the distance. Eagerly you row your lifeboat towards the island. When you get off on shore, you are delighted to find that a few herbs had survived the flood. Also, there are some springs providing fresh water. After several days on this island, one morning you notice that another island has emerged in the distance. You get into your lifeboat and row toward the second island. On this island you discover that there are pineapples, scrub trees, and more varieties of vegetation. After spending close to a week on this second island, one day you see a third island. Like before, you row your lifeboat over to explore this new island that has even more lush vegetation than the other two islands. As you look across the sea to the first islands, you realize that they are, in fact, now connected by a strip of land. Now, as the days go by, you begin to see land all around as the flood waters recede further. Now the land is almost all connected, with some remaining areas of sea shrinking gradually. And so, with solution-oriented therapy, we begin by finding islands of security in a sea of chaos."

This is one of my common motivating metaphor stories for clients who are currently feeling overwhelmed, flooded, and hopeless to change their situation after repeated failures. In solution-oriented therapy, it features a "path out of the forest of failure" with small but manageable stepping stones. We start with questions like "Are there any times or situations where the problem does not exist?" Then we begin the process of management-by-exception, gradually increasing the scope of the area in which the problem does not occur and shrinking the zone of its influence in our client's life. In Mike's case, I knew he does not drink in a work context, nor does he drink a lot when life is orderly and organized, but he grimly copes when life is chaos and retreats into an alcoholic fog of entitlement.

In Debbie's case, it was hard to imagine her escape from Mike's derision. Even when he did not verbally criticize her, his derision had thoroughly contaminated her self-esteem and led her to the depressive mantra of "what's the use of trying." Perhaps this cascade of internal discounting could not be abated, but maybe if Mike made a decisive shift, she could surface from the debris of the marriage and her depression. For me and them it was worth a try.

I asked the couple about their reactions to this motivating metaphor. Their comments matched what I had noticed in their body language while I told the story. Mike was looking forward to any change that could move the couple forward out of its misery. Debbie was more subdued and sceptical but really wanted to save the family and the marriage. When I asked them to propose small but significant changes that could make a difference, they reverted to blaming each other for previous attempts that had led to disappointments and failures. After a few minutes of observing this enactment of how they undermine initiative with blame and despair, I stopped that train of communication with a proposal to them:

> In the coming week, I asked Mike to refrain from criticizing Debbie about her shortcomings. Furthermore, he was tasked to compliment Debbie on at least three things she did that day, no matter how small. He found that assignment almost impossible to contemplate, and Debbie rolled her eyes with a look that said: "This won't last a day!" I asked them both to reserve expressions of their contempt for the duration of the week, allowing Debbie her first island of peace from Mike's usual sarcastic put-downs. Then came my assignment for Mike's island. The couple were to designate an area of the house that would remain clean and uncluttered. The children were to keep their toys and clothes away from this area, regardless of how untidy and chaotic the rest of the house looked. Mike could go to this area to retreat from disorder and his feeling of distress and despair.

A week later the couple were more relaxed and optimistic. Mike followed through with his assignment, with no violations. He complained it was a huge effort, but the results were significant. Debbie now was looking after her badly neglected personal hygiene by showering, brushing her teeth, brushing her hair, getting dressed daily out of her pyjamas, and even taking on some light housework and cooking two meals. Her severe cloud of depression had lifted, and she was no longer feeling so overwhelmed by life. Beyond their normal cooperation in parenting, which remained at a high level, Debbie felt more like Mike was a contributing partner. She noticed how much more attentive and helpful he seemed to be. Although he still did the majority of the meals and household tasks, Debbie took more notice of his help in the household. Most noteworthy of all, Mike had sharply curtailed his use of alcohol, limiting his consumption to one or two beers per day on the weekend. While they were both enthusiastic about the lift from the oppressive atmosphere of their family, they found it hard to resist reverting back to the blaming game about why the positive change happened. Was Debbie's lift from depression because Mike finally curtailed his drinking, or was Mike's reduction of drinking because there was more order and peace in at least part of the household? Again I had to intervene to stop this death spiral of attribution. I encouraged them to focus instead on moving forward rather than drowning in the tsunami of past earthquakes. I asked them about how they could carry the positive momentum forward. Interestingly, Debbie wanted to establish her own area of organization in the household. She wanted a desk area of her own that would be clutter-free and organized. Mike agreed and said he would continue his muzzling criticism and continuing with compliments. He commented that he was now finding it easier to note Debbie's positive changes because they were continuing to be more sincere and appreciative as he watched Debbie restored to the wife he loved and cherished. Still the couple were worried that this week was merely an illusion, a honeymoon phase that would collapse back into the misery of the past.

Next week the couple returned with another report of success. Debbie was becoming more energized and optimistic. Mike's drinking alcohol was now stabilized again at a light moderate level satisfactory to both. An interesting development was that now each of their children wanted to have their own uncluttered territory in the house. They wanted to have their own toyboxes and even agreed to return each toy to their own toybox before taking out another toy to play with. The parents could hardly believe that their unruly and boisterous children could actually request such an arrangement and abide with it, but they followed through, as did their children.

By week five the couple continued with their program, and the children cooperated by cleaning up after themselves and putting their toys away as promised. The parents could hardly believe it. Even the whole family pitched in so that the common areas were less cluttered and more organized, not perfect, mind you, just significantly better. After congratulating the couple on their great success, I recommended no further improvements, other than the usual guidelines recommended by Dr. John Gottman and his associates. These are well-documented elsewhere but make for good marital therapy and relapse prevention strategies. They include such techniques as soft start-ups, five to one ratio of compliments to corrections, the five magic hours per week that the couple invests in their marriage, the use of a list of rescue attempts when couple communication breaks down, and avoidance of intimidation, disgust, disrespect, stonewalling, and defensiveness in talking with our spouse. As you probably have detected, I had already integrated many of these themes in previous sessions as well.

However, in this case the almost fairy-tale results were outstanding. The couple never dropped back to their former misery. Their habits of mutual support and teamwork consolidated to become a new way of being for the couple and the entire family. I believe that starting with small stepping stones that were achievable, with the scaffolding of therapeutic support for these changes, was the crucial element that turned this case around from its hopeless beginning. Within six weeks our therapy ended. A six-month follow-up confirmed that the positive results had continued to consolidate.

CHAPTER 21

OLD DOG, NEW TRICKS

ANOTHER STORY HAD ITS ORIGINS in the small community outreach clinics our mental health team did on an almost weekly basis in southwestern Ontario. As a mostly urban professional with limited experience in small communities, I had underestimated the role of social and church organizations in not only the social fabric of the community, but also how they were vital and integral to each person's identity and social status.

At that time I was early in my career, barely in my thirties, when a 76-year-old female client presented with substantial levels of depression. She was not suicidal, and displayed few vegetative signs, but still was distressed, agitated, irritable, and highly conflicted about her situation. She asked me through desperate tears if I could "teach an old dog new tricks." I replied likely yes, if the old dog was willing to consider possibilities for new ideas and courses of action. Up to that point, I had never treated an elder, and was wondering if I was over my clinical depth, but I agreed to try helping her.

Through social skills, altruistic spirit, and diligent effort my client had over the years become a "pillar of the community" in her small-to-medium sized town. Everybody knew and admired her untiring efforts in the service of several organizations she chaired. While she was well-respected, she was becoming increasingly aware that many people were frustrated with her power and rigidity and her reluctance to delegate, even in situations where she was overwhelmed with the volume and complexity of situations she handled.

In several campaigns, it seemed as if very few people would volunteer to help, and at the last minute there were barely enough to get the job done. After years of these projects, my client was overwhelmed with cumulative fatigue, almost at the point of exhaustion, and yet she felt unable to stop running for president in these organizations.

After empathizing with her, and literally drooping in my chair with the posture of her load, I asked her about previous attempts to let go of these responsibilities. There were several, but in each case community people would cheer her on and she would again be voted into these positions by overwhelming acclamation. She was not motivated by power as much as a need to maintain high standards about the performance of each role she served and supervised.

Using my background in Zen and the Martial Arts, I told her "He who rides the tiger dare not dismount." She pondered that saying carefully. After further conversation, it emerged that the constraint that held her back was her feelings of low self-esteem and unworthiness. We did some brief therapy work to examine the origins of "unworthy" and "never good enough" messages from her childhood and family-or-origin, using Gestalt empty-chair techniques to process and resolve these script messages. I will not elaborate on these techniques, since most of you know how well they work. Here I am merely laying out the scaffolding of the design of therapy, not the crucial welds that enable its effectiveness.

The main constraint that held my client back from changing was the fear that she would be rejected if she stopped performing. She had become a human-doing rather than a human-being. I pointed out that she would never be able to discover her true worth and lovability unless she cast off the cloak of her roles and social utility to the community. In her fear scenario, she would walk around the houses of her town in the early evening. Rather than being welcomed where she went, almost none of her neighbours or town folk would invite her up on their front porches to chat. In her darkest fears, she would be discarded, scorned, shunned or ignored, rather than the feigned and mildly uncomfortable social chatter she now encountered. We talked further about how to manage her expectations. We predicted together that there would be people that would ignore her, but perhaps some would welcome and cherish her company and conversation. She would then be able to distinguish between true friends, versus those who merely talked with her to leverage their social position. We collaborated on the concept of social courage in testing these distinctions, using imagery and stress inoculation to deal with potential rejections and loss of relationship.

After several spaced sessions over the course of months, my client began to offer notice to several organizations that she would be retiring and not seeking re-election. In subsequent months she did, in fact, either leave these committees or act merely in an advisory capacity. After several months, the predicted results happened. She became a great deal more popular and approachable now that she had relinquished her positions of authority and was no longer an impediment for needed social change and younger leadership in the community. She went on as a kind and gentle soul and a cherished person held in high regard for her lifelong contributions.

There is no magic in this case, merely standard workmanship in the design and working of the therapeutic alliance to effect a positive life change for my client and her community. It still seemed to me a story worth telling. As a young clinician, it is easy to be intimidated and humbled when dealing with clients that are senior and seasoned in life experiences you can only imagine or know from textbooks. Nevertheless, if your empathy and compassion are strong, and your therapeutic method is sound, you can help clients who are far older than you. Coming back to this story, going forward I was never again overwhelmed with the prospect of working with elderly people, although now I am cautious about my limitations in dealing with the onset of their dementia. That will be told in future stories.

Part Four:

HYPNOTIC INTERVENTIONS

And now what many of you have been waiting for: stories that actually talk about the use of clinical hypnosis to solve a problem situation. In several instances the targets of the intervention are multiple. That is, the therapist is using hypnotic trance in one individual in a family or group. Simultaneously, the therapist is working with others to reshape their own orientation to their own problems as well as their relationship to the symptom-bearer. These were rather complex interventions.

CHAPTER 22

THE MAN IN THE BLACK COAT

WITH A FAMILY in the chaos of multiple and cascading crises, drowning in despair, it is often best to start with a solvable problem. This problem may seem minor and by no means the core issue. The narrowness of its scope of influence may render it more accessible to change. If this peripheral problem can be solved, the therapy itself gains momentum through credibility and effectiveness. With hope reinstalled, the family can now tackle more core problems with greater resolve and energy.

A metaphor I use for this process is tangled fishing line. Suppose you are fishing and your line becomes tangled in multiple knots, a huge mess. In spin-fishing, we call this "throwing a loop." Suppose further that you do not have a spare reel or spare line. This tangled line is all you have to work with, so you begin the tedious task of working out the knots. You could go directly to loosening the core knot, but you would soon find that this process is futile, because you need to separate all the loops, and once straightened, rewind that line on to the reel with proper tension. You must begin at the periphery, carefully teasing out those knots and loops first. Those ones are easier to see and pull apart. Eventually the whole mess becomes simplified, and finally the core knot can be resolved. Family therapy does not have to go that way. Sometimes if you can resolve the core issue, the others resolve themselves. However, in severe and complex cases, starting with a solvable problem is often the best way to go. One prominent example of this principle was a multi-problem family.

Over 20 years ago, I was a clinical supervisor in a mental health services clinic associated with a community hospital in Calgary, Alberta. On Tuesday mornings, the entire multidisciplinary team of a dozen clinicians would observe the live screening of a difficult case for team consultation. On this particular morning, we were observing a large family that was being transferred to our clinic by a local children's hospital who found they were unable to help the family. The multiple problems of this family were complex and chronic. There had been 17 previous therapies, all with little success. Perhaps with a fresh approach our team might do better, but it felt to most of us that this case was dumped on our laps because the other hospital was fed up with trying to help this family.

Andre, a 38-year old janitor of a high school, seemed to be sincere and caring, but helpless in knowing what to do beyond his role of sole financial provider. Helene, his wife of the same age, was the stay-at-home mother of this large Roman Catholic French-Canadian family. There were eight children in all, mostly girls, ranging in age from 16 to 4. The teenage girls were still in school, but frequently truant and involved with street drugs and minor delinquency. Several of the middle children had learning difficulties and were behind in school. The eight-year-old Julienne was developmentally delayed. There were also some chronic respiratory problems in two other children. To make matters worse, the youngest, Celeste, had leg deformities that required several surgeries to correct, but now still walked with a mild limp. Thus there were multiple interventions from the medical system, the school system, and the legal system. A year previous there had been an investigation by child welfare following odd and sexually inappropriate self-touching by Julienne. An investigation of possible sexual abuse and incest revealed nothing, although child welfare investigators had suspicions that Andre could be a perpetrator, as he was often overly affectionate with the children and overprotective of them. Julienne had denied that she had been sexually molested by anyone and was upset at the embarrassment to the family that her self-touching had precipitated this investigation. The family was also supported by their parish church as they were among the working poor in their community.

As the team observed the family in this intake consultation interview, we too were overwhelmed by the sheer volume of 32 stated problems. Still the family seemed honest, motivated, close-knit and mutually caring for each other; even the teenage girls seemed helpful and involved, although all of them did not know what to do about their situation. I placed a call through the telephone intercom into the interview room. I wanted to know: was there any problem that had remained untreated in all their years of interventions and family therapy. Helene, the capable but over-burdened mother, said that no one had treated her persistent nightmares.

Further questioning revealed that she had persistent bad dreams, several per week, for most of her adult life, but especially in the last three years. In many of the most vivid dreams she was being stalked or pursued by a man in a black coat. Most of the settings were in the dark, so she never got to properly see his face, but glimpses seemed to show that he was white, middle-aged, dark hair, medium to large build. She did not know why he seemed to be menacing, although his inviting gestures implied the threat of a sexual attack, but it never actually happened. Either she outran him, or the dream would fade before anything bad happened, but the anxiety was terrible. In the dreams she was typically walking alone at night, and nobody was around to potentially defend or rescue her. It was important to note that there was no known or at least reported sexual abuse in Helene's past, according to the case history forwarded to us. We asked her about this in our present interview, but again she denied any previous sexual abuse, nor did she believe that any of her children had been molested. Nevertheless, she was still nervous about the future possibility of this happening, largely because of her disturbing and persistent nightmares with that theme.

When we went to the mid-interview break, the team discussed several treatment options, but none of us had much optimism that we could help the family in any significant way. However, I was curious about the nightmares, and why previous therapists had neglected to address that problem. Perhaps there were too many other real and regular crises for the family to face, that there was no time or energy left help Helene with her private hell. I ventured that perhaps, with hypnosis, the nightmares could be cured, but the rest of the team thought that this was the least of the family's problems, again to be put on the shelf of low priorities. But in the absence of any other clearly delineated plan, the team drifted back to perhaps treating the nightmares. The team looked to me, given my background skills in hypnosis, to provide the treatment. I hesitantly agreed to do so, but only in conjunction with a co-therapist who would undertake the role of case manager. After some initial reluctance, my colleague Terri Sullivan, agreed to take on the role of case manager.

This splitting of roles proved to be a wise choice. Although the family agreed with the plan, it took over three months to finally organize the members to come to a family session to plan the hypnotic treatment. Meanwhile there had been several crisis intervention interviews dealing with school truancy, medical crises, and other issues. Just trying to get the whole family together in the same room was like herding cats. Nevertheless, we finally got together for the group hypnosis planning session.

I instructed the family that their mother needed to feel in her dreams that she was not alone, that they as a group would ward off the man in the black coat and defend mother from any possible threat. The plan was that I would induce a hypnotic trance in Helene, then on cue Andre and the children would read from their scripts assuring mother that she would be safe and they would help to protect her. Then I gave each family member a paper and pencil to compose a list of ten statements of encouragement and safety that they could say to mother to reassure her that she would be safe. Of course, I had to edit them, to ensure they would have the desired effect. For example, wordings like "No one is molesting the children," would likely activate Helene's distress, so the rewording "The children are safe," was a necessary edit. The planning session was rendered more chaotic by the hyperactivity of two of the children zooming noisily but not destructively as we were trying to get the family organized for their scripts. We all took a short break, the family, my co-therapist Terri, and myself. Then we went back to begin the actual family hypnotherapy session.

For those of you who are not familiar with dual or multiple hypnotic inductions, I'll take a moment to give you a primer. Trance is any state of sustained focused awareness, where the attention is so focused that other thoughts or sensations are far in the background, almost as if they do not exist in consciousness. Hypnosis is the use of words and/or repeated actions to attain and utilize trance states. Dreams can be altered or even transformed by mental rehearsal of the dream, especially if such rehearsal is in a trance state. In trance clients can rehearse their responses to threatening situations, so that when they occur again in dreams, they will have several effective responses prepared to use to deflect the danger and transform the dream. This is almost like training for lucid dreaming, although the client does not have to fully be aware that they are in a dream for the strategy to work. Another key point to remember is that dual or multiple inductions are unusually powerful, in that they induce confusion in the listener and greater imprinting of key messages in the client's subconscious mind. Dual inductions typically begin with the primary hypnotist doing the beginning induction primarily on the left of the client, then a second hypnotist begins talking on the right side of the client. The two alternate several sentences back and forth, then both hypnotists begin simultaneously talking their individual scripts of messages to be imprinted by the client. After several minutes of simultaneous speech, gradually the prime hypnotist prevails and ends the trance session with a proper reorientation of the client back to normal waking consciousness.

In our family hypnosis session, I began by settling down the family and placing them in two semicircles, some on the right of Helene, including Andre, and some on the left. In each group there was a mixture of ages and sexes. Terri and I were seated in front of Helene. Terri's role was to help settle down all the children so they could focus on their mother. I began the trance induction with eye fixation and many holistic statements, truisms, and utilizations typical of Ericksonian hypnosis. A short time after her eyes closed, I had Helene imagine she was in her dream and awaiting the appearance of the man in the black coat. Within a minute or so, the man began approaching her in her dream image. Then, on cue, I directed that Andre read his first two messages from his list of ten. Then I cued oldest daughter, on Helene's left, to read her first two messages. Next, I directed another child to read her first two messages from her list. It was important that we used two messages, so that Helene could get the location and identify the speaker and decode the meaning of the messages. One by one, alternating in this manner, the entire family read their messages to mother in groupings of two messages per child. Finally, on cue from me, the entire family began simultaneously reading all ten messages of their scripts, repeating their lists several times. After several minutes of all voices blending, I cued them to say the messages more quietly, as I resumed talking over them, gradually silencing them as I finished off the trance and began reorienting Helene back to our interviewing room.

We asked her what her experience was like. She reported that she at first relaxed into a pleasant trance, as her eyes started to blur, and her eyelids became very heavy, and her body seemed to float in space after her eyes closed. Then in the dark grey mist The Man in the Black Coat began to emerge, but suddenly she could hear Andre's voice reassuring her that he was close nearby and would protect her. Then she heard, one by one, the voice of each child. As she felt the presence of her entire family with her, the Man in the Black Coat walked more slowly and hesitantly, seeming to diminish in size as well. In the next phase, as the family talked together gathering around her, The Man seemed frightened and turned shyly away, slowly disappearing in the mist, by now small and faint. Then she focused on my voice in the trance, saying that her family would support her and protect her in future dreams. I asked her to retrace her emotions during trance. The sequence was: anxious and unsure about a new and strange experience, relaxation and relief, apprehension about The Man in the Black Coat, surprise and warmth hearing the voices of her family, amazement when she saw The Man cower and turn away, relief then triumph, and finally, confidence. The rest of the family reported feeling it was a strange and novel experience, but once they got into the spirit of the exercise, they felt strong and helpful, and proud of being in this family supporting their mother, who always had taken care of them. Andre felt strong and confident being the father of this family and helping his wife, instead of his usual feeling of not knowing what to do.

The family and the therapists all left on a high of mutual accomplishment. I think all of us were exhausted by the high level of focus required by the task.

Of course, all of us wondered what would happen in Helene's dream experiences the following week. Owing to other problems and scheduling difficulties, we had to skip that week, but the telephone message was that Helene had no nightmares that first week after the family hypnosis session. The week after that, only Helene and Andre could make it in for their session. They reported that there was only one nightmare. Helene was disappointed that The Man had returned. However, she heard the voices of Andre and the children, and The Man in the Black Coat turned hurriedly away. Helene felt stronger and more confident than ever. I did a briefer version of our dual induction, using the voices of Andre and my co-therapist Terri to do a brief recap and reinforcement of the messages of protection and safety. The couple left feeling steady and confident. At the end of the session they also reported that the children's health had improved, and even the two teenagers had settled down more in school.

It took another month, but finally we were able to reassemble the family for another session together. By this time Helene had experienced other dreams, far more pleasant. The nightmares had vanished. She no longer felt over-burdened; her mood was far more optimistic and cheerful. The children all seemed to be functioning better. Like before, some of them still needed tutors, but these children were now paying more attention and working harder at their studies. The teenagers were now attending school regularly and no longer hanging out with the druggie crowd. In other words, the multiple problems of the family seemed to almost melt away. Although they still had their challenges, it seemed they faced them as a team, a coordinated and caring family. They always seemed to be caring, but now it seemed as if they knew how to care effectively. In order to reinforce our former work, we asked Andre and the children to get out their message scripts, and we did a re-enactment of the original family induction to face The Man in the Black Coat. This time the whole production took far less effort, and was effective, but perhaps less dramatic than our first session. After all, we were merely replicating the same process. Still, all involved felt satisfied with our session and fairly confident that the good results attained thus far would hold into the future.

That session was our last. In the six-month follow-up telephone call, we found out that the nightmares involving The Man in the Black Coat never returned. Helene seldom had bad dreams, and when she did, they were only of mild intensity and relatively easy to resolve. The family had now been functioning well with no involvement with other helping systems except tutoring for the children and some supplemental financial support from their parish. The children's health and school grades were better and stable. We closed the case successfully.With the family's permission, we had signed releases so that we could present their videotape clips at an at the annual conference of the American Association for Marriage and Family Therapy in Chicago in 1986. That session was well-received as an example of family hypnosis. I will remember this story as a difficult but rewarding piece of family hypnosis involving dual inductions. I will also savour the principle of working with a solvable problem first. But most of all, I will remember the warmth and sincere dedication of this multi-problem family pulling together as a team to go beyond their difficulties.

CHAPTER 23

Hypnosis in Symbiosis

OCCASIONALLY I USE HYPNOSIS in a family therapy context. At times it can be difficult and complex, but often it is very creative and rewarding work. In this case I was using a series of dual inductions, rotating family members as my co-therapists, utilizing their mutual co-dependency as a therapeutic asset.

Sharon was a 45-year-old accountant who came in with Cheryl, her 25-year-old severely bulimic daughter. Cheryl worked as an administrative assistant. Recently her bulimia nervosa had escalated in severity such that she vomited on almost all eating occasions. She was acutely depressed but not suicidal. Currently she was on medical leave due to the severity of her condition. Sharon had been anorexic as a teenager and young adult. Her condition improved only slightly around the time of her engagement and marriage to Paul, an engineer. Two years after their wedding, Sharon gave birth to Cheryl. She was a good but overprotective mother, and her food restriction began to get worse in Cheryl's early years. Although Sharon had been treated in hospital in her teenage years, she refused treatment now, saying she could overcome her condition by herself. After years of putting up with Sharon's rigid thinking, mood swings, food and figure obsessions, anxiety, depression, and other symptoms, Paul could not stand it any longer. Despite his caring for Sharon and Cheryl, he left them in Calgary to take a well-paying job in Toronto. The couple went through a separation and divorce when Cheryl was age eleven. Surprisingly, after Paul left Sharon realized that, as a single parent, she would have to recover from her anorexia. After a few brief sessions with a counsellor, she began eating normally and her symptoms subsided. Essentially, she made a full recovery with minimal support.

However, for many years she still remained hypervigilant about her only child, fearing that her parenting might lead to Cheryl developing similar tendencies as a teenager. Cheryl seemed to be an ordinary adolescent although overly dependent and very emotionally close with her mother. In high school Cheryl was an average student despite working very hard for her grades. She was shy and had few friends. She was often moody, depressed, and obsessed by appearance. In an effort to politely break away from her well-intentioned helicopter mother, Cheryl decided not to go on to university but instead do several business courses, enter the career world, save some money, and find her own apartment.

By the time she was twenty, Cheryl was living on her own, but her mother called her several times a day and visited many evenings a week, being so involved that it was difficult for Cheryl to find time to develop her own friendship network, despite Sharon's urging to do so. Mother and daughter were symbiotically joined in closeness but repressed resentment that neither was truly autonomous. Finally, by age twenty-two, Cheryl's well-hidden eating disorder emerged. She had been secretive about her bulimia nervosa for years, making excuses for her brief trips to the washroom shortly after eating, and wanting to spend more evenings alone with seemingly little to do in the way of activities or hobbies. Whenever Sharon would confront her daughter about her suspicions, Cheryl would find alibis and excuses, denying that anything was wrong; she was just tired from working hard, or had a stomach flu, or whatever. Finally, after more than two years of these patterns becoming more frequent and severe, Cheryl finally admitted to her mother that she was bulimic. Sharon was guilt-ridden but relieved that her daughter had finally broken through denial, deceit, and isolation. Still, Cheryl wanted to solve her problem without therapy, feeling she could do it for herself. Within several months it had now come to this: she was unable to concentrate and function properly at work and was now on medical leave. She accepted her mother's invitation to move back home for a while to work on her recovery. With her mother's urging, Cheryl reluctantly admitted she was ready to give therapy a try.

In their first session, both Sharon and Cheryl were trying very hard to be polite and respectful with each other, but the frustration in their relationship was palpable. Mother felt somewhat betrayed that daughter had been secretive about her disorder for several years, allowing it to fester and worsen. She also felt embarrassed at being naive and being duped for a while by her daughter's denials. Cheryl was embarrassed by her condition and how severe and constant it had become. Mother wanted to be as helpful as possible in promoting her daughter's recovery. Both had relatively few other friends and activities, except working out frequently at local fitness centres. Mother had heard from my former clients how I used hypnosis in helping eating disorders and was hoping we could use this approach with her daughter. Cheryl also was intrigued with the idea of hypnosis. After interviewing using the standard protocols for assessment of bulimia nervosa, I highlighted how enmeshed Sharon and Cheryl seemed to be. Cheryl was concerned that her mother seemed to be obsessed with Cheryl's eating disorder, asking endless questions and voicing worried concerns. I told them my comment about over-involvement.

Q: "How do you know you are co-dependent?" A: "When you are about to die, someone else's life flashes in front of you."

Then I proceeded to outline an interesting approach to help them help each other. We would use mother and daughter's enmeshment as a strength rather than a liability. With my help and instruction, we would do rotating dual inductions. That is, in one session I would be conducting hypnosis with Cheryl as the subject or client, with the assistance of her mother as co-therapist. In the alternate session, I would have Sharon be the subject or client, while engaging her daughter as my co-therapist. At first, they were somewhat overwhelmed with the requirement of being a co-therapist, but I reassured them that they would be more than adequate reading scripts that we would prepare in advance of the hypnosis segment of each session.

For those of you who are not familiar with dual or multiple hypnotic inductions, I'll take a moment to give you a primer. Trance is any state of sustained focused awareness, where the attention is so focused that other thoughts or sensations are far in the background, almost as if they do not exist in consciousness. Hypnosis is the use of words and/or repeated actions to attain and utilize trance states. Another key point to remember is that dual or multiple inductions are unusually powerful, in that they induce confusion in the listener and greater imprinting of key messages in the client's subconscious mind. Dual inductions typically begin with the primary hypnotist doing the beginning induction primarily on the left of the client, then a second hypnotist begins talking on the right side of the client. The two alternate several sentences back and forth, then both hypnotists begin simultaneously talking their individual scripts of messages to be imprinted by the client. After several minutes of simultaneous speech, gradually the prime hypnotist prevails and ends the trance session with a proper reorientation of the client back to normal waking consciousness.

Each session featured a dual hypnotic induction following the first part of the interview where we would talk about the key theme that had emerged for mother and daughter that week. Although we tended to alternate the roles between Sharon and Cheryl, we used some flexibility in case either of them had the primary concern for that week. Of course, we addressed the usual eating disorder themes: distorted body image, obsession with slimness and weight, identity, self-esteem, worthiness, distorted thinking patterns, black-white thinking, mindfulness, balanced nutrition, protein and blood sugar regulation, emotional regulation, communication, validating oneself and the other, tolerating differentiation and separation, appropriate boundary management, mind state management, etc.

This written description does not do justice to the beauty and care with which mother and daughter nurtured their greater sense of helping each other while growing a sense of individual identity. It was easy for each of them to come up with ten supportive and insightful statements which they would then read on cue for their part of the dual hypnosis section. As I conducted these sessions, it was like a sequence of rotating duets with two different voices and perspectives on life. It was an honour to be part of this mutual collaboration of all three of us.

Over the course of several months, Cheryl got progressively better. By week four, bingeing and purging episodes went from nearly all eating occasions to perhaps two per week. By week ten, these episodes had ceased altogether, so Sharon had gradually let go of her policewoman role in attempting to control her daughter. Of course, that ease of tension led to further affection and validation between mother and daughter and greater confidence that Cheryl could continue to get better without intense supervision. Despite Sharon's misgivings, Cheryl was able to remain stable living in her apartment. She returned to full-time work without incident. After three months she had continued to be symptom-free. Our individual sessions were now down to once per three weeks. She continued to do favourably, and all seemed well until the next crisis loomed.

Now that her daughter was in therapy and recovering, Sharon was ready to take her next step. She listed her house for sale, and she bought a condominium in Victoria, B.C., a warm and friendly community in which to retire. But this change would mean she would now be living away from her daughter, a long day's journey by car and ferry, and a one-and-a-half-hour flight. You might think that Cheryl would be happy for her mother. Although she was excited for her mother, the thought of separation haunted her day and night. She became deeply depressed, almost suicidal, again retreated from work and back to her bulimic symptoms, but this time not as frequent or severe.

In response to this crisis of perceived abandonment, I decided to re-invoke the dual induction format that had been successful earlier. Within three sessions, Cheryl's symptoms had resolved. Her depression lifted; she returned to work and stabilized. Within a month her recovery was sustained, and this continued even after her mother moved out to Vancouver Island. After several well-spaced follow-up individual sessions, we mutually agreed to close the case successfully.

Two years later I received a surprise gift from Sharon. I wish you could see it, but I never took a picture of it. Nevertheless, I had it mounted as an art piece on my office wall for more than five years. With wear and tear, it fell and broke several times during moves and temporary storage, eventually beyond repair. But first you need to know that a significant theme in our therapy and our dual inductions was overcoming the addiction to perfectionism that mother and daughter both shared. We applied the pattern intervention "whatever you do, from now on, do everything imperfectly as an act of homework to break your perfectionism." As you have read in other chapters, this homework is quite effective in cases of perfectionism. Mother and daughter both applied this task exactly as given (well, not really exactly as given, or that would be violating the rule itself). The perfectionism dwindled and eventually vanished.

Coming back to the gift itself. It was a wall-hanging relief piece consisting of elongated small pieces of driftwood, each with two plastic googly eyes, with the markings in the wood forming heads and chins and sometimes shoulders of strangely lifelike comic figures. Assembled together, they looked like a gathering of strange people, a good-natured but goofy-looking choir. Burned into the small cross-piece sign was the inscription: "Nobody's Perfect." It was a fitting reminder of the fun work we had done together.

CHAPTER 24

THE WELL OF ANGER

(Ed. Note: This is quite a long chapter. Be prepared. Pack a lunch)

THIS STORY MAY BE remarkable in that, in our more recent codes of conduct for psychologists, its process might constitute a violation of professional ethics, in that it involves a potential dual relationship. The fact that it was fully contractual with informed consent and due diligence brings it into the realm of good and effective psychotherapy, as I see it. But it sure was an amazing process. Working with extremely angry and violent people is tense work, far from easy. You are almost like a demolitions expert attempting to defuse a bomb that could blow up in your face or in assault or homicide against someone else during the course of treatment.

There were four phases of this treatment, each offering a contribution to the effectiveness of therapy. There was the preparation phase and the therapy contract. Next was the therapy itself. The third element was the selection and editing of key sessions. The final element was the public presentation of the case.

Section one: The Contract. At the time of this story, I was somewhat early in my career, having just returned from a training stint in Judo in England for a year in 1975, practicing family therapy there, and returning to London, Ontario, to eventually find work in a mental health clinic in a provincial hospital for mentally ill people. My particular strength was in Cognitive Behavior Therapy, assisted by Gestalt and hypnotic elements. Owing largely to the clientele I served at that time, I accidentally became known for my effective treatment of anger management cases, a dubious honour. As a result of this reputation, and my waiting list, I was referred a very difficult and sensitive case.

A community psychiatrist referred Barry, a 32-year-old truck driver who had aspirations to become an EMS ambulance worker. His career desires were a perfect match for his ego fantasy to become a protector and rescuer of innocent victims. As we know from martial arts philosophy, our greatest strength can also be the source of our greatest weakness, and so it was with Barry.

In his teenage and early-twenty-years, Barry repeatedly got involved in assault and battery convictions, but most of them were in conflict situations where he was attempting to intervene as the peacemaker, separating the combatants and being caught up in the fray. However, he often let his anger overcome his good intentions, and several males were beaten badly, although not fatally. However, by this time in his criminal record, not guilty by virtual of temporary insanity had become a thin-ice defence. The ultimate verdict was, if Barry did not reform in his next treatment, he would be confined indefinitely under a Warrant of the Lieutenant Governor in Oakridge Hospital for the Criminally Insane in Penetanguishene, Ontario. For those of you who do not know what that means, you are incarcerated for a lifetime, pending annual reviews where you are assessed about your likelihood to reoffend. Barry was headed towards a sentence similar to that of the movie "One Flew over the Cuckoo's Nest" in which Jack Nicholson played sociopath Randall Patrick McMurphy, champion of the oppressed. This was a nearly perfect representation of Barry's life drama.

Barry's psychiatrist implored me to treat him. He surmised that Barry was just a nice guy compelled by the affliction of vigilante justice idealism. He was not a sociopath. He had genuine remorse for the fights he fought and the harm he caused; it was just that his emotions took over his behavior, and his rage against injustice was like a volcano running over, destroying everything in its path, other than innocent by-standers. In other words, he could channel his aggression sufficiently that no innocent person got hurt. Nevertheless, he was dangerous enough to warrant the attention of authorities, who rightly judged his violence could not be tolerated. This referral was deemed to be his last chance.

Normally it is wise, if you can ethically refuse it, to not accept a referral where the client or others are claiming that you are his last chance. The performance characteristics are overwhelming, and the onus is typically placed on the therapist to deliver a miracle. The therapist needs to deflect this potential success on the client's commitment to build a therapeutic relationship that can lead to the resolution of his dilemma. Typically, I refer to all previous failed therapies as "latent learning," meaning that they were not a waste of time, merely instances of unconscious learning before the client was ready to be responsive to their hidden meaning. All that is now needed is the catalyst that will suddenly bring these latent learnings into focus. Such is the metaphor I use to help people who have not responded to previous therapies, whether sloppy or expert in delivery.

My future client was abundant in terms of latent learnings. He had wiped out of many previous anger management programs. None of them seemed to engage his system of internal righteousness and justice, the seeming source of his rage. While acknowledging his response was overblown, he seemingly could not resist the urge to right injustice wherever he perceived it, and could not resist the compulsion to be the champion of the oppressed.

Partly out of empathy, I agreed to treat this long-suffering man. However, I laid down some conditions that I thought might bias the result in terms of success. First, I could not accept him immediately; I had a waiting list of people who wanted to see me. Second, there were many people I could see that had a higher prospect of successful treatment. For me to see him, he would have to sweeten the deal. I would agree to treat him on several conditions:

1. We would have a maximum of ten sessions, although these might be more than an hour.

2. These sessions would be videotaped with his signed permission.

3. If his therapy were successful, we would co-present the edited videotapes of these sessions and his successful therapy to a local audience of health care professionals in London, Ontario. The objective would be to show the technical aspects of a thorough therapy for anger management so that other community professionals could use aspects of it in their own work.

4. Barry and I would work together to edit the videotapes so that no material objectionable to Barry would be presented.

5. Barry's last name would not be divulged, and any who might know it were constrained from its publication.

Barry agreed to these provisions. Two months later his therapy with me began. Actually, before this happened, the first and crucial intervention was the therapy contract itself. I knew from his referring psychiatrist that Barry had a strong sense of altruism and the persona of a hero, a rescuer, a champion of the underdog. This contract utilized Barry's signature strength. He would now be entrusted to show other angry people how to channel their anger into acceptable channels of action to rectify unfair situations. His story and case example would also illustrate how a person who had been unresponsive to many previous treatments could now see his way clear to form a strong therapeutic alliance to turn his life around. Furthermore, he would indirectly provide help for many misunderstood angry men by illustrating the technical aspects of a multidimensional treatment that could be learned and applied by many health professionals in the southwestern Ontario region. For me, as a presenter, I might be relieved from my long waiting list if other regional practitioners could step up to take on these difficult cases. For Barry, he would be a leader by example. Because the stakes were high (incarceration versus freedom, a failure figure or a courageous hero facing his demons), such a contract was biased towards success.

In addition, to commit to this contract required Barry to imagine his future success, so the power of imagery and future pacing was already beginning to work even before our first session. Also, the work of collaborative editing further cemented the therapeutic alliance, as we could discuss the evolving nature of our relationship as it developed by commenting on the process. Another crucial aspect was the degree of control given Barry in the process of our co-editing and his sense of veto as to what would be displayed in our presentation. Because I thoroughly believed in Barry's editorial right of veto, he felt fully respected as a mutual collaborator in his success and the subsequent presentation of his recovery. Finally, because of his desperation and my local reputation as a skilled therapist, a strong placebo effect was well-established before our first meeting. I am grateful for this, because it took all of my best efforts and skills to turn this case around in such a short time-frame.

Section two: the therapy sessions. Barry was referred to me by psychiatrist Dr. B.K. to assess his suitability for cognitive behavior therapy. Throughout the first interview Barry was over controlled in his monotone voice and rigid posture. He showed a great deal of muscular tension, and was quite verbally guarded and defensive while outlining his problem and growing tension. In relaying incidents from his remote and recent past we both noted with concern that Barry will resort to the use of firearms if necessary. However, it is significant that he typically fires at objects and not people, more as a threatening gesture, less as an act of destruction. These gestures remind me of gorillas, very peaceful and caring animals.

It seems that when Barry does hurt people physically, firearms are not involved. Another pattern that is a source of considerable concern is his tendency to dissociate during periods of blind rage. It is crucial to note that he does not dissociate in expressions of rage in which he was the original instigator. Barry showed himself to be rather compulsive in his routines, somewhat perfectionistic, and having unrealistically high expectations about himself and others, especially regarding doing a job properly and treating people fairly. He was uncommonly sensitive to criticism or perceived rejection by others. Sometimes his irritability became worse during weeklong episodes of insomnia and intermittent binge drinking of alcohol. At that time he had been treated with SSRI antidepressants in a bid to suppress his angry outbursts.

Barry seemed very interested in the program of anger control that I outlined, which featured relaxation training and cognitive restructuring of ambiguous experiences. He was receptive to the discovery of personal identity apart from the tough guy or nice guy roles he often played. We would use assertiveness strategies to diffuse of disrupt the angry situations in which he typically would feel compelled to threaten or carry out vindictive actions against potential threats. I also pointed out how his demeanor would likely cause others to be afraid of him, a reaction which would likely contribute to his feelings of dangerous omnipotence which no one could control. This therapy would allow him to experience his anger as having real limits through the practice of controlled blow-ups. We would arrange for a padded cell to be available for Barry to have these exercises of controlled rage. I also expressed my contention that his problem was so powerful that only Barry with all his powers would be capable of surmounting it. That is, drug induced restraints would only forestall and postpone the necessary confrontation between Barry and the limits of his rage. Strategies of self-control that work consistently would be the only way to maintain Barry's self-esteem and confidence so that he would no longer have to threaten others to protect himself.

As the interview progressed, I increasingly felt that Barry would be a good candidate for this kind of treatment. He showed high motivation, concern for the welfare of others and himself, willingness to make a commitment involving considerable work and emotional vulnerability and trust in the therapeutic alliance. He said that he wanted to make a better life for himself and to prove to others that he was basically a nice guy. He maintained rapport even in one or two situations where I challenged him with mildly provocative questions and probes.

With the approval of our staff psychiatrist, we negotiated with the referring psychiatrist to wean Barry off antidepressants during the two-month waiting period before he could begin his treatment with me. This move was a bit worrisome, as the removal of a chemical control might precipitate an outbreak of violence by destabilizing Barry's supposedly delicate emotional balance. However, I was confident that he would be able to hold on until we began his CBT treatment with me. As it turns out, this period went by with no critical incidents (possibly reflecting his high motivation and a beginning sign that the therapeutic contract was now taking effect).

The first taped session was perhaps noteworthy because of a malfunction in the microphone system. We had no cameraman, and the mike seemed okay at the beginning, but it was battery-operated and the batteries ran down before the midpoint of the session. We had no way of knowing this until we reviewed the session at the end. When I became aware that the tape was unusable I cursed briefly, expressing my disappointment and frustration. Barry seemed amused that his therapist was also human and subject to these situations as well. We used several clips from the session, where I did a voice-over while observing Barry's obvious muscular tension with postural and gestural rigidity.

In session two, we began to deal with Barry's self-criticism whenever he made the slightest mistake: for example, his inability to remember angry incidents thoroughly. I reminded him that his standards of performance and his expectations regarding his abilities were grandiose and unrealistic, and that being hard on himself served little positive function and perhaps maintained his anger rather than lessening it. I also offered that the fog of vague memories of angry incidents would lift if he had compassion for his inability to control unjust situations; in other words, he would have to let go of his omnipotent and righteous moral posture, and acknowledge his impotence in changing the world to his ego-image of fairness and goodness. This posture does not require passivity in the face of injustice; merely, it means accepting our limitations, and having compassion to work within them to support social and humanitarian change. Barry still had difficulties with this notion and any limitations on his abilities to change the world for the better according to his rules of fairness. Compassion for short-comings in himself and others seemed outside his perspective.

Also in session two, I outlined for Barry a form for charting incidents in which his anger arose. This is a typical CBT homework assignment. Back in those days, we used what we call ABC charting. A stood for Antecedent, that is, what was going on before Barry was aware of his anger. This would include where and when it happened, who was present, what was said, who did what to whom, and what thoughts or feelings preceded the anger. B stood for Behavior, and included what Barry said or did, and how long the incident lasted. C stood for Consequences, including how others reacted to his words and behavior, was there any penalty or sanction or encouragement, and how did Barry feel about what happened. In this kind of charting we are looking for emotional triggers, patterns of reaction and response, and changes in the level of mastery of anger, as well as other people's help in settling down after an angry outburst. I also encouraged Barry to become an observer in watching and later analyzing the development of his anger response, especially identifying what he was saying to himself about his predicament. His perception of what was happening and what would be his best response was the cognitive element, a crucial aspect of emotional experience, perceived threats, and most useful responses. (In my current practice with angry people I just use the categories Before, During, and After, to eliminate the psychological jargon but get at the same information.)

We prepared for session three with a short editing of session one, focusing mostly on how Barry looked and moved. He was impressed by how serious and rigid he appeared to be and also how much more relaxed he became as the session went on. Our spirit of collaboration extended into session three, where I introduced him to a small hand-held biofeedback device. This machine, made by Thought Technologies, is quite simple. It measures galvanic skin response, or skin conductance, as your fingers sweat. It is remarkably sensitive to activation or stress, sending the tone to a high pitch. As you relax, the tone ramps down gradually. But even if you have a moment of tension or doubt, the tone jumps up again. It is a wonderful Zen learning tool, because the harder you try to control it, the higher the tone goes. When you give up and focus on something more relaxing, the tone gradually falls. In effect, you learn to control your emotions by not trying so hard to control your emotions. The lesson: do not try to control; merely allow, and all will eventually work out.

With Barry, the predictable happened; he tried to fake that he was mellow, but he was battling to suppress his emotions. The tone went up. He got visibly more frustrated. The tone soared to a high level. I told Barry to stop trying to dominate the machine and instead, to shift to a vacation or pleasant time he had experienced. The tone fell gradually and jaggedly, but agreeably. Barry learned something important in that moment. At the very moment when you are most angry, the primitive brain takes over. Fear of loss, isolation, and abandonment, are like a death threat to the amygdala, which shuts down the cortex. At that moment it is best to switch channels and begin soothing that primitive part of the brain. Anger cannot be defeated by trying to suppress your anger. Instead, anger and other strong emotions can be muted by "switching channels" in your brain. This does not mean ignoring the problem and denying it. It means learning to mark and park the problem and that you momentarily acknowledge that this is a problem which you agree to address later, when you can think more clearly. The crucial aspect is to agree to commit to addressing the problem and its resolution at a near point in the future (usually, within the next two weeks, when you can discuss the incident with others). Barry began to learn how to suspend problem-solving when overwhelmed with frustration, and instead bring his activation level down with imagery.

The next part of the session involved Barry reviewing with me his ABC charts of the previous week. Actually, he had done quite well in handling work and social situations where his emotions ran rather high. Barry was a member of a day program in a therapeutic community featuring a lot of group therapy and communal activities. Again the main situations in which he became frustrated involved the themes of unfairness or people acting in an uncaring manner towards less fortunate group members. We did not go into extensive reframing of the meaning and perceived wrongs in these situations yet.

Cognitive reappraisal works best after the trigger situations have been diffused, one element at a time. This is the behavioral aspect of cognitive behavior therapy. The ABC charting showed that Barry is sensitive to raised tonal patterns in other people's voices. This is somewhat interesting because Barry himself has very limited tonal range in his bass voice and tends to speak in a monotone drone. Perhaps this tendency arose in his attempts to suppress affect and its expression in his own voice, to keep it in a narrow and manageable range, never betraying nervousness or fear. Nevertheless, when I tried to make him talk with his voice high and squeaky, he was unable to do so. So I modelled a greater tonal voice range, while Barry attempted to remain calm. It helped that I expressed no verbal content, saying the same phrase "words, words, words" repeatedly in a wide tonal range. After about two minutes of this exposure, he was surprised to find that he no longer had any emotional reaction to my tonal range.

The second aspect, and one which is much more sensitive for Barry and for others, was loudness. Using a range of words from angry to neutral content, I had Barry shout progressively louder with some words and then progressively softer with others. At some points he was disturbed that his heart was racing quickly and that he was sweating with the heat of the studio lights augmenting his emotional body heat. Still, he was able to notice a progressive increase in control and a desensitization of his reaction to loudness. He was also learning how to tolerate an increased range of activation and expression of affect without as much fear. It is said that when you are up to elbows in alligators, you forget that your job was to drain the swamp. It is also this way with a progressive anger management program. First you turn off the taps (ongoing triggers); then you empty the flooded basement of your unconscious.

At the end of the session, Barry mentioned that he wakes up in the middle of the night, sits bolt upright in his bed, heart pounding, as if startled. He was wondering what this was about, and I told him we would be getting into this when we come to the phase of emptying the well in a future session, that I would respect his unconscious mind in not rushing his awareness prematurely. He said he appreciated the respect with which I was pacing his sessions.

Session four followed a particularly bad week for Barry. He was a member of a therapeutic community, an ongoing non-residential group therapy immersion program in which he had been enrolled for two months. Recently there had been a greater than usual change of people in the program. He was noticing that some members were getting worse during the course of the program. Some were graduating into a better life, but Barry seemed to be among the members who were deteriorating. He was becoming restless, going two days in a row without sleep. He became increasingly agitated, arguing with others, shouting and name-calling, and hitting boards, trees, and mailboxes. He was suspended from the program for a day for self-destructive behavior, hurting his hand punching a tree.

In our session Barry was tenser than ever, as we went further into the exercises of controlled discharge of anger. He was talking about feeling dissociated and in an altered state, although his behavior still seemed to be coherent and in control. When he expressed his anger by wringing towels and smashing boxes in our exercises, he was amazed that he was letting his expression be far louder and more extreme than he thought he would. This type of therapy, inspired by the techniques of Gestalt therapy and psychodrama, was part of a strategy called catharsis, the equivalent of "blowing off steam" from a boiler so that it does not explode. While it seems to make excellent intuitive sense, the anger-catharsis hypothesis was later dismissed in research by Berkowitz and associates at the University of Wisconsin. It is now no longer practiced in most anger management programs, but it seemed to work well for Barry. He seemed exhausted but somewhat relieved at the end of the session, feeling the validation of having some sanctioned and non-destructive way of venting his anger. I felt tired, as the emotions we witnessed were intense and sustained through most of the session. I did not, as I would likely do now, go beyond the anger to get at underlying emotions likely related to fears of abandonment. Barry was just too depleted, and so was I. Although concerned that this session might now be enough to settle Barry down, I had a sense of confidence that he would not continue to act out in the coming week.

As it turned out, Barry was okay in the following week. On one occasion when he became frustrated, he took a time-out from the group, then took the towel that I had lent him and twisted it in a knot like he had in the last session, then returned to the frustrating situation and worked it through appropriately. However, in the days following that event, Barry seemed to withdraw into a detached dissociated state, numbing himself from both negative and positive emotions.

In our session five, he was berating himself for wasting a week of potential recovery by withdrawing. I instead reframed this time as a period of regrouping his emotional resources before reaching out to others.

In this session we also had Barry twist his towel while screaming as he imagined angry situations from his recent past as well as far back in his history. What was different this time was that Barry did not try to retrain himself or hold back in any way. He was able to feel the full extent of his emotion without the fear that it would go out of control or overwhelm him. In a sense, he broke through his grandiosity, and felt his anger as a human rather than a beastly emotion. We followed this exercise with the behavior therapy part of the session wherein we anchored several deeply relaxing scenes from his childhood in Northern Alberta. At the end of the session Barry told me that, for the first time, he no longer had a tension headache during our time together. I directly related this relief to the fact that he was no longer struggling to restrain himself. He was beginning to feel acceptance and compassion for himself and an emerging sense of confidence in managing his emotions.

Session six followed a week in which there were only two circumstances involving Barry's anger, situations in which the other people were reportedly quite provocative. Once again the predominant theme was Barry's identification with oppressed people who were suffering unfair treatment at the hands of others. I reframed Barry's rescuing stance as having a potential flaw. That is, he might inadvertently be robbing victims of their initiative to defend themselves if they became conditioned to wait for Barry to champion their cause. This reframe gave him some pause to reassess the value of his righteousness in rescuing others.

In the behavior therapy part of the session, we gradually desensitized Barry's fear of having others behind him and out of his vision. I circled behind his chair, lightly touching him on his shoulders and head in a random sequence, but only when he announced that he thought he could handle it. It should be noted that my touches were gentle but firm so that he could feel the warmth of my hands, but none of my movements were fast or abrupt. This method allowed Barry to get beyond his automatic stance of defence and hypervigilance.

In the subsequent two weeks before session six Barry had no incidents of rage. Instead of his former passivity and "nice guy" persona, he was now becoming appropriately assertive in defining his boundaries. He reported that he felt profoundly relieved from the pressure of carrying the burden of anger. Furthermore, he received a lot of encouragement from others in assertive confrontation situations that let him know that he can be accepted while being firm and outspoken rather than aggressive. Also, he enjoyed that now persons found him more approachable now that he was no longer scaring people away. He was no longer storing the anger from previous situations to contaminate the present dilemma and negatively cloud his judgment and emotional reactions. Another change was that he was now able to listen to others and recognize when he was drawn into identification with their negative cognitions and emotions. Now he was becoming more able to assume a therapeutic role of empathy, allowing others to solve their own problems. In group situations he was able to be more effective by sometimes relinquishing the role of group saviour, instead settling back, observing, and supporting. He was now finding that his former power by physical threat and intimidation was being supplanted by group consensus and acceptance, so that he was gaining much more than he was losing.

Another huge change was that formerly he was perceived as an independent pillar of strength of his group. Now he realized that he was able to admit that he has needs and vulnerabilities. He could now ask for help in companionship and support while he was going through personal difficulties. As we celebrated this change, we developed the metaphor of spreading the trust umbrella. Another even more appropriate metaphor was the image of a tower supported by many guy wires grounded in different places. Barry really resonated with this image. He also talked about how he had expanded our desensitization exercise of the last session to include his group, milling about behind his chair and then randomly coming up and touching his back, shoulders, and head. He could now do this in the absence of any anxiety. In fact, he recounted one instance where he was able to sleep while others were behind him talking. This ability was a major contrast to his previous life where, for example, he could only relax on the back seat of a bus.

Another interesting development was the variety and detail of content we covered in this session. Barry talked about his difficulties in previous psychiatric hospital admissions under certificates of mental illness, about his struggles with authority figures, demanding bosses, and his distrust of others that likely contributed to the breakdown of his marriage over a year ago. It was as if Barry was examining and reviewing the self-destructive patterns of his former life as he emerged from the shadow of rage. He now could see more clearly his perfectionism, distorted thinking patterns, and compulsive defences. No matter how hard he tried, he could not control his world, and the behavior of those around him.

In regard to the need for control, Barry told me of another key decision. He had decided that now he was ready to leave his therapeutic community. However, the rest of his group thought that his date of December 10 was too early. They felt that his positive changes, though welcome, were still too new and tender, and that he had still further work to do on himself. It seems that Barry was quite disturbed by the group going against his judgment. At first he was quite moody and withdrawn, resisting their collective influence. However, the more he thought about it, the more he remembered our talk about his rigidity, and the idea from judo of formal integrity with positional flexibility. This metaphor helped him resolve the dilemma and go along with the group members and delay his leaving the therapeutic community for another month. Upon making this decision he felt even more grounded and relaxed.

In view of all these encouraging developments and Barry's assertion that he now felt no fear or threat of going into an angry phase, we decided to re-examine our therapy contract. That is, the original therapy goals had already been met by only our seventh session in a scheduled series of ten. Under the circumstances I proposed that we keep the remaining three sessions in a bank for Barry to follow-up with any future situations in which he was unable to use the strategies and techniques we had developed together. Barry appreciated this approach and especially my vote of confidence that he had turned a crucial corner and was now in the consolidation phase of therapy. He also wondered that if anger were no longer an issue, we could use a session or two about his idea of getting back together with his former wife. I thought this would be fine. Meanwhile, we could now get together to edit video clips of our seven therapy sessions and begin thinking about our partnership in presenting his case at a professional workshop. We agreed to begin that work in the coming weeks.

Although it may have seemed a little premature to terminate our first therapy contract as a mission completed right after a crucial turning point, I had another rationale. I thought that in Barry's case in particular, it was a good idea to let him do as much integrating as possible on his own so that he could identify his achievements as being self-initiated and fulfilled, rather than under the guidance of therapy. Furthermore, we had the advantage of indirectly reinforcing the therapy lessons in our editing sessions, monitoring to make sure integration was proceeding. But most of all, both of us had trust in the therapeutic alliance and the way Barry was utilizing these techniques regularly in his life.

Section Three: consolidation in the process of editing. In our editing sessions we had a lot of fun picking the clips for our workshop. Barry reacted well when I shared with him the technical aspects of his treatment that I thought were important to present. He got to select some special scenes that were his favorites in terms of turning points. During our editing Barry updated me on his progress, graduating from the therapeutic community and taking upgrading courses at a community college to become an EMS ambulance and first aid technician. This career choice was a perfect match for his intellectual level and his sustained interest in being a rescuer, but now in a more contained and useful way. He spontaneously noticed himself using patterns of flexible thinking when in awkward interpersonal situations. He reported one incident of anger over the holidays, but he was easily able to overcome and re-channel his emotions using the techniques he had learned in therapy.

In session one, we featured primarily Barry's rigid face and posture, muscular tension, hypervigilance, and distrustful guardedness. My gestures and posture were slower and more reserved than I normally am, and my voice tones, although not monotone, were flatter and more subdued. Barry relaxed a bit more as the session progressed. Session two was rather unremarkable as we began more behavior therapy techniques to help Barry lower his activation level. Under my instruction he learned belly breathing, progressive muscular relaxation, and other specific techniques to self-soothe and generate a state of reduced tension and greater relaxation.

Another clip featured the metaphor of "The Well of Anger." In my hand-scribbled cartoon sketch, I drew a picture of Barry's Well of Anger. It seemed to be seething with anger, hatred, rage, resentment, depression, hopelessness, righteousness, power, scariness, and almost any caustic emotion imaginable. (I deliberately left out possible underlying emotions such as fear, anxiety, insecurity, loneliness, and anything implying the shame of vulnerability, things his ego would reject at this early stage of therapy). It looked like this caustic acid of bubbling hatred would explode like a volcano at any moment boiling over to hurt and possibly kill family, friends, and even nearby innocent bystanders. Barry was seen as trying to keep a tight lid on this caldron of anger, but occasionally the lid would blow off and people would get hurt. Barry identified with this metaphor, and felt genuine remorse for the harm he inadvertently inflicted on others, even sometimes those who deserved it. His empathy and humanity were great strengths that would form the core of our therapeutic bond as we worked together. I offered the idea that this therapy would provide a flexible cover for the well, perhaps more like a flexible plastic barbeque cover that would flex at the sides allowing steam to escape regularly and in a harmless way. We would also use the idea of channeling off some of the elements so that they could be useful in dealing with frustrations and injustices, instrumental anger fueling assertive responses and constructive negotiation.

The main clip we used for session 3 was a demonstration of awareness from the philosophy of judo, which I call Judo-awareness. On a smooth table top I pushed an empty inverted styrofoam plastic cup with my finger in several directions. I asked Barry, since I was much bigger and stronger than the cup, why did it not collapse and break from my force.

Barry replied that, because no matter where I forced it, the cup yielded space, or spun slightly off centre so that my finger rolled around its curves and went on past it. So the lesson was that the empty cup preserved its formal integrity by offering spatial flexibility, yielding to or spinning away the forces it encountered. Of course, there are limitations to this model. If the cup is full of liquid or sand (ego attachment and prejudice) the cup will be so heavy it won't be able to glide over the table (friction or stuckness, positional rigidity), so my finger could dent the cup. Or perhaps the cup might run out of space to manoeuvre, and be pushed off the end of the table. So the cup in a sense needs to know the boundaries of the field, and circle within those limits. Yet another limiting case happens when the cup is caught in the middle of two opposing forces. It will be crushed unless it spins out from the middle and allows the opposing forces to meet each other directly. Thus the peacemaker between opposing forces often gets crushed, unless he moves with grace and skill. Barry was quite fascinated with this demonstration, and at perhaps an unconscious level was becoming more aware of the dangers he exposed himself to by being a champion of the oppressed, carrying the flag against any injustice he perceived.

As that session progressed, Barry and I established boundaries of safety for our work together, such as the signal "Time Out" if ever I might push him beyond his limit of tolerance. At several points in the session, I encouraged him with the attribution, "You already can do it. It's just that you don't believe it yet." We were already transporting his belief system beyond despair and desperation into a sense of belief in his ability to master his emotions.

In session four, as Barry was reviewing his charting for the week, the clip we used was one of "the gathering storm" where Barry is sinking into depression. Disappointed with himself, and in an insomniac funk, at one point he wants to quit the therapy and leave the session. He is afraid that he will descend into a "tunnel of rage" and go out f control if he starts to express his anger in the session. He is also afraid that, when these things happen, other people withdraw and reject him. I reply that I am there for him; I am confident he can do the twisting towel exercise, and remind him that he can use our "Time Out" code if he needs a temporary break. I sit nearby Barry, and I model twisting the towel and screaming at it. Barry does likewise when it's his turn, but very tentatively, afraid to fully release his anger. Each time I ask him to push it further and yell louder. Finally he does it completely. He looks exhausted, but relieved. After helping to talk him down with belly breathing, he is visibly more relaxed. I end the session with the words "you will see me when you are farthest into your own space. Our work will come to mind." This statement had the effect of a post-hypnotic suggestion.

Although we did not do any formal hypnosis, some of the words I spoke when Barry was in extremes of agitation, exhaustion, and subsequent relaxation had enduring impact, so that he was readily able to apply them in his life between sessions. Another informal technique was my frequent use of reframing the meaning of situations to include patterns of possibility excluded by his pre-judgments. One further technical aspect was my use of attributions about Barry's strength and resources, and especially his sense of kindness that extended beyond merely rescuing the oppressed.

Section Four: The Workshop Presentation. As we presented his therapy it became increasingly clear that The Well of Anger treatment combined many aspects of a multimodal approach. Engagement was firm and sustained throughout treatment based on mutual respect and trust in the therapeutic relationship. Cognitive elements challenged and reframed his thought and perceptions. Affective strategies in managing emotions were central to this therapy. Behavioral sequences became assertive responses. There were also features from semi-hypnotic communication. Among these were attributions, reframing, pacing, leading, utilization of strengths, metaphors and stories.

The only elements that were missing were humor and softness. While I tried several times each session to entice Barry to see the irony in his life situations, he would sometimes respond with a wry smile, but never the belly-laugh I usually like to evoke in my client. Although he loosened up a lot as the therapy progressed, Barry still remained a rather serious guy. In most anger management cases, I can usually get to tender emotions underlying the tough displays of anger. While we did discuss elements of hurt, guilt, jealousy, envy, loss, and threat, and we certainly talked about fear of rejection and abandonment, we seldom unmasked the softness and tenderness of the inner little boy under the tough guy shell. Still at some level I held that frightened boy in my arms, and respected his vulnerability. We both deeply trusted each other, and even had feelings of affection that we never fully liberated. Perhaps the appropriate expression of those feelings might emerge in some other venue of Barry's life.

Three months later, over 200 psychiatrists, psychologists, social workers, and other helping professionals from across southwestern Ontario assembled for a day-long presentation on 'The Well of Anger," the long-awaited workshop by the author and a rather nervous Barry. It was his first professional presentation, and he was not used to public speaking, especially about his own treatment. He felt relieved and more comfortable as I took on most of the talking, and he filled in with occasional color commentary.

Now that this therapy was completed successfully, Barry

was free of the threat of further incarceration and mandated treatment. He was well on his way to career and relationship rehabilitation. And he presented himself well in our workshop. In the closing questions and remarks, the audience asked him more about his experience, as they had done earlier. The main theme for him was the transition from despair and hopelessness into calmness, confidence, and mastery of his emotions. When asked about whether he was fully aware of the techniques I was using, he said not entirely, but he didn't care. He trusted me implicitly, and that was all that mattered. As we edited together and selected scenes, he became increasingly aware of the method underlying many of our therapeutic interventions, but that was not as important as the experience he had being a client. As we ended our day-long presentation, we received a standing ovation from the audience. Strenuous work, but a job well done.

CHAPTER 25

ALLOWING FOR A REMNANT

A POLISH VETERAN of the Second World War was referred to me for a serious problem of muscular rigidity. He walked like the Tin Man in the Wizard of Oz, and even lacked any facial expression other than a rigid mask of tension. There was no known physical reason for this tension that began and persisted from his war days onward. His condition was severely impairing his life. This was years ago before the full recognition of Post Traumatic Stress Disorder as a diagnostic category. He was treated with several anti-depressant and other medications and insight-oriented psychotherapy with no improvement of his condition. He was on a permanent psychological disability pension, could hardly speak through his clenched jaw and jerky movements, was barely functioning socially, and had little family support other than a brother and sister-in-law. The doctors involved, including his psychiatrist, referred him to me for cognitive behaviour therapy. Even in the early 1970s, CBT was still perceived by the psychoanalytic therapy establishment as unorthodox and experimental. Nevertheless, the Tin Man was not responding to conventional therapy, so perhaps CBT might work; it was worth a try.

In our initial interview, Viktor was in his early 70s, and spoke with a heavy Polish accent. He was striking in his appearance, tall, gaunt, rigid in gait and posture, choppy in words and gestures, with a frightened and weary look in his eyes. After the usual assessment questions and establishment of rapport, I asked him why he kept himself so rigid, assuming there was a voluntary component to his symptoms. His answer confirmed my intuitive guess, and I was glad I worded my question that way. He responded that he kept himself rigid to stay alive and sane. He was convinced if he let go of his rigidity, he would die, or worse still, he would lose his mind. I asked him the standard CBT question about what data he had for this notion, and he replied with certainty that he was alive and sane, apart from this disabling problem; therefore, his method was continuing to work.

As you know from previous stories, I was familiar with neuromuscular rigidity as a treatable disorder, and the role of paradoxical avoidance in validating and empowering a problem pattern. Rather than challenging his irrational thoughts, I began a process of utilizing them. I asked him if he had to remain rigid while sleeping (looking for management by exception). He responded that in sleep, he went from one tense posture to another, awakening to stiff sore muscles and another day of the strain of vigilant rigidity. I asked him if he would be willing to do a mild experiment that would not have to force him to abandon his survival strategy of rigidity. He agreed to do the experiment with me.

I asked him to remain totally rigid in his entire body, except the muscles and flesh underneath the fingernail of his left baby finger. Could he allow that? After a half-minute in which I matched his choppy breathing, he announced that his left baby finger tip could relax while the rest of his body remained vigilantly rigid. I then asked him: could his left hand teach his right hand baby finger tip to do the same thing? He closed his eyes, and within a minute, he was now able to accomplish the same result. Then we went through relaxing each finger tip under the fingernail for each finger, then transferring that experience to the corresponding right finger. Then we went beyond the first knuckle joint to the second knuckle joint in each finger.

In each part of this progressive sequence, I encouraged Viktor to still hang on to the survival tension in the rest of his body, but to be curious about how easy and wonderful it was to no longer have to hold tension in his hands. As we moved beyond his hands to his arms and shoulders in the same methodical manner, my client became more excited and happy about each new revelation. In each discovery, I urged caution and told him to keep tension is his remaining body so that he would not fall apart, especially now that we were working on muscles and tissue in his body core. As he occasionally opened his eyes, he would see me pacing and leading his breathing, which by now had become deeper and more rhythmic. He felt better and more relieved, but still I cautioned that he should retain his survival tension in his legs. We worked from the quadriceps down to the calf muscles, keeping residual tension in his ankles, then the soles of his feet. As we got closer to the soles of his feet, I observed that the Tin Man was becoming more worried, with an anxious look in his eyes that I had not seen since the beginning of our session.

I assured him that I would not, and he would not, remove the anchor or lynch-pin of his survival. As we got to the toes, I had him relax each toe separately, except the flesh underneath the toenail of his left baby toe. I insisted that he should keep this area as the spot where he would remain tense day and night, while allowing the rest of his body to relax as much and as long as he wanted. A relieved and knowing smile came over his face, and he shook my hand with both his, tears of gratitude flowing down his animated face. That was all it took. In the coming week and months, I followed up on his happy personal and social life and pleasant retirement lifestyle. The rigidity symptoms never returned. I kept asking him if he could still feel a remnant of rigidity under his left baby toenail, but he felt it didn't matter anymore. I wish all my sessions could be miracle cures like that one.

Milton Erickson often spoke about the advisability of allowing clients to retain a harmless vestige of their symptom, even if only in symbolic form. This prescription of maintaining a remnant allowed clients to retain their dignity and integrity as people. It also enabled them to surrender a problem pattern that had been their difficult-but-known friend and constant companion for many years, so that they could abandon the problem without negating a part of their identity. Prescribing the keeping of a harmless remnant is a nicely respectful master stroke of gentle therapy.

Walking By The Graveyard: Left Brain and Right Brain

FOR SOME BRAIN FUNCTIONS, we use brain circuitry that is limited to a relatively small part of the brain. In the interests of economy of space and energy, some functions are almost like autonomous circuits. We use them but hardly think about them, like the coordination involved in drinking a glass of water. Some more complex patterns, like choreographed sequences in a dance, often involve many parts of the brain. With practice, these moves are committed to motor memory, and can be executed with minimal involvement of our conscious analytic mind. In fact, our left brain (at least, for most right-handed people) chatter and thinking often can interfere with the execution of these right-brained visual-spatial abilities (e.g., analyzing while doing a golf swing).

We also observe this functional autonomy of the right brain when a gifted young athlete comes off the playing field after a personal-best performance in which she did an outstanding play or move. Her coach or a media interviewer might ask her "How were you able to do that!?" She might answer," I don't know. I was just 'in The Zone', describing her alpha-brainwave Flow state. It was a trance-like experience where she was totally lost in the focus and integrity of the moment, The Eternal Now, with no thoughts blocking her experience, followed by a sense of wonder and awe in its mystery. However, if we were to interview a world-class athlete after a similar moment, the person would note the Zone state of consciousness, but also be able to describe in technical detail exactly what their body was doing and how they were able to execute the difficult play. In other words, both their right and left brain were involved, but the left descriptor-analyst was muted or relegated to observer status during the move. After the move, the left brain might be activated for a moment to help the athlete remember the crucial factors, then go into "Mark it and Park it!" mode quickly to get with the next task with full attention. In *Mind State Management: The software of the mind*[2], we select the brain wave state that best facilitates the task at hand. So also, in hemispheric coordination, we engage those parts of the energetic reptilian brain, the emotional limbic system, and the hemispheres of the cortex to produce a symphony of synergistic excellence.

In his book *Flow: The Psychology of Optimal Experience*, Mihalyi Csikzentmihalyi (1990) outlines the characteristics of Flow states. More importantly, he outlines strategies of attitude and preparation that optimize flow in sport, relationships, and life in general. In other words, Flow, like good luck, is the result of the intersection of opportunity with a great deal of prior preparation and practice, in which positive imagery often plays a key part.

Psychotherapy and counselling can also generate similar peak experiences, when everything in the therapeutic alliance "clicks" and a beautiful moment of connection and transformation occurs. As in the attitudinal and philosophical preparation witnessed in other flow situations, counselling and coaching key moments are often preceded by the preparation and attitudes of openness of the therapist. So here is a short form description of one of the strategies I often use.

I assign to my left analytic brain the task of setting not only the goalposts, but more importantly the boundaries of the playing field. I use all available knowledge gathered

---

[2] This program can be downloaded from www.solutionorientedcounselling.ca

in this case, comparing it with research and knowledge of best ethical, effective, and efficient practices that bear upon this client situation. I also assess client motivation and preparedness for an array of possible interventions, which I also discuss with a client to ensure informed consent and full collaboration. These boundaries of possible action determine the pegs in the corners of the playpen. My left brain, in discussion with my client, might help me determine which approach or strategies we might employ in what sequence. For example, with a client suffering from PTSD, I could use EMDR or other desensitization approaches, or MBSR or other mindfulness-based interventions, or even Acceptance and Commitment Therapy, or other channels based on examinations of meaning and purpose, or perhaps an amalgam of several of these elements.

I look at the boundaries of the playpen as if they were three dimensional, containing all possible options as if they were the toys. Then my client and I engage in play with these myriad patterns of possibility, floating them up gently like thought balloons. It is in this spirit of serious play that I allow my intuition, largely a right-brain and limbic-system function, almost free liberty in coming up with ideas and metaphors of meaning that might provide the clues to solve the puzzle. I encourage my client to play with these possibilities until a recognizable and agreeable pattern emerges to guide our subsequent actions. It is as if the playpen of logic provides the safety of length, width, and height, leaving my intuition to push and probe as it may. If anything my intuition comes up with seems too obtuse or absurd, I check it out with my client with an empathy query "does this have any resonance or meaning for you, or am I way off-base?" We either drop it or carry on that line if the client feels it is productive. Even if the client's defenses may choose not to proceed, I watch for non-verbal cues that perhaps the notion was relevant but premature, storing it for possible use later in that therapy if a coachable moment arises along that path. Generally, these guidelines of optimal therapist brain function serve me and my clients well, but sometimes I am not too sure, and I even climb out on a limb to present a strong unconscious intuition for which I have almost no supportive data. Let me tell you a story about this.

Bob was an engineer, and Susan was a psychotherapist. They were happily married in their early 30s and parents of two young children. Jared, age three, was reportedly a delightful and easy-going child. Daphne, now aged six months, also was cheerful and engaging. Nevertheless, Susan developed a strong phobia about Daphne dying of SIDS, Sudden Infant Death Syndrome. I think it is even called by another name now, but it happens when the child accidentally ceases breathing and suffocates, often in her sleep. It is a rare condition, and Susan had Daphne checked out medically and there were no problems identified. Furthermore, Bob and Susan had a microphone crib monitor installed so that they could hear sounds in the nursery room to detect any audible signals of baby distress. Nevertheless, Susan could not shake the obsessive fear that Daphne might die suddenly. Susan had not experienced any depressive symptoms post-partum, and there was no family history of heart or respiratory problems. Susan did recall that a distant friend of hers had a baby that died of SIDS two years ago, and the entire friendship network had shared in her grieving and recovery, but that seemed in the distant past.

Being a therapist in our medium-large city, Susan knew of my work as a psychotherapist and had attended several of my workshops featuring hypnotic techniques and strategies. She also had heard of several professional people in the city who had favorable outcomes as my clients, so my reputation already had a placebo effect when she asked if I could treat her obsessive phobia with hypnosis. After checking out with her all the possible safeguards and assurances to avoid dual relationship potentials and ways to overcome them, we agreed that I could ethically treat her condition. We had a few preliminary sessions to check out possible unconscious material in her family background and current marriage, and no pathology emerged.

By session three Susan was adequately prepared and eager to go into trance. Although she seemed to be good hypnotic subject, I worked carefully in extra detail and slowness throughout the induction and deepening procedures. Then out of nowhere, a powerful and strong image came into my mind. I saw Susan walking peacefully by a graveyard in the dusk of evening, not in darkness, just in the purple shades of twilight just after sunset. For a slight moment I was struck with the horrible thought that, if I voiced this image, I would be inviting the iatrogenesis of introducing the element of death (and therefore possible activation of fear of death) into our very first hypnosis session. What if she went into abreaction? Well, I suppose that might get to the heart of the matter, the core of her fear, and I knew how to help people through abreactions and negative reactions quite smoothly anyway, so my moment of doubt was replaced by calm confidence. But first I would need her consent, so I asked her unconscious mind if it would be okay to introduce an image that I thought might help her in dealing with fear of death. Through our previously arranged process of ideomotor signalling established earlier in that trance, her right index finger jerkily raised momentarily, indicating a "yes," so I calmly went on to describe the imagined scene in a leisurely stroll, ending with her returning home relaxed and confident after her evening walk. Then I ended the trance with the usual reassuring messages, and she opened her eyes slowly, with a wide smile on her face.

"How did you know to pick that image!?" she said in astonishment.

"I don't know. It seemed to come out of nowhere, but I felt compelled to tell you about it and work it into our first trance, if that was okay with you." With this reply she was bubbling with excitement and enthusiasm. She then proceeded to tell me that one of her favorite childhood memories was walks in the evening with her father when she was about eight or nine. It was the only time she could have his full attention, with just the two of them together. He was a man of few words but a warm listener and validator of her world. Those were magic moments she cherished. So when I described the scene to her, even though I did not include her father, she "coloured him into" her image making it became more special and calming. Also, at that moment in her trance, she knew that she was okay, that Daphne was healthy and okay, and she could relax that her daughter's safety was assured.

Susan checked her feelings about Daphne after the trance and thought that she was okay now. No further work was needed. I applauded her confidence and said that sometimes, especially when there is no complicating pathology, a simple phobia could be cured in one hypnotic session. However, just to be sure in case she needed further support to consolidate our hypnotherapy, I invited her back in a month for our follow up session. Sure enough, in that session she confirmed that the fear had vanished, and she had returned to being a happy mother and wife.

As I saw her in various professional meetings later, I learned in our side conversations that her positive results had consolidated, and the problem was no more and never returned. What joy! And so I learned to trust my intuition, with the proviso of checking its hunches out with my clients.

CHAPTER 27

What Colour Is Your Migraine?

EVEN THOUGH I OFTEN use variations of clinical hypnosis in psychotherapy, I do not consider myself an expert in pain management. For clients who want strategies to deal with chronic pain, I can use standard hypnotic techniques like turning down the thermostat or changing the channel, or using an imagined hand going numb in cold water and transferring the numbness to the afflicted area. Another favorite way is to have the client displace the pain from the center to the periphery of his attentional field, almost like a picture-in-picture visual shrinkage of the pain. My clients and I have had some success with these methods over the years, but there are some others that I have been unable to help, such as one man with phantom limb pain. This was before the technique of mirror imaging was developed for this disorder.

Nevertheless, I have developed a method of helping clients significantly diminish migraine pain. Once again, this facility developed almost by accident by a client teaching me about her symptom. Ruth was a 46-year-old married mother of two children referred to me to help her overcome her flight phobia, a relatively standard presenting problem. One day, however, she almost cancelled her appointment when she developed a very strong migraine on her way to our session. Although not nauseated with pain, she was in considerable discomfort, which she rated as 9 on a scale of 10. I commended her for deciding to come to the session despite her distress and asked her if she would like to try an experiment to deal with her migraine so that she could have an easier drive home. Ruth replied that any technique that would relieve her pain would be worthwhile to try. So we began an unusual experience together.

We started with the same mild trance we had done in her two previous flight phobia sessions, an eye fixation induction. I then invited Ruth to imagine her headache was positioned in an empty chair about four feet to her right. As she looked slowly at the chair, I asked her to describe what she saw. She envisioned a big orangey-red blob pulsating violently and erratically. I repeated her words with a slightly subdued tone and slower pace as I asked her to merely wait, while expecting some kind of change to occur. She was directed to be especially curious about any change that might be interesting or unusual. Sure enough, the intensity of the orangey-red color began to diminish, and the pulsations became more regular, although still jerky and violent. This was the first indication that Ruth would be capable of trance-forming her pain.

Gradually over the next several minutes she noticed that the blob was becoming smaller and paler in color, almost a metallic grey. Meanwhile I kept reflecting her own words back to her in a slower, softer, rhythmic cadence in a manner similar to what Ernest Rossi and other famous hypnotists use with their clients. The blob was now changing form into two sets of angry steel teeth, biting and clashing with each other, sending off metallic sparks as they viciously attacked each other. Becoming a little more directive, I asked Ruth if she could imagine the teeth themselves becoming slightly paler while the surrounding gums might become still steely, but with a more rose or pink shade. Gradually, with no further guidance by me, the teeth were becoming whiter, and now the gums were becoming a more natural pink. As this transformation developed, she also noticed that the biting was not as fast and vicious. If fact, Ruth was fascinated as the two mouths developed lips, and they were playfully engaged in what she called "love bites and love nips." The softness and gentleness of their love play was now becoming light kissing. Ruth was amazed at what was now developing. However, this imagery action was still seeming to occur several feet away from Ruth in the empty chair she was looking at.

The next intervention was especially important. I asked her to imagine that the two nipping and kissing mouths could leave the area of the empty chair and come back to Ruth's head. For a moment she hesitated, fearing the return of her migraine, but with some reassurance on my part that it would be okay, the two mouths began kissing each side of her forehead at the temples. They were warm, gentle, and soothing. I then invited Ruth to gradually come out of trance. When she reoriented to the present room, I asked her what had happened to her migraine. She answered that it was completely gone and that she felt relaxed and mildly tired. She was totally amazed at what had just happened, but wondering if she could ever replicate this process. We then did a brief trance induction, followed by a quick review of the changes that had occurred, with a post-hypnotic suggestion that next time she experienced an aura or the beginning of a migraine, she could go into trance and repeat this process to transform the metaphor of her migraine.

In our follow-up session three weeks later, Ruth reported she had one mild migraine which she was quickly able to dispatch using our technique. Furthermore, she now felt a surge of personal confidence and well-being, and felt she would be able to fly without anxiety. A month later she told me she had flown from Calgary to Victoria for a getaway weekend; the flights went smoothly with no anxiety. That was our last session, so we ended the therapy successfully. A two-year follow up revealed that the migraines had not returned, a very welcome outcome for our work together.

Empty Chair Technique. In other cases where there is an involuntary symptom, including psychophysiological disorders such as ulcers or skin rashes, I often have my hypnotherapy clients interview the somatic self in an empty chair. The somatic self is an imagined part of the person that is in charge of running the symptom or presenting problem. It often has its own biological unconscious wisdom, a hidden message or cosmic lesson for the client. The client is encouraged to interview this part of themselves with interest and curiosity, rather than the typical anger and accusatory tone they usually employ when considering their problem pattern. This reshaping by the therapist might take a few repetitions before the client is ready to adopt this more neutral and detached stance. Here we are invoking the natural phenomenon of dissociation in therapeutic hypnosis. Usually the client is ready to adopt this stance within several minutes after beginning the empty-chair role play. Of course, readiness to engage in this intervention is prepared in advance by the therapist.

Having your client talk in an animated way to an imagined part of themselves sitting in an empty chair sounds absurd to most lay people. They might think it is crazy or hokey, and that there is no way they could identify or get into this process on an emotional level. However, almost everyone has had a training experience where they had to role play in order to learn a skill. At first they were tentative and stilted in their talk, but in a short while, they were truly surprised at how free they were to engage at a fully emotional level in that training exercise. This process would be similar, except that they would be switching positions from time to time, talking to and with their somatic self and their executive self as they came to understand the role of the symptom in their lives.

We therapists know this as a standard technique of Gestalt therapy, adapted in emotionally focused therapy (EFT) and self-relations psychotherapy. It is a powerful process for releasing many unconscious but strong constraints against change and personal growth. The client switches places and is now talking for the somatic self, (with some coaching and encouragement by the therapist nearby) making sure (s)he is not ignored, dismissed, abandoned or banished by the client until the client fully understands her (usually) protective message. Then the client shifts back to her original chair and again becomes her executive self, learning from and forming an alliance with her somatic self, with whom she now has some empathy. The therapist coaches and shadows each switch between the two parts of the self. The exact timing of these switches is a judgement of therapist skill, but often follows where the emotional energy is strongest and the possibility of reconciliation best. After several switches back and forth, the two selves usually find a way to honor the message of the somatic self without having to perform the symptom or problem pattern. At that point the client is ready for other methods such as exposure and response prevention to extinguish the anxiety associated with the problem pattern, which typically resolves fairly rapidly now that the unconscious obstacles are removed.

These therapeutic strategies can be used with many disorders, but are especially effective with psychophysiological disorders, or problem patterns that seem to be involuntary or compelled. However, returning to migraine pain, there is a more recent case that I would like to discuss.

Caitlin. Caitlin was a 20-year old university student who had to withdraw for medical reasons midway through her second semester. She had experienced moderate and at times severe migraine headaches throughout high school, but now they had become so prolonged and severe that she was unable to study or concentrate. She returned home to her parents to convalesce, but her symptoms hardly subsided at all.

Furthermore, she felt embarrassed and defeated by this problem that medications could not help. Her previous talk therapy experience did not work at all to relieve her symptoms. She and her parents were desperate and helpless when a family friend, a clinical nurse, told them about my unorthodox but seemingly effective methods. With nothing to lose, they decided to give this therapy a try.

In her initial interview Caitlin presented as an intelligent, kind, dedicated but overwhelmed young woman. She was desperate to try anything that might work to break this cycle of false starts of clarity followed by the crushing disappointments upon the return of her migraines within several days. Although having no previous experience with hypnosis, she was curious and interested, and responded well to a mild-depth practice induction. She was intrigued by the story of how Ruth had learned to trance-form her migraine into a manageable metaphor, and was eager to begin projecting her headache into an empty chair.

In her second session, we began with a brief review of her progress. Her headaches and migraines were daily, but usually not as severe. Then we did some exercises in trance. Despite my attempts to improve deepening, Caitlin could only attain levels of mild to moderate depth in trance. However, I then told her of several cases that had successful resolution of the presenting problem even in situations where only mild depth of trance was ever obtained. Caitlin then felt more relaxed as she went into a mild trance and projected her migraine into the nearby empty chair. The subsequent changes were relatively small diminishment of size, intensity of color, and slowing of throbbing in the pulsing empty chair. She felt tired at the end of our second session, but experienced a slight level of relief from her migraine. In the subsequent three days she was symptom-free for the first time in a month. Encouraged by this success, she was not blown away by the return of her symptoms that weekend. We had prepared her for this, predicting that now she would be able to handle relapses better because of the temporary days of relief she would now experience.

In our next session, Caitlin experienced only slow and slight variations in her projected headache, so at this point I introduced the idea of an empty-chair discussion with her somatic self, the part that was running the migraine. Caitlin was eager and animated as she became that part, telling the executive self that the headaches were her reminders that overachieving to please others and gain their approval was a deeply flawed and unsustainable mission. She needed to learn how to please herself, to cherish her own regard and selfhood rather than looking to others to define her worth and identity. This message would be appropriate for anyone her age, but in Caitlin's case, it was far more precise and poignant. In fact, many migraine sufferers are overachieving dedicated martyrs to social or corporate causes such that they neglect their own fulfilment and personal peace. Often they punctuate dedication to others by retreating and collapsing into a shell of misery after the completion of a big project or tense week at work. Eventually their personal resources are so depleted that they are chronically impaired and have to take time off work to nurse their migraines, becoming all the more frustrated with their sporadic inability to perform their high level of skill and service to others. As they finally hit the wall, it is nice for their migraines to speak up in a commentary about a personally unsustainable self-sacrificing lifestyle and mission. And so it was for Caitlin. Her migraine now had a voice, and a strong one, with a message of spiritual wisdom.

She now could go for weeks without a migraine. She stopped taking her pain medications, and found she could think more clearly. The former joy and enthusiasm of her pre-teen years had now returned. As predicted, when her migraines did return, they were now of diminished frequency, intensity, and duration. Encouraged by her recovery, she returned to her university, did make-up assignments and exams, completing her year and keeping up her high academic record. She also was more assertive with her roommate, her social group, and her boyfriend, so she had more time for herself. Ironically, she found studying and schoolwork easier as she took more time for fun and took her life less seriously. She is now almost through her second year of university and doing well. The migraines are not totally gone, but thus far they are mild and occasional inconveniences, rather than a central feature defining the parameters of her life. In her increasingly rare follow-up sessions, it is wonderful to hear about her personal development as a young adult, one of many clients that make my professional work so enjoyable.

CHAPTER 28

CLEARING THROUGH CLOUDS

JOHN WAS REFERRED by his psychiatrist, a colleague known for his gentle supportive Jungian therapy augmented by various combinations of medication. After many years of coping with severe chronic depression, John wanted to try something different. He had read in the clinical literature that Cognitive Behavior Therapy combined with hypnotherapy was often a highly effective approach for treating depression, and so he wanted to try it.

John was a middle-aged engineer working in design of various plant structures in the oil and gas industry in Calgary, Alberta. He was highly regarded and cherished for his creativity, technical brilliance, and diligent work ethic. Nevertheless, he would frequently experience "crash days" where he was unable to concentrate, flooded with ruminations and narratives of worthlessness and despair. It seemed as if there was a panel of judgemental voices that he called the "Old Men". This invited him to judge himself as an imposter of adequacy, and any day he would be fired for his poor performance. This event would herald the rejection of his supportive wife, who by that time would have exhausted her patience with his negativity and dour moods.

In our emotionally focused sessions, we placed the "Old Men" in chairs on the other side of the room and had him alternatively be the voices of the Old Men, then be himself countering their almost outrageous claims and the certainty of imminent catastrophe. While he was effective doing this in my office, he had more difficulty practicing the same retorts back at home between sessions, especially if he had difficulty sleeping because their voices were so loud and unrelenting most of the previous night. He felt as if he no longer had the strength to argue against them. While these voices were not hallucinations, they were nevertheless very prominent, commanding his attention and overriding critical reasoning and work-related tasks.

Using hypnosis we were able to reduce their loudness, and relegate them to the periphery of his consciousness, but they could not be silenced. We used the example from the motion picture "A Beautiful Mind" wherein the actor Russell Crowe plays a Nobel Prize-winning mathematician tormented by delusions and hallucinations; he eventually learns how to live with his demons, not by dismissing them, but merely relegating them to the periphery of his social and mental life. He learns not to fight their voices and entreaties to engage, but instead disidentifies and detaches from them. He knows that they will always be convinced that they are right, but he has chosen to embrace a different and more healthy and balanced perspective of his professional and personal worth. Similar to the movie, John is learning to let The Old Men grumble their condemnations and obscenities in the background rumble of his life narrative.

Still there was the crippling effect of his "crash days." Thankfully, his employers allowed John to miss work on these days and work on the days when he could function properly, knowing the net effect would be favorable and fair for all concerned, as he was still a well-regarded and cherished key professional in his firm. Still, his crash days were a devastating experience for him; his moods and thinking would go almost black on those days, with the depressive "Why bother?" mantra keeping him locked in a prison of inactivity. Thankfully, even on crash days he would make it to our sessions, and hypnosis would help him break free of their negative spell. In the first of these crash day sessions, one metaphor had special and enduring significance for him.

I told him I had been on a fall vacation on Saltspring Island, one of the Gulf Islands on the West Coast near Victoria, British Columbia. In the autumn it rains frequently in November, and that year was no exception. On one of those typically foggy days, for some crazy reason, I decided to drive up the road to the summit of Mount Maxwell for the first time, maybe to see the sun above the low clouds shrouding us in thick fog. At the end of the road was the trailhead in a ghostly forest where all you could see was the cedar bark path framed by tree trunks, the bark path itself, and exposed rock.

It was wonderful and peaceful with the fragrance of cedar everywhere.

In one part of the trail, there was a thousand-foot cliff with a rather high fence with warning signs along the way.

I sensed we were at the edge of a steep cliff with probably a 500 metre vertical drop or more, but that idea was only because of the contour lines on the local topographical map. All I could see was a grey haze of fog, becoming much thicker about 10 metres away. Then, suddenly within moments, the clouds began to clear.

Now it was as if a visual miracle happened. Looking down, I could now peer through the clouds and see boats in Burgoyne Bay, way down below.

And so it was. In the previous moment there was nothing I could see, just fog. In the next moment it was clear that many feet below, there was a harbour with boats and people. Then, mere minutes later, there was nothing to see except thick fog. But now I had a mental picture (and a physical photo to match it) of the reality that a bay community existed beyond that cliffside fence.

I suppose I told John this story as a metaphor about our knowledge of implicate reality (underlying form) just based on a story or a topographical map, versus explicate reality (what we can know through our senses, such as sight). The important point I was conveying was that once reality is verified through our senses and cognitions, we now have the basis of knowledge that the bay and harbour are there, even on days that are so clouded in that all we can see is fog. Thus, even though the fog of depression may cloud our vision, we can still know with a great deal of certainty about the reality beyond the fence of our limitations. Ordinarily, this therapeutic metaphor with its accompanying photographs would be compelling enough, but somehow I sensed it would have special significance for this Alberta client. As it turns out, I had no way of knowing it at the time, but John had lived two years in nearby Victoria, B.C. and had been on Saltspring Island, although never at that lookout park.

After that session, that salient personal metaphor had the effect of helping John remember, even in his worst crash days, that another reality still exists, even if the cloud of his depression obscures it temporarily. That idea, plus practices of Mindfulness, reinforce the conviction that moods come, moods go, emotions come, emotions go, perceptions come, perceptions go, judgements come, judgments go (no matter what their spell). Our enduring reality is that we are not our thoughts, and our emotions, our perceptions, our fog, but we can be grounded on the idea that we create our world.

"I am not what happened to me. I am what I choose to become." That is a mantra that clears an opening in the clouds of depression, into the clarity of patterns of possibility of how we want our lives to be. In his foggiest moments, John is still guided by the foghorn and lighthouse metaphor of a reality beyond the fog of his current transient state. As his therapy progresses, the fog of depression is lifting like a cloud in the late morning sun.

CHAPTER 29

HERE'S LOOKING AT YOU, KID

IN MY EARLY YEARS as a therapist, I did not take notes in the session. I thought it was disrespectful not to observe and engage my client with eye contact at virtually all times. However, there are many people for whom sustained eye contact or intense observation can be a threatening and invasive experience.

One such person was Anne, a somewhat attractive 24-year-old single university student finishing her B.Sc. in biology. She had been shy most of her life. There were no clues in her personal and family history as to where, why, and how she had developed her aversion and fear of eye-contact. She just felt intensely uncomfortable and strangely vulnerable when people looked at her. Her parents were supportive enough, and so was her outgoing sister who excelled in sports, but Anne would just focus on her studies, reading, and other mostly solitary pursuits. Like many shy people, she was often considered by others to be "stuck up" and "above it all" when the opposite was true. She saw herself as socially awkward, inept, and unworthy. After many times when people would invite her to join them and she refused, gradually they left her alone and gave up on her, confirming her self-fulfilling prophesy of their rejection. She had one close friend from high school days. They were both shy and kept largely to themselves while attending university.

In Anne's assessment interview, I asked her what would be so terrible if another person looked at her and she returned the look. She squirmed uncomfortably in her chair, alternating looking down at the floor, sidelong to the walls, and some-times at the floor. She could find no credible reason why eye contact was so intensely uncomfortable, just that she was now in the lifelong habit of avoiding it. I tried to find out what she thought would happen if she violated her rule, searching for some horrible and unbearable catastrophe that might result. Once again she could not imagine any terrible outcome, but she just had this enormous dread. For the brief times she could look at another person in the eyes, her anxiety would very quickly ramp up to panic proportions. She had been so embarrassed about her "silly, stupid problem" that she had never broached the subject of getting treatment for it and had strongly resisted help when her parents suggested it. However, she now realized that she would be graduating in a few months and looking to start a career as a lab techni-cian, so she needed at least enough coping skills to handle job interviews. She agreed that now was finally the time in her life where she could not continue trying to ignore this problem. After I described the process of systematic desensi-tization, she agreed to begin treatment in our second session.

We did the usual steps of constructing a hierarchy of scenes that for her triggered increasing anxiety. Using belly breathing and imagery, Anne found it surprisingly easy to enter into and maintain a relaxed state. Then we began graduated brief exposure of the scenes, starting from the easiest and working towards the most difficult. Surprisingly, she was able to handle all the scenes with virtually no anxi-ety right from the first exposure. Throughout the hour, she remained moderately relaxed and found the little surges of anxiety very brief and easy to manage. At the end of the hour, she felt relieved and successful. I congratulated her on her courage and thoroughness in following through with the desensitization procedure to its successful conclusion. Of course, I wanted to have her return the following week to see how this experience would transfer in her daily living in the coming week.

In her third session, Anne came in with large changes to report. Yes, she was able to look at people on the bus riding home. Nothing bad or unusual happened externally. She had similar experiences on the university campus. She was able to see others and others see her, and make brief eye contact with no negative repercussions.

However, now she was blown away by the implications of this new experience. She came to realize that all the problems she had been carrying in silence for years had been impressions and illusions of her own making. People were not staring at her. No one seemed to be malicious, judging, or rejecting her; they were merely going about their business, barely noticing her, but basically neutral or mildly friendly as they made brief eye contact. Moreover, feeling no threat, she experienced no anxiety symptoms related to eye contact. However, she did feel very weird and decentred about the reorganization of her experience of reality. That is, nothing seemed real; it was all surreal and other-worldly. It was if she was groggy, awakening from a dream, but still not quite trusting her new waking reality. She was not paranoid but quite disoriented about her reality anchors living in a world where she could now potentially function normally. Still, the experience was disconcerting, so much so that she wondered how she could integrate and feel comfortable and confident about her new world. I suggested that perhaps, if she wished, we could reinstate part of her former eye-contact phobia, rendering her somewhat shy once again. Then in the coming weeks we could have her recover more gradually, integrating her new perspectives in a less upsetting way. She heartily embraced this new slower pace of therapy. Of course, once Anne accepted the idea that she could control the pace of her progress, her return to partial shyness was only half-hearted and relatively brief. Within a few weeks she was on her way to becoming her new confident self. She never had problems with eye contact again.

Among the lessons I learned from treating Anne was a fast cure is not necessarily an optimal cure. I was so eager to help Anne quickly that therapy had destabilized her experience of reality and meaning. Part of recovery is the integration of the client's world when the old problem pattern is removed. This principle applies even more strongly if the client is living in a family or other intimate relationship. Systemic loops that had formed the context of the symptom now need to be rearranged and perhaps renegotiated to ensure the problems do not return to their former host.

The second lesson was for me to reconsider my own use of eye contact in psychotherapy. At times eye contact can be threatening. Of course, there are many examples of this phenomenon in the animal kingdom, where sustained staring by another animal can activate the amygdale and even result in displays of aggression towards the offending animal. This display is most often seen in apes and monkeys and in dogs defending territory against intruders. Perhaps my emphasis on acute and continuous observation of my client was in some cases intrusive and disrespectful of my client's privacy, especially in the early phases when the therapeutic relationship was being established. Perhaps I could still observe, track, and pace a client's experience by listening to the breathing, tone, and voice inflection patterns while occasionally looking elsewhere. Now, I am quite confident that I can observe sometimes without watching. I can even take notes in the session, using them to mark what is important to emphasize. I now use my gaze more sparingly, to selectively note what my client considers to be important, and to mark analogically the connection that helps move my client in a therapeutic direction.

Part Five:

CHARACTER DEVELOPMENT

The following stories are a little longer to read because they took a lot longer to develop over the course of therapy. Yet, they are no less inspiring because it took a lot of gentle but firm guidance to achieve the favorable results that developed.

CHAPTER 30

Liver And Onions

DURING THE COURSE of my career, I have helped quite a few people deal with life-threatening illnesses, including cancer. Mostly they want to use hypnosis and guided imagery to shrink or kill cancerous cells by building up the strength of their immune system and using T-cells to combat the disease. We know that there is anecdotal evidence that imagery can assist in the healing of cancer. Now, of course I am not a medical doctor, so I have barely more than a layman's understanding of how imagery does this, but typically my clients have some sensible theories and strategies.

The most obvious idea is that T-cells can be programmed to seek out and selectively attack only cancerous cells, leaving healthy tissue surrounding them unharmed. For example, one of my clients used the metaphor that T-cells were actually navy SEALs, specially trained scuba-diving technical warriors armed with deadly spear guns. They would seek out the cancer-fish and kill them effectively, with no damage to the other fish and the marine environment. Our imagery sessions were exciting: searching, hunting, and finally spearing and killing these cancer cells. Most of my clients, especially males, featured aggressive imagery. Even most female clients used these metaphors because our culture is taught to fight destruction with even more potent aggression, a winner-take-all paradigm. This is a prevalent strategy, and sometimes it works brilliantly with a remission of the cancer. On some other occasions it does not work; the cancer may be suppressed but not cured, and my clients may move on to more aggressive surgical and chemotherapy strategies. In a few cases the illness progresses and the psychotherapy shifts to a more spiritual level as my client goes into a hospice and we help in the process of acceptance and peaceful abiding. This grief work is actually quite beautiful, and I can see how many therapists are deeply rewarded for the privilege of accompanying their clients on this final journey.

However, returning to the topic of imagery approaches to defeating cancer, a few of my female clients used even more interesting and intriguing strategies. You can kill a cancer cell, or any cell for that matter, by cutting off its blood supply. So supposing you coated the membrane of the cell with a gum or cream so that it could no longer absorb the nutrients that sustained it? Of course, that coated cancerous cell would wither and shrivel up, and be sloughed off with other body waste tissue, only to be replaced with healthy cells growing in its place. One of my female clients used this kind of imagery with an infrared super-detector that could sense overheated cancerous cells, then squirt them thoroughly with suffocating foam that would cover the entire membrane with an impermeable jell. We would return to their withered shells by the wayside in our next hunting expedition. She fully recovered from her cancer after ten sessions.

By now you are probably wondering about the legitimacy of the title of this story. Well, as you know, there are many layers of an onion skin, and many layers beneath it as you peel the crusty layer away. My client Uriel was a 56-year-old married accountant with two children, a boy and a girl, who were grown up and thriving. He was very active in the Jewish congregation to which he devoted his volunteer time as a treasurer. However, like most accountants he was exacting and mercilessly precise in his demands of the synagogue and its members. Furthermore, he was, to put it flatteringly, a crusty S.O.B. He was typically cynical, distrustful, sarcastic, patronizing, angry, bitter, and seemingly miserable to all those who knew him. Nevertheless, his long-suffering wife was loyal in her support for him despite his public reputation and received sympathy from the Jewish community for putting up with him on a daily basis. Even his children learned how to get along with him. They knew he was fair. More than that, they knew his tender and affectionate side that the community seldom saw. However, even at home his characteristic cynicism often poisoned the family atmosphere and stifled the sharing of joy. It seemed that nobody really liked him: they just put up with his negative diatribes because he was a loyal and dependable person, a sensitive soft soul under a bitter crust. Porcupines are lovable once you get past the quills.

Then came the sudden discovery of his liver cancer and his referral to me by his family doctor. Now, I don't know that much about cancer, but my understanding is that liver cancer can develop quite silently, with little discomfort until the condition is well established. In Uriel's case it was said to be so virulent that it was likely terminal. Our first session I suppose was characteristic of his first encounters with any male potential authority-figure: he would be the alpha male by intimidation. What did I know about cancer? How could the hocus pocus of hypnotherapy do anything to reverse the trend of a terminal illness? What were my credentials and record about using imagery to cure cancer? I told him that my professional code of conduct as a psychologist precluded the use of testimonials of previous successfully treated clients (geez, I wish they would change this code provision). Uriel continued with his attack about the stupidity of this referral and my inability to help him. I responded with my sense of curiosity: if it were at all possible to use these techniques, even if ineffectual, wouldn't it be better than to not even try them at all? He softened with my non-confrontational craftsman approach, and decided he might give it a try. The conversation was not as easy as that; there was a lot of gentle motivational interviewing, where I played devil's advocate and discouraged him from even attempting such a ridiculous treatment, and you know how that goes. Eventually he was intrigued with an approach that was so off-beat and seemingly irrational, with only a smattering of empirical research in its support. Nevertheless, he had heard of people using imagery to defeat cancer, and my intrigue had engaged his strong fighting spirit. In that first session, we progressed from being confrontational opponents into united allies in combating a common enemy.

Our sessions began with me deconstructing Uriel's myths and fears about the nature of trance and hypnosis. It is not a matter of the hypnotist's control; it is the hypnotist assisting the client in developing his own trance to use imagery in a manner that better serves his own purposes. The therapist is merely a consultative guide in discovery, not a director of destiny. We then began with Uriel's favorite metaphor. He loved late World War II newsreels showing the strafing runs of P-51 Mustang aircraft fighters blowing up German tanks, trains, trucks, and other supply logistics to aid the Allied effort in ending the war and Nazi Germany in 1944-45. Uriel just loved to imagine himself as a fighter pilot rocketing and strafing Nazi tanks of cancer and blowing them up. We had a lot of fun flying low over France and Germany on these sorties of destruction. Even better, the Luftwaffe had been virtually eliminated as a counter-threat, as was minimal antiaircraft ground fire, so the aggression against cancer cells on the ground held virtually no threat to our safety. It was pure unadulterated forceful aggression and destruction of the enemy, a testosterone dream mission. Even my feminist and pacifist tendencies were overwhelmed by the pure exaltation of victory on these imaginary sorties.

Week by week, as the therapy progressed, Uriel became slightly softer to other people, beginning with his wife and sons. His bitterness was replaced with a mild sardonic spirit of acceptance, and at times, even moments of the joy of being alive and sharing experiences of wonder and gratitude. He even became more mellow in his community, more accepting of others' shortcomings and failures. He became more compassionate and accepting of frailties of himself and others. People in his Jewish community noticed the welcome difference in his demeanor and attitude. He was showing the true menshe underneath the crust of mean bitterness that he had shown over the years. His reputation was vindicated by some who had told others that deep down, under that crust, was a warm and sensitive person. It's just that few had tolerated enough of his character armour to wade through it to find the value of the soul it sheltered. Uriel became more popular as people felt more at ease in his presence. Although at first uncomfortable and shy, he came to like this new way of being in the community.

This kind of shift towards a kinder more mellow and compassionate posture is quite typical of clients with a terminal illness that have come to terms with their mortality. They adopt a position of acceptance which we call 'peaceful abiding.' As their ego melts away and their transcendent self emerges, they come to see themselves as one with others and even the universe. It is quite a spiritual transformation, and one of the aspects that makes hospice work so rewarding. In my work with clients with cancer, I help them come to a position of acceptance even as they continue combating their illness with imagery and other aggressive medical treatments such as radiation and chemotherapy. The rationale of this complementary hypnotherapy treatment is to relieve the suffering and anguish in the initial phases. Then I can assist my client my client to hang on loosely and not overplay their recovery or progression by forcing it too intently, instead merely allowing their healing capacity to gather strength and resources to effectively combat the cancer. This was Uriel's process as well, as we met weekly for eight weeks for our "tank-busting" imagery sessions, seasoned with some philosophical and spiritual principles such as mindfulness.

Then a strange thing happened. His terribly advanced cancer went into remission. His pain and discomfort steadily declined then vanished altogether. It was too soon and sudden to celebrate a victory over his cancer. Nevertheless, we both became more optimistic that something was working in his recovery. We proceeded with hypnotherapy on a bi-weekly basis, then monthly for two more months.

Then an even stranger thing happened. As he recovered from his cancer, Uriel returned to his former personality style! I could hardly believe it. Uriel did not quite revert to his former nasty bitter cynicism and despair, but he again acted rather harshly towards his family and others, frequently using sarcasm and criticism. Once again, many community members turned away from him, incredulous at his seeming lack of gratitude for his recovery and the support of others during this process. It seemed that this way of being was ego-syntonic for him, a familiar way of keeping other people at a more comfortable and less intimate distance. He was unwilling to consider throwing off this armor, even though he had enjoyed much of the cheerfulness of his recovering self. As he ended therapy he thanked me for our sessions, and the tank-busting was fun, but still it was just hocus-pocus, a silly diversion. He recovered because the chemotherapy was finally working; that was the only reason. All this other soft stuff was for sissies, and I was a pleasant enough fellow, but our work really was irrelevant as far as he perceived it. I took that dismissal with a grain of salt. After all, there are many people who would still rather perceive themselves as independent and not needing any psychological help, even after a successful process and outcome. In my follow-up phone calls two and four years later, Uriel was still cancer-free, and from my informal connections in his community, as feisty as ever.

For me awareness is a one-way street. Once you have experienced a better way of living and seeing your reality improve, why would you ever want to revert to a less adaptive and lower quality way of life? I suppose it might have to do with not reshaping your inner self, so going back to the old way is more familiar and comfortable. We certainly see this phenomenon in relapses in addictions work. I was unable to engage Uriel in doing that inner work, so it was a less than satisfactory outcome for me in terms of my wishes for Uriel's functioning. However, as I still learn in my work, sometimes our clients see us only in terms of the functionality of meeting their goals within their life paradigms, reaching for nothing more than comfort in improving how they use their neuroses. As the expression goes: when the tailor meets the saint, he is only interested in what the saint is wearing.

CHAPTER 31

Therapy By Changing Your Sense Of Humour: from cynicism to silliness

A FAMILY DOCTOR referred a couple to me for marital counselling. They were both locked in a death spiral of blame, projection, defensiveness, contempt, and utter disgust for the other that had begun many years earlier. It is often cited in the marriage therapy literature that the typical couple does not come in for marital counselling until they have been dysfunctional for the previous six years. To their credit, this couple did not engage in physical violence, but the verbal wounds they inflicted on each other were far worse, with sarcasm and sneering cynicism dripping from their pursed lips in our first two assessment sessions. Both expressed a need to end their 12-year marriage; they only attended therapy to prove to their respective families-of-origin that reconciliation was hopeless, that they had given marital therapy a chance at repair. I told them that their collective mental set precluded that possibility, but that at least they could agree on their hopelessness, if nothing else. Thankfully, there were no children involved. Also mercifully, they were both somewhat successful in their respective careers, in which they buried their lives and their identities, him as an accountant, her as a school teacher. We agreed to end the consultation at that point, with the couple headed full speed for divorce.

About a year later, the now ex-wife contacted me requesting individual therapy. Although she had disliked the previous marital sessions, she liked my spirit of fairness, respect, and optimism with which I had conducted them. So I agreed to see her as a client. She began the first session with a monologue of bitterness, cynicism, and vitriol about life, injustice, suffering, entitlement, and general rage at the world and her lot in negotiating through its injustices. After patiently listening to this spew of invective for 20 minutes, I stopped her and told her to end this verbal abuse. She was shocked at my label of her behavior. I pointed out that, for her to rant and for me to merely listen passively, was for me to condone her verbal abuse of our time together. Furthermore, therapy would not accomplish anything if this pattern became our standard format of communication. Then she said, "but if I don't tell you how I'm thinking, how can you possibly help me? This is the way I talk to myself all the time. I can't stand it!"

I again told her that this room was for psychotherapy, not verbal abuse. (At that point I was mentally returning to the script of an ancient Monty Python sketch, called The Argument Clinic, in which a patron of the clinic accidentally goes in the wrong door and is harangued by the counsellor verbally abusing him rather than beginning an argument.) I told her to remain silent unless a positive or at least neutral thought entered her mind. Another 10-15 minutes of silence ensued, then she broke the emptiness by saying how sorry and sad she was that her mind was so negative and entrenched in hostility towards life. This statement of sadness was our first point of engagement on a new course of therapy. I had remembered from our marital sessions that she had at least one redeeming feature: she was highly intelligent and pointed in her use of sarcasm and cynical wit to encapsulate hopeless situations in vicious black humour. I intrigued her with the possibility of utilizing that strength in a therapeutic collaboration around changing her personality by changing her sense of humour from cynicism to levity and frivolity. She at first recoiled from this proposition, but was intrigued by my attribution of the strength but misuse of her sense of humour. I asked her to consider this proposal over the next two weeks. She returned for her appointment, agreed with the premises of our therapeutic contract, and we began our work.

We met once every two weeks for about eight months. You might think that our work involved watching humorous DVDs of comedy films and sketches, and analysing why and how they could be funny, thus indirectly transforming the prevalent attitudes, perceptions, and conceptions of my client. That would have been enormous fun for me, and little work. Unfortunately, I work in private practice, and charging my client more than $100/hr to laugh is not ethical, even if potentially therapeutic. No, this therapy was far more mundane. Each session, my client had to present to me her worst encountered situations in the previous two weeks. She would first describe them from her usual perspective, dark glasses. Then I would ask her to reframe each incident from an alternative perspective.

This viewpoint is represented in a story about two children and their Christmas presents. One was perpetually pessimistic and negative. Her name was Char. Her twin sister, Lena, always saw things positively. Their differences became so widely extreme that their parents decided one Christmas to rig the presents they bought them in a more biased way, in an attempt to balance their outlook on life. On Christmas morning, they watched as Charlene unwrapped her presents. In typical fashion, Char was critical of the colors, sizes, and shapes of the toys and clothing gifts. Nothing satisfied her, and she was grumpy. Her parents then watched Lena open her two presents, both large bags of horse manure. To their amazement, Lena started throwing the clumps up into the air giggling merrily. They asked her, "How can you be so happy and joyful?" She said, "With all this poop, there must be a pony nearby somewhere!" I call this attitude "looking for the pony," and it prevails in a lot of my therapeutic outlook. Others call it "making lemonade when all life gives you is lemons." You know what I mean. Well I would insist that my client could not leave the description of a negative vignette until she had come up with at least a neutral reframe. For her it was a work of mental gymnastics, and these mental muscles were indeed out of shape. After my allowances for awkward and effortful silences, she would come up with some favourable and occasionally brilliant captions. Some of them even used my philosophy of life, that "irony is the driving force of the universe."

Gradually her humour conveyed a self-reflexive sense, incorporating some acceptance and even compassion and kindness, toward herself and other actors and forces in our great cosmic dance. Eventually, she even began to giggle in her appraisal of truly ridiculous and absurd situations she encountered. She even at times became child-like and silly, repeating little children's jokes like "How do you catch a unique bunny? You 'neek up on it! How do you catch a tame bunny? Tame way! You 'neek up on it!" You need to be in the mind of a child to appreciate this whimsy and fanciful humour. By the time her humour had evolved, there were far fewer situations that required reframing. In fact, her professional and personal life had by now become happier and more joyful. So we agreed this therapy had come to its proper conclusion.

In our final, 18th session, we mutually rejoiced in our therapeutic collaboration, which had become an increasing pleasure over the months. In her token of affection for the help, my graduate client gave me a lovely book, called *Today I will Honor my Inner Martyr: Affirmations for cynics* by Sarah Wells and Anne Thornhill (Prima Publishing, 1998).

This hilarious small book features mantras that sometimes seem to be the main underlying schemas for some people's lives. Some examples are:

- Today I will provoke a loved one's anger just to assure myself that I still have an effect on him or her (p.13).

- Today I will remind myself that my friends and family are just waiting for me to fail (p.20).

- Although everyone pretends not to realize it, they know I am superior to them (p.28).

- Today I celebrate my ability to verbally support others while mentally judging them (p.38).

- Today I will cultivate a relationship with an especially needy person so that I can fulfill my need to be needed (p.48).

- The best years of my life are over. They weren't exactly good years, but nonetheless, they are over (p.52).

So that was my client's graduation present to her therapist. As we laughed together at these mantras of cynical humour, we affirmed that it was not our intention to eradicate all forms of vicious humour of superiority, but merely to indicate other ways of framing situations in humorous form that featured self-reflection, irony, and even whimsical silliness. Thus ended one of the most interesting therapies I have done in my career.

CHAPTER 32

TREATING A BULLY

QUITE A WHILE AGO, in the mid 1980s, I was the chief instructor of a small community judo club. Most of the members were children, plus a small group of adult upper belts who also assisted in the teaching. Among the judo students and good tournament fighters were our son, Mark, and daughter Sarah. After a few years their interests drifted in various activities away from judo. For this and several other reasons, we decided to fold the club and send our remaining students to another more distant community club. It was a fun judo club while it lasted, but we needed to move on to other things as well, and running a club is a great time drain.

As a sensei, I impressed upon my judoka that they were not to use judo off the mat, unless in a life threatening situation. I enforced this and other rules of the judo code of conduct strictly, so my students knew that if they used judo in the school yard or anywhere else off the mat, they would be expelled from the club. However, I later discovered to my horror that my regime and enforcement of them was way too strict. It was early in the 1990s that Mark came in one day from school quite upset. He was the victim of bullying by two boys who ganged up on him and beat him. He was bruised and contused, but there were no serious injuries. On the other hand, the emotional wounds were far greater. Mark felt frustrated because he could have easily dealt with them if only he could have used his judo skills. He was embarrassed that he was being picked on and did not fight back. I wanted to call the school and the other boys' parents to discipline these bullies, but Mark wanted to settle the matter himself for his own honour and reputation. I apologized deeply for the rule that would not allow him to defend himself. I told him that, going forward, he could use his judo skills anytime he felt he needed to defend himself. Mark nodded his head knowingly. I don't actually know what happened, but the bullying problem never came up again. Perhaps there were one or two scuffles where Mark used his judo, and the other boys quickly broke off; I think it went something like that. But I will never forget the anger I felt towards those bullies, and in fact, towards all bullies and cowards.

At about the same time Mark was dealing with his situation, I received a referral to treat another 12-year-old boy at a different school. This guy was himself a bully. He and his friends picked on other weaker kids in his class and the neighbourhood, using the threat of force to extort small amounts of money and toys for "protection." They were, in effect, beginning to practice racketeering in their junior high school. Although Jason had been suspended and expelled from a previous school, and now was suspended from his current school, he had avoided the juvenile justice system with warnings and mild reprimands. The scale of his misdemeanors was deemed small, and after all, he came from "a good family." As it turned out, Jason did come from a lovely family. His father was an engineer working in an oil company. His wife was a geophysicist, working for another oil company here in Calgary. This couple balanced their busy dual career lives with the demands of child rearing. Their 10-year-old daughter had always been easy, an A-student with lots of friends. Jason had always been somewhat compliant and no trouble at home, other than a few incidents where he was teasing or cruel with animals. However, at school he was bored and restless, often inattentive and distracting other students in class (not a good sign). He liked to tease and make fun of other children, especially the shy ones. Each year as he became older his nuisance and cruel behavior escalated. When confronted by teachers and his parents, he was somewhat ashamed when caught, but could offer no reason or excuse why he did these rather hurtful things. When forced to do so he might offer a shallow apology to the kid he bullied, but was sometimes later known to hunt down and corner that child for "snitching" on him. Only recently had the behaviour escalated to the point of minor extortion and consistent intimidation of others.

I treated Jason with a combination of individual and family therapy. In family sessions, I encouraged his exasperated parents to be kind but firm in their dealings with Jason, enforcing losses of privileges after each reported incident. Jason's behaviour settled down somewhat as the firmness persisted, and the threat of imminent expulsion from his current school hung over his head.

I had a worse time trying to engage with Jason in individual sessions. He was superficially cooperative and engaging, but he exuded a personal style that was slick and polished. I had seen this kind of display earlier in my career when I was working with psychopaths and sociopaths in a hospital for the criminally insane. It was hard for me to keep an open mind and a kind heart, as I listened to Jason describe his pleasure when other children feared him and deferred to him. It might have been easier to understand if he had some history of being abused or a victim of some kind of childhood trauma, but instead all I noticed was a pervasive attitude of entitlement, with relatively low levels of empathy for others. He did not seem to care that he was unpopular, because the power of the fear he inspired in others was sufficient for his teenage ego. What was even more galling was his derision for children who did not fight back when he hurt them; their passivity stimulated his disgust with them, and he would show even less mercy for them. Of course, it was even harder for me knowing that two months earlier my son had gone through such an experience on the receiving end. It took all the self-discipline I could muster to resist the counter-transference feelings I was having before each session.

Family therapists frequently go through a phase of "being stuck in the family position," that is, temporarily feeling what it must feel like to be in this family dilemma. In my case, it was feeling almost helpless overwhelmed by anger towards my client and his cruel behavior. Deliberate cruelty against innocent victims is still a hot-button issue for me, so I have to remember that anger is a secondary emotion, covering another layer of more primary emotion.

I reached through the anger to sense sadness that Jason felt so powerless that he felt he had to subjugate others to have a place in this world. I'm not sure if this formulation was accurate, but it did allow me to listen to Jason in a spirit of loving-kindness and let go of my judgements. I continued to listen with empathy and calmness, reflecting back whatever emotions he shared. After five sessions, he started to open up about how he loved his family and was deeply embarrassed by the trouble and shame he caused. He was seriously per-plexed about why he felt he had to control others with power. He felt confused and lonely, socially awkward and unwor-thy, so I suppose this was what he felt was his only option to have any sense of identity and importance. Nevertheless, he was not making the connection that his antisocial behavior was further eroding whatever possibilities he might have in forming true friendships. He knew that his gang buddies only liked him because he was tougher than they were, and would likely abandon him if he showed any weakness.

Gradually Jason became less disruptive in class and the schoolyard. He even started playing sports and other activ-ities. Others got over their initial fear and mistrust and started to like his natural athletic skill. He learned to move beyond being merely competitive and started to become more cooperative. His family was cautiously optimistic that he was getting better. There were a few minor setbacks, but far less severe or often, more like shoving matches rather than actual fights. (On hearing about these events, I positively connoted the self restraint involved.) Thankfully, the teaching staff and Jason's family cooperated with firmness rather than panic and alarm, seeing these slips in the context of overall improvement. Occasional family sessions were helpful in maintaining this stance toward Jason. After two months, we tapered off our individual sessions to once every three weeks, and family sessions once every five weeks. Towards the end of treatment I no longer held any negative feelings or dread in our sessions. Jason still carried some aspects of narcissism and entitlement, but they were now within the range of typical teenage disrespect and mildly rebellious attitude. Even though he no longer got into trouble, It seemed as if Jason hardly had any mirror neurons, and empathy for others was still not easy for him to master, but at least he was starting to develop some companionships, if not friendships.

Looking back on this case, perhaps I could have used my feelings in a different way. I could have, as I often do with adult clients, revealed to Jason the kinds of emotions I was going through as a way of working on our therapeutic relationship. However, I felt that, at least in our earlier sessions, such self-disclosure would have been met with his sneering derision. He likely would have disqualified me as a therapist. I felt it was better to hold my ground, deal with my emotions internally, and maintain a steady posture of firm loving-kindness and understanding. I think I created a caring space that gradually allowed him to explore, question, and emerge as a more normal and balanced teenager. Regardless of what happened with Jason, I do remember my internal struggle in dealing with him as one of the hardest situations of counter-transference that I have encountered in my career.

CHAPTER 33

SELF-HANDICAPPING

A 20-YEAR OLD BOXER referred himself to me for help with sport psychology to overcome his problem in professional prize-fights. He was regarded by his manager and his sparring mates as a tough and skilful club fighter, but most often when he got into the ring in a prize fight, he would pick up warnings and penalty points from the referee for low blows, also known as hits below the belt. This was not dirty fighting, merely sloppy hits that inevitably meant that he would fall behind in points. In this situation he would fight more freely in a come-from-behind position, now a definite underdog, more desperate, but at times, more effective. Most of the time, however, he would wind up losing the match on points. He would leave the ring convinced he was the better fighter and only losing because of penalty points and getting behind in the score.

This pattern is a good example of what we call self-handicapping. A person who often uses this pattern can defeat himself repeatedly and sometimes win big when most of his supporters are starting to give up on his chances. While he can be occasionally heroic, most of the time he winds up protecting his ego by saying to himself, "I know I'm a better boxer than him; he was just lucky to beat me." The life script of underdog was his mantra. He even liked his nickname "Slammer" from his brief encounters of incarceration for petty theft and minor assault. He wore his jail-time as if it were a badge of honour. Although he projected an image of aggressiveness and belligerence, it was no more than a mantle of machismo. Inside he was unsure of himself, trying hard to prove his toughness. According to the dictates of machismo, it is not sufficient to prove yourself once; you must continuously defend your image and reputation, at risk of being shunned and disrespected by all the people you put above you, especially aggressive males.

As you are reading this, you are probably expecting to hear about an abusive childhood with parents of unrelenting standards and cruelty in their enforcement. No, this was not quite the case. Slammer was actually the middle child in a working class family. His parents argued frequently, but not violently, about his father's alcohol dependency. On a few occasions, Slammer took his mother's side and defended her against his father's emotional abuse and implied physical threats. His father eventually left when my client was seventeen, but was diligent in child support, if not family involvement. However, the crucial element was that he was emotionally distant and uninvolved in the child-rearing of the children, focusing instead on his career as a welder and financial provider, and friend to his drinking circle. Slammer's other two brothers went on to groom themselves for careers in the trades, but Slammer didn't fit the family cultural mould. He was quiet and shy, and liked art and other pursuits and interests, for which he seemed to lack talent or the courage or support to try beyond his first fumbling attempts. He was not a bright or successful student, and dropped out in grade eleven to do odd jobs and work part-time at his great ambition, to become a prize-fighter for a living.

There is a noteworthy characteristic that sometimes happens in males. There is a syndrome that has been described as "absent fathers, lost sons." That is, there are many young males raised in situations where their father was physically or emotionally absent by virtue of his career or other emotional distancing. These sons often acted as if lost, certainly not validated and supported in their struggles to emerge from adolescence into adulthood. Of course, many of these young men are prone to joining gangs, where they can enact shows of machismo in front of their male peers for status, power, and approval. Whether in gangs or alone, many become enslaved to the wheel of Samsara, having to prove themselves worthy of being men over and over again, chasing the approval of an unseen but ever-present ghost of their absent father.

To cite a more poignant variation of this script, we need to descend into the realm of psychoanalysis. According to this paradigm, if a son is his mother's favourite, they form a coalition of affection to the perceived exclusion of the father. The son enjoys being exalted, but is constantly in unconscious fear of the father's retribution. To defend against an unconscious but symbolic counterattack by their father, these Momma's Favourite "Oedipal Triumphs" unconsciously lower their profile by failing in life. It is as if they fear that, if they succeed, they will further incur the wrath of their displaced and defeated fathers. If you subscribe to psychoanalytic theory, this formulation makes reasonable sense. We call it "fear of success," manifested in a pattern of just-missing calls to greatness, failing in crucial tests to graduate to a new level of success. Even though I am using the example of males, a similar dynamic can also occur in females with the lifescript "whatever I do, it will never be good enough."

Regardless of its origin, self-handicapping and other forms of self-sabotage have the effect of cementing a self-script of inadequacy and anxiety, while feeling the pressure to prove oneself. Slammer needed the support and validation of his therapist, his manager, and his club-mates and friends. However, it was hard for them to get onside with his repeated failures. Furthermore, with his limited financial resources, even though I was seeing him on a reduced fee basis, there was little time to do an in-depth therapy to address these issues properly in the five sessions we had.

Nevertheless, we were able to accomplish one worthwhile goal. Slammer had come to realize that his self-handicapping was protecting his ego, but avoiding his date with destiny. As long as he held back, or self-sabotaged enough that he could not win, he would never know if he "had the right stuff." Sometimes in life it is more peaceful and authentic to come to a position of Zen acceptance. In this context, you truly try your hardest, not holding back. If and when you do not win, at least you gave yourself every chance of succeeding. If your best was not good enough to carry the match, then you can deal with the verdict of fate; today was not your day. You can learn to accept temporary defeat, take a hit, and come back next time wiser and stronger. This is the athlete's code. But you cannot follow this code if you protect yourself from the consequences of competing to your best ability. Learning to live with our limitations and strive to go beyond them is a spiritual endeavour requiring courage and hard work. For all his bravado, Slammer was lacking the courage to put his full skills on the line.

In the following months, Slammer succeeded in stopping his self-handicapping. As you can imagine, he won more fights over equally skilled and determined boxers; he lost to superior fighters, and became well-respected among his peers and handlers. He never reached the Big Time; almost no boxer does. But at least he had the satisfaction of giving it his all, and accepting the verdict of authentic competition.

BIG JOHN

GROUP THERAPY is especially effective with people who have interpersonal problems, or personality disorders that tend to get them into tangles in their relationships. In the mental health clinic where I first worked after graduating with my Ph.D., I was working in a civic hospital in London, Ontario, where the group therapy component was a strong part of our therapy program. We ran open psychotherapy groups, didactic groups, behavior therapy groups, and groups for specific populations, such as those suffering from obesity. It was in one of the psychodynamic groups, co-led by myself and psychologist Dr. Arnie Slive, where we met Big John.

Big John was an unhappy person. In his late twenties, John was a former heroin addict, a heavily tattooed biker gang member with a criminal record for assault, break and enter, possession of stolen property, and several other offences. He was a rather imposing physical presence, with his six foot five inch frame supporting a weight close to 300 pounds. His gruff manner and coarse language and threatening stories of his gang life were merely character armor for his desperate sadness and loneliness. On several occasions he had attempted suicide, including the more innocuous methods of overdoses and other more dramatic gestures. He was skillfully inept at brinksmanship in arranging his own staged demise. In one instance, he tried to kill himself by shooting a .22 caliber rifle into his chest. The bullet missed his heart and exited cleanly through his upper back, causing amazingly minor tissue damage. Despite his skill in surviving suicide attempts, John seemed to be clumsy and a failure at many of the things he did. He worked as a construction laborer, having few skills or education after dropping out of school in his teens. He was also a recovering heroin addict and member of a biker gang. Yet with all of his failings and troubles, he was morosely engaging as a sensitive lost soul, and from the beginning of his therapy group he managed to elicit the care of his fellow members.

John was adept at emotional extortion, using his obsessions with death and multiple suicidal gestures as a way to manipulate attention through drama and suspense. Group members would try to persuade him that life was worth living, which only reinforced his comfortable rebuttals with "yeah, but..." disqualifying statements "you just don't understand what's it's like in my world" until he finally and triumphantly exasperated those who were trying to reach out to him with his caustic put-downs to their street naivete. After several rounds of this kind of interaction, the group became more aware of the insincerity of his ploys. On one occasion John upped the ante by being absent after a session in which the group had called him out for his negative attention-seeking. He had made some veiled suicidal threats, saying the world would be better off without him, but the group and the therapists were unable to make him promise he would not try to take his own life, although he repeatedly said he had no plan or intent.

Nevertheless, he was absent at the beginning of the next session. Despite other concerns involving motivated people ready to work on their issues, doubt haunted the room as we all speculated on whether John was alive, and how would we all feel if he suicided The predictable outpourings of helpless guilt abounded. Now bear in mind, the role of co-therapists in a psychodynamic group is not necessarily to confront credibility gaps, but to facilitate the group process and allow the group to come to its own consensus, so that it can learn from its successes and mistakes. So just imagine now, as the group had spent over 60 minutes wringing their hands, in walks John, vaguely apologizing to the group for being an hour late in a 1.5 hr. group therapy session. The uproar that ensued took most of the rest of the session to settle down and integrate. Working it through, the group came to realize its process in being caught in The Rescue Triangle. For a while the group felt like helpless Rescuers of Victim John, then felt themselves victimized when John made his entrance, then finally started to Persecute him for setting up their excessive care for his well-being. This is how the myth of "we all care for each other regardless of their self-destructive behaviors" becomes a learning laboratory for the group. They begin to discover that the ethos of unconditional positive regard, to which they all subscribe and wish to attain, becomes much more difficult to apply in real life. The group then comes to a more realistic ideal of "non-possessive caring" or caring with adequate boundaries.

There is yet another dynamic in the suicidal gesture ploy: the worry about accidental suicide. That is, sometimes people stage elaborate overdoses in which they rely upon a family member coming home just in time to see that their family or friend has overdosed, calling the ambulance and getting the drugs pumped out before they are toxic enough to cause death. Occasionally this strategy misfires, in that an unexpected delay results in the friend or relative arriving too late, and a help-seeking gesture becomes an accidental suicide. This eventuality is very difficult for a therapist, and not much better for a group member. Unfortunately, there is a gambit played by desperate people. It is based on a perverse sense of forgiveness. That is, if I offend you, and you forgive me, I guess I must be loveable. If, however, I offend you more greatly and you forgive me, I must be that much more loveable. So, the higher I raise the stakes, the more lovable I must be. When the stakes are life or death, the game of ego gratification becomes potentially more deadly, and all participants are ensnared in its trap. This dance of terror is what we call emotional blackmail: "love me, care about me, or I will kill myself." Thankfully, the group was able to survive this trap and move on, learning their life lessons about the traps of rescuing.

Several weeks later, the group had disbanded after its course of twelve sessions. My co-therapist, Arnie, and I inherited the loose ends of all unsolved cases. John was still alive, but constantly obsessed with death, so I had the job of treating him individually. I decided to apply the boundaries I needed to work more comfortably. I offered a non-suicide contract. That is, in addition to the usual clauses about prompt and regular attendance at therapy sessions, I required John to commit to no actions, words, or gestures that would indicate his desire to kill himself for at least six months while we worked on his therapy. Violation of these terms would result in his treatment with me being suspended for 30 days after the incident. I would refuse any contact with him during this period, even if he were hospitalized. Those were my terms as his primary therapist. Predictably, he rebelled against any constraints against his emotional and behavioral freedom, and left my office in a huff.

A few days later he called for an appointment. He said he was willing to sign the anti-suicide contract. I looked forward to working with the part of him that was willing to reform. So he came in for the session, willing to commit; however, there was "a minor glitch." He had accepted a contract to enforce a gambling debt owing to his former biker gang, for which he would be paid $1500. He accepted the assignment without protest. He agreed to break the hold-out's legs. I asked him how he would do it. He said he would blind the victim with pepper spray, then beat both his legs with a baseball bat. I told him that, although I accepted the professionalism with which he might execute his crime, I could not agree with his personal ethics. I asked him if he could release himself from this contract, but he said: "You don't understand how the mob operates. If you refuse a contract that you accepted, the same fate happens to you!"

In a flash I was caught in conflict: do I save engagement or enforce boundaries and accountability? Of course, the latter considerations won hands down. I told Big John either he renounces all gang affiliations and obligations, including this contract, or I would no longer be his therapist. His response to confrontation and limits was predictable: he rejected me with all kinds of angry expletives. He threatened that I better look over my shoulder down every alley for the rest of my life, because he would be waiting for me. Looking back, perhaps I could have taken legal action regarding his threats. Instead I closed the case as unresolved, but for many months, I felt unsure about my personal safety.

Meanwhile, about this time I was arranging for my leave of absence to develop my judo skills in England prior to the Montreal Olympics in 1976. As it turned out, I did not compete for Canada in that Olympics, but settled back in London, Ontario, to await the arrival of our first child, Mark.

Here is the amazing epilogue. It was two years later. We had returned to live in London, Ontario, to resume our life in Canada after a year's absence. To tell you the truth, I had never extinguished my mild but persistent worry that Big John would suddenly attack me after all these years, as he had threatened to do so for my supposedly abandoning him in his time of need. It was not foremost in my mind, but a lingering unclosed theat. As luck and circumstance would have it, my wife and I were looking through furniture in a store in east London when a large sales person approached us. I did not recognize him at first, but Big John asked to take me aside to explain his fate. He said that after the shock of his being rejected by his therapist, he went into a dark depressive phase. Then, seemingly out of nowhere, he found Jesus Christ! Now he was truly a born-again Christian, and his entire life was saved. He thanked me profusely for helping him find a way to the grace of Jesus in his life. I shook his hand in mutual thanks, and breathed easier thereafter.

CHAPTER 35

THE CAROTENE KID

KRISTEN WAS A 19-YEAR-OLD university student when first admitted to our inpatient unit for a severe case of anorexia nervosa. At five feet, six and a half inches, she had gone down to 86 lbs. and was losing rapidly. Her grades had fallen miserably, as she was unable to concentrate, despite numerous hours studying and working on assignments. She was now hospitalized on medical leave, her school year in jeopardy. The color of her skin on admission was an unusual shade of orange as if jaundiced, but actually a result of overdosed carotene from her diet, which was almost exclusively carrots - huge amounts of carrots.

On the ward when I met her, she was nervous, anxious, and agitated, wanting to escape this prison and return to her studies as soon as possible. She was not focused on her anorexia, yet she was desperately obedient to the rulebook of anorexia that had had driven her to this state of emotional and mental paralysis. She was unable to sleep much at night on the ward. We pointed out to her that her insomnia was not because she was crazy but because she was hungry. The early phases of the starvation syndrome feature hyperactivity as an adaptive reaction designed to help starving animals to further explore their environment, thus discovering unexpected caches of food. Our anorexic patients are often late-night walkers for both conscious and unconscious survival needs. Kristen was now on a weight gain program wherein she earned ward privileges contingent on weight gain, so even her late night walking was now restricted.

As she began to respond to the weight gain program, she started to confide in me as her primary therapist, who would guide her through both the inpatient and outpatient phases of her treatment. Upon talking with her, I discovered her first rule of being and personal worth: she judged herself to be overweight as long as her belly protruded beyond the top of her hip bones when observing herself in a standing position looking sideways in a mirror. I challenged her that no woman or man alive or in history could satisfy that rule. By that rule, all human beings that have ever lived were overweight. In my challenge, I said she could set her own target weight if she could find evidence of anyone having a convex or hollowed-out belly while in a standing posture. As she had ample spare time on the ward, and loved to prove authority wrong, she set out on library and media research in search of data that would support her point. After three weeks, she conceded my point, and I had established some validity against the relentless and unfair rules of anorexic thinking.

After her inpatient stay, she was released at a weight of 118 lbs., on the road to recovery but still below the minimal healthy weight for her height established and reported by Garner and Garfinkel (1985). Using empirical tables, the minimum healthy weight for her height would be 126 lbs. She protested that she would be fine at 118 lb., and asked that I trust her judgment that this would be enough? Because she was an otherwise cooperative client, following through on most treatment compliance and homework assignments, I relented and let the minimal weight be set at 118. Despite many positive breakthroughs on a psychological and emotional level, in the coming months she was unable to give up her hyper-vigilance against weight gain, and would not allow herself to fluctuate in weight like normal people do. She was doing fine in her academic grades, although she had to work longer and harder to concentrate and perform than her intelligence would indicate. She continued to experience relatively persistent levels of anxiety and food and figure obsessions, amounting to one to two hours total a day. After trying every known intervention to help Kristen to lower her anxiety, I finally told her something major needed to change. She would have to change her minimal healthy weight target to 128 lbs, plus or minus 2 lbs. She would need to demonstrate this for more than three consecutive months, and especially she would need to show allowance for fluctuations, rather than weighing in weekly at the exact same weight as she had in previous months.

At first she balked at this requirement. I reminded her that we had agreed to let her try stabilization at 118 lbs. with the provision that if this did not work to resolve her anorexic symptoms, she would have to accept the best practices minimal healthy weight specified in the anorexia research literature. Rather than end therapy with her anorexia still prevalent, Kristen relented and agreed to the new regime. At first it felt like a personal defeat, an acknowledgement of failure, but that was just her ego talking. When she came to a position of true acceptance, she stopped over-control of eating and began to allow her weight to float upwards. Then an amazing thing happened. Her prediction was that when she stopped "watching her weight" it would balloon uncontrollably higher and she would become overweight. My prediction was that because there was no history of obesity in her family, her weight would stabilize at the criterion weight. This prediction was accurate. Kristin, despite abandoning her vigilance, and even having forbidden foods such as hamburgers, maintained her weight at her biological set point, which actually averaged around 226-229 lbs. What is more important, she could do so with no control! She could finally trust her appetite and sense of satiety to her body, rather than the over-ride of her mind. That is, she would stop eating, not because she should, but because further eating no longer interested her; she felt full and satisfied. Kristin abandoned her previous regime and now was free to pursue her life goals. As expected, she soared through her undergraduate marks, so much so that she gained an entrance scholarship to graduate school in a prestigious university in Eastern Canada. As luck or fate would have it, her absolutely bound-for-success boyfriend was going to go to a prestigious law school in the same city, so they could continue a divinely blessed upper middle class romance to the delight and dreams of parents from both their families. Their romance was seemingly a match made in heaven, with perfect career planning on both sides so that she would finish her Masters degree in Sociology around the same time he would be finishing his law degree. One factor was missing: Kristin's assent to this perfect plan. Alignment to a perfect corporate script was not quite a part of her life plan. In her therapy session, she asked for my advice as to what to do. I kept on redirecting it to what she should do given the scenarios we mapped together about her future. She kept pushing it back to me. Finally, I said: "Listen, Kristen, you haven't lived until you stared Success in the face and said 'F*** You!'" She laughed and thought that was the wonderful answer to her dilemma. She turned down the post-grad scholarship while her boyfriend moved on to law school. She spent the next year in light and frivolous opportunities in art and business, all very successful, which set the platform for her next academic project.

She moved on to completing a degree in law herself. She is now happily married and mother of three delightful children. I see the family occasionally at local folk festivals, and she reports being really happy in her career and family life. With her kindness, wisdom, and razor sharp wit, she continues to be a delight to have known.

One thing in this story remains. Kristen's therapy with me lasted almost two years, including spaced follow-up appointments. Finally, it came down to our termination appointment. She had by now been free of anorexic symptoms for more than nine months, so we decided to end therapy. In the exit interview, we exchanged mutual admiration and thanks for this great learning experience together. I asked her, as I often do on exit interviews, "Is there anything I could have done to make this therapy better or more effective?" Kristen replied without hesitation that I should have enforced the 126 goal from the beginning rigidly. She said that, because of my willingness to do it her way, she went through about six months of what she called "permanent PMS." This was her way of saying that her maintenance at a sub-healthy weight resulted in a temporary period of control conflicts, obsessional thinking, anxiety, irritability, and mental misery that might have been avoided in her therapy. I asked her, would she have gone for my rigid goal at the beginning of therapy? She stated she might have resisted the entire treatment regime, knowing how oppositional she was, had I not given into her initial demands, and letting her try it her way for many months to see how it worked for her.

Although I would like to draw from this case a definitive conclusion, I am still uncertain how rigid I should be about my terms for accepting a new case, especially as I now operate exclusively in private practice. For eating disorders, now I will not accept a case unless the client will consume and digest at least one nutritionally balanced meal per day, and agree to move towards best practices minimal healthy weight as soon as possible. Without this assurance, and medical monitoring support, recovery is so remote as to be unproductive. Unless I have these safeguards in place, I typically will not engage these difficult cases. I now determine my operating parameters for success in treatment. This is what I have learned from Kristin's teachings.

CHAPTER 36

THE PASSIVE PRETZEL

SEVERAL YEARS AGO, I had a client called Karen. She was a dynamic attractive interior designer who had recently left an unhappy marriage featuring verbal and emotional abuse that occasionally erupted in physical struggles as well. She was glad to be out of that relationship of six years. Thankfully there were no children and thus no further need for contact with her ex. Her grieving the end of her marriage went relatively smoothly, and she focused on rebuilding her life as a single person in her early 30s.

She was not at this point interested in dating. However, one idea was strong in her mind about the kind of man she would like in her future. He would not be an alpha high-achiever, controller like her ex. As Karen herself was quite assertive and outgoing, she felt that an easy-going agreeable man that would love her and love the activities and values she cherished would be just right for her. For now, she parked this idea and just focused on herself and her career. After about ten sessions she left therapy quite satisfied that she was now able to cope and thrive in life with the support of her friendship network.

It was about ten or twelve years later before she contacted me again. After several years of single life, she had fallen in love with Joe, a carpenter, a casual and happy low key fellow who loved and appreciated her. He was always kind and never complained or tried to boss her. Joe was a handyman and good at renovations, a natural match for her career in interior design. During the six years of their marriage they had collaborated on many projects, including buying and flipping three fixer houses. They worked well together. They never fought, and hardly ever disagreed. Joe loved her with all his heart. But Karen was becoming increasingly frustrated with him because of one pervasive problem.

Joe was passive. He was totally content to stay at home in the evenings and watch TV and cuddle on the couch. Whenever Karen wanted to go out, Joe would happily agree to take her wherever she wanted to go and do whatever she wanted to do. He seemed to have no opinion or preferences of his own. He seldom showed any initiative or interest but would gladly comply with Karen's ideas and requests. Their relationship was very peaceful, very agreeable, in fact boringly agreeable. Karen came to resent that she was almost always the leader, the one who had opinions and interesting things to say, while Joe was happy to merely listen and follow. It was as if she had married an adoring puppy dog. Whenever she was frustrated and unhappy, Joe would just be confused and not know what to do. She could not get him to voice opinions, let alone argue. At least in her former marriage there was the excitement of two wills contesting each other. Fighting Joe was like fighting a pillow, a marshmallow, sickly sweet but no substance. As time went on in the marriage, Karen found that Joe's passivity was driving her crazy. Joe remained confounded to understand how to satisfy the seemingly irrational demands of his wife. They were at an impasse.

There were three conjoint sessions in which their dilemma was repeatedly enacted. Karen was frustrated with Joe's passivity, to which Joe confusedly but clumsily apologized with promises to try to do better to be her spouse, but wanted guidance as to how to do it. He wanted a plan, a structure to follow. He could not understand that Karen wanted someone to generate her structure so that she would not have to fill the constant role of leader. She wanted a relationship of two contributing adults, and Joe seemed bewildered and almost unable to comprehend her need or how to begin to fulfill it. Even when we did some communication exercises in the sessions, when it came Joe's turn to lead, he became flustered and could not seem to go beyond a few short and simple sentences. It's not that Joe was verbally impaired, it's just that he seemed to run out of ideas, especially in the absence of structure. We had to conclude that marital therapy was not turning the corner, so I saw Joe for two individual sessions, again with no discernable results. Karen heard of a brief men's assertiveness group in the city. Joe dutifully went to all six sessions but could hardly recall what was discussed in those sessions. Throughout these interventions, Joe was agreeable although still awkward and unskilled. The couple dropped out of treatment.

Two years later Karen returned for a follow-up session. By this time she had divorced Joe, but they still remained friends. Sometimes she would ask him to do handyman repairs and renovations in her condo, and they got along well, but she felt she needed to move on. She regretted trying to turn Joe into someone who would be unrecognizable to himself. Joe was willing to try to twist himself into being Karen's pretzel but could hardly sustain any of her desired changes for more than a few days. It just was not in his gentle and passive nature to be a take-charge dynamic guy. Karen felt better to be on her own, still looking for an ideal mate, one who would not be into domineering, but also a man who would be interesting and show initiative as well as love. Again she seemed calm and well-adjusted in her new life. In a summary of what she learned in her marriage with Joe, with his safe and cloyingly agreeable passivity, she said, "be careful about what you ask for; you just might get it."

At this point, I am asking you to consider some philosophical points. The first is the conundrum of what we call "the be-spontaneous paradox." The minute I command you to be spontaneous, in the next moments, if you act unpredictably, you are still following my command to be spontaneous; therefore you are engaging in a controlled act to follow my command rather than spontaneity. A similar bind happens when I insist that YOU TAKE CHARGE! Whatever happens in the following minutes, even if you are acting in random ways, this performance is still under the umbrella of my demand that you take charge. From a meta-perspective, you cannot insist that another take charge of the relationship, as that would be a hierarchical inversion where their performance would be under your orders. Even when I pointed out this absurdity to the couple, they still needed a practical escape from their logical box. This would have been possible if Joe were able to sustain the requirements of leading without structure. Unfortunately, it seems he could not. However, in his new life as a single guy he seems unconflicted and well-adjusted, no longer trying to be a person he could not become.

CHAPTER 37

And Then Something Happened

(Ed. Note: This is another long story, covering eight years)

MANY YEARS AGO I ran an eating disorders treatment centre out of mental health services in a civic hospital. The Bulimia and Anorexia Program was quite successful but did not have a budget of its own, and it gradually starved due to funding cuts where it was made the sacrificial lamb so that other general services could remain open.

One case I saw under the auspices of this program was Carrie, a 34 year old single mother of two daughters, ages 7 and 10. Carrie was 5'3" and 85 lbs. when we first saw her for assessment. Although she had been chronically anorexic for several years, her weight had recently plummeted to a dangerous level. In the clinic we recommended hospitalization and placement on a weight-gain program, but she adamantly refused. The only available treatment was outpatient psychotherapy, but in order to safely qualify she would have to ingest the equivalent of one balanced meal a day of adequate calories to maintain her weight. She reluctantly agreed to this regimen and to a modified home-care program run on an honorary basis.

The home-care program required weekly weigh-ins by a nurse at her doctor's office in underwear and a hospital gown at the same time each week (in this case, Monday mornings at 10:00 a.m.). If a gain of two pounds or more, unlimited mobility was permitted. If the gain were zero to two pounds, she would be restricted to home, except for child-care responsibilities and doctor's appointments, with no further exercise permitted. Weight loss would restrict her activity to child-care and doctor appointments only; otherwise bed rest and no exercise was permitted. Of course, other than weigh-ins, this program was almost impossible to enforce. From previous experience with these programs, I advised the nurse to be watchful but not tyrannical about weights hidden in undergarments, even vaginal and even rectal weights to fudge the program. I told the nurse that such strategies, even if undetected, would only work in the short run for that week because it would establish a new baseline for the following week, so no need to monitor for hidden weights. As predicted, Carrie barely complied with the minimal requirements of the program. Of course, there was no one at home to restrict her movement or enforce bed-rest, and besides, she had two school-age children to care for.

In those beginning days, Carrie was overwhelmed with anxiety about weight gain on every eating occasion. For those of you who have not treated anorexia nervosa, you might think that all the therapist needs to do is to teach the client to lower her anxiety level, and all will be fine. There are two problems with this idea: due to a phenomenon called the starvation cycle, the underweight condition itself generates high levels of anxiety that will not subside until adequate nutrition is restored. Secondly, the generalized tyranny of anorexic rules become so compelling to the victim that it is like the grip of a python. It strangles logical thinking and reduces the suffering person to a brain ruled by the brain-stem amygdale. Cortical functions are so limited so as to be totally disqualified in a flood of terror and paranoia about possible weight gain and the collapse of this pseudo-control anorexic rule empire.

While strangling in the grip of anorexia, there was only one way to open the jaws of the beast, and that was through the therapeutic relationship. We had to have a beginning point of trust in the effectiveness of therapy, and it needed to be a concrete demonstration to inspire hope. Thus it was that every Tuesday, my first appointment, Carrie would bring a breakfast for two, which we would eat together. It was important that she would prepare it and provide it. I did not want her to be dependent on me for her nutrition. My calmness became a positive model and cradle of safety where she could eat with a temporary respite from the tyrannical rule structure of anorexia. From this containing net of safety, Carrie learned to trust in the prospect of her eventual recovery. Gradually and erratically, she began a painfully slow march to a healthier weight and state of nutritional and mental functioning. However, this lifeline of trust was quite weak and tenuous, as she presented many tests to see if she could have confidence that I would support her total recovery.

As Carrie recovered from her anorexia she became emotionally alive, and the genie of her extreme moods was now out of the bottle. Despite all the strategies and techniques I had prepared her for in terms of emotional regulation for this phase, we were both surprised by the extreme fluctuations in her mood and mental functioning. Her family doctor was also concerned, but the three of us thought that it would be better to ride out those storms without antidepressant medication. That decision seemed sensible at the time, but now I'm not so sure.

Also, it turned out that this was coincidentally a time of challenge for me professionally. The Bulimia and Anorexia Program staffing allocation was being reduced, and our program waiting lists were growing. We were becoming a crisis-generating system, because we had no choice but to treat the most severe and potentially lethal cases, while parking the more treatable cases. Realizing that the situation was now untenable, I gave notice that as of that September of that year I would be accepting no new interns or practicum students. Further, I threatened to resign within a year if there was no adequate funding and staff resourcing of the program. I was ordered to refrain from taking the matter to the media, and as an obedient employee I remained politically silent while the program starved for resources. By the spring of the next year I resigned to go full-time into private practice. Within a year other key staff left and the Bulimia and Anorexia Program, once one of the best-regarded programs in Western Canada, folded.

While some of my higher-functioning clients were able to afford my private practice fees and continue treatment underway with me, many had to stop and fend for themselves, or be reassigned to general therapists with no specific expertise in treating eating disorders, a hit and miss proposition. I felt generally okay with these arrangements but ethically obligated to continue treating Carrie. In the previous year she had been making some steps towards a promising recovery, but trusted no one except me and her family physician and her nurse. So I made a fateful decision, based partly on ethics and perhaps hubris. After all, a vast majority of my clients with eating disorders had made very good recoveries, so I thought that with a little more support, Carrie would be able to turn the corner on her anorexia. Carrie was a single parent with a deadbeat ex-husband barely making erratic child-support payments As she had almost no means of financial support, I decided to treat her without charge. Many professionals agree to do this out of their generosity for worthy cases. This was my turn. There were several other cases I treated this way that are not included in this book.

As it turned out, Carrie had many more problems than merely a case of anorexia. She was multiply addicted, probably related to her previous sexually and physically abusive childhood and adolescence. As the anorexia subsided, her borderline personality disorder emerged in full bloom.

Her emotions ran rampant, only minimally managed by the techniques we practiced and rehearsed in sessions. Carrie smoked cigarettes frequently, over a pack a day. She used pot when she could get a source for it, alcohol whenever she could afford it, and sometimes when she couldn't. Still, she managed to be a loving, if inconsistent, mother for her daughters. Both of them sensed their mother's instability and rallied in loyal support of her as she cared for them the best way she knew.

A key source of stress in Carrie's life was her relationship with her ex-husband Jim, a municipal policeman. After the birth of their children Carrie had become increasingly child-focused, perhaps because of her own sexual abuse by her father many years before. Furthermore, she had come to develop vaginal dyspareunia, a condition whereby the vagina has difficulty lubricating and in fact tightens into spasms and cramps at the very prospect of intercourse. On the few occasions when it happened, intercourse was very painful, an act to be avoided. Faced with this dilemma in her marriage, the couple did not seek counselling. Jim, a macho male, was embarrassed to talk about this problem, let alone asking for professional help in dealing with it. Instead he became more frustrated and physically and emotionally abusive with Carrie. On one occasion, Jim raped her with his service revolver, lacerating her vagina with the protruding gunsight. At that point, scared for her life, Carrie just went to an Emergency Room in a local hospital to be stitched up; she was too scared and embarrassed to tell anyone the truth of her trauma. She knew if she reported the incident that her policeman husband would deny it as the preposterous ramblings of an obviously deranged woman. So she dropped it, and waited in fear until the moment where she developed the courage to leave him but not challenge him.

In the years after she left with the children, Jim kept trying to prove that Carrie was an unfit mother because of her multiple emotional and psychological problems. It was at this point that I began treating her and nurturing her back to physical and psychological health. However, this conflict was continuing at several points in the two years of her initial recovery from anorexia. With my coaching, she was able to withstand the challenges to her ability to parent, although I stayed clear from court testimony on her behalf. I steadfastly kept the roles of therapist and advocate separate.

During this time, every week I would save a special appointment slot Tuesday mornings for our breakfast session, now in private practice. But then, something new was happening with Carrie. Through a mutual friend, she had met and fallen in love with George. George was also a member of Carrie's church community who was attracted to her kind nature, humor, and fun-loving disposition as a single parent of two daughters. He also found the daughters to be engaging. Pre-teen Amy was basically a nice child despite obvious developmental delays that made her the butt of jokes and teasing by the other church children and well as her schoolmates. Teenager Hilary was a brash and mouthy tomboy, spirited and unpredictable. Although both had minor but frequent behavioral problems at school, they were obedient and loyal to their mother, even somewhat protective of her and her frequent personal problems. Carrie herself had become more socially active and attractive as she moved beyond her anorexic phase. Shortage of money was perhaps the only factor that suppressed her frequent consumption of alcohol, pot, and cigarettes. She also had a raging obsession towards her ex-husband and her ongoing battle about his access to the children for visitations. Carrie added fuel to their conflicts by her extreme emotional outbursts in community contacts and parent-teacher interviews, whereas her ex appeared more rational though frustrated by their mutually negative portrayals of each other.

Despite my attempts to help her get beyond her self-portrayal as a helpless victim of circumstance, Carrie commanded a great deal of church and community social support by this posture toward life. Also, her stance of a damsel in distress was the perfect match for George's rescuer fantasies. He had been raised by a mostly absent and ineffectual father. His mother was still alcoholic, as was his sister, both living at close to subsistence level in a nearby rural community. Like Carrie, they were partly supported financially by their local church congregations. George, on the other hand, was financially self-sufficient, with a steady union job as a lineman for an electrical utility. He would be the steady rock on whom Carrie could depend to give her emotional support and forgiveness when she got into "situations" with interpersonal conflicts and episodes of erratic behavior.

In her former anorexic phase, Carrie had a habit of projection and distortion of external blame while conveniently "forgetting" or not quite telling the truth in a passive-aggressive undermining of her therapeutic recovery. As her recovery team suspected, she did use hidden weights to pretend she was gaining weight, whereas she appeared to look the same. When the scales eventually caught her out she would collapse in tears and admit she lied to her medical team and myself. My general stance towards lying is that I can only work with the best approximation of reality that my client is ready to face and share with me. This naive stance can leave me vulnerable to client claims of progress while an actual relapse is underway, and several weeks are lost proceeding on false data. Nevertheless, it allows me the opportunity of consistent support for my client, even if her momentary behavior does not warrant it. That way, I am not caught in uproar as the drama triangle rotates on the discovery that I have been misled. As I look back on these years of treating Carrie, I know, as I did at the time, that we were involved in behavioral sequences that are best described by Dr. Eric Berne *Games People Play*, in that we were transfixed in roles and sequences of possibly predictable outcomes. Yet, in order for me to be that fixed security anchor for Carrie's recovery, I needed to play the role of steadfast supporter, hoping not to become an enabler of her problem patterns.

Carrie's repeated deception was likely her way of slowing and recalibrating her therapeutic recovery, such that success did not elevate her too high above her low self-esteem life scripts. In the few selected times I broached this idea with her she at least partly agreed. However, she was shame-ridden after "something happened" and she temporarily relapsed. She wanted badly to be a good client for herself, but mostly for me, the Good Object in her attachment to therapy. As she slowly progressed in her erratic recovery from her multiple addictions, her swings in moods and behavior became more extreme as she battled in a borderline way with her impulses for self-sabotage. She would cover her slips with denial so that sometimes they would become breakaways into slides of several days avoiding her support net, not answering voicemails, and angrily isolating herself in shame and severe depression. The antidepressants she was prescribed seemed to have no effect on her, other than adding to her dysregulation in wild interactions with alcohol and other street drugs. Her self-injurious behavior also included wrist-cutting and several suicide attempts by overdosing on her prescribed medications, street drugs, and alcohol.

There is a pattern that I have seen in similar cases that is quite unnerving. I don't like to pathologize, but I must admit it is behavior frequently seen in more severe personality disorders. The pattern goes like this: I make a mistake and apologize to you, and you forgive me. I guess I must be acceptable, because you forgave me. Later, I make a similar but slightly bigger mistake, ask for your forgiveness, and you forgive me after my apology. I guess this proves that I am more loveable. In each instance, I might learn the lesson from that mistake, but now there is a pattern where the next mistake I make is even more costly for everyone who loves me. Nevertheless, all of you rally to support me. I become even more convinced that I am lovable because all of you have rescued me, forgiven me, and accepted me as a person, even though you strongly disapprove of my actions. Finally, in an ultimate attempt to retrieve and prove my worthiness, I attempt suicide in a gesture, usually an overdose timed so that a caring person discovers me before the drugs totally overcome me. (Sometimes this strategy misfires in a case of truly accidental suicide, when the gesture and subsequent rescue is mistimed because the rescuer arrives late due to unforeseen circumstances.) In a perverse reality, helping professionals and friends sometimes inadvertently reinforce the escalation of severity in the gestures of these clients.

According to theory, we are supposed to ask the client to stop apologizing, because we are henceforward going to label the next mistake as deliberate provocation of our patience and acceptance. This is the dictum of confrontation. Research has shown that this approach does not assist clients towards recovery. Moreover, we know from addictions counselling experiences, that most relapses are inevitable. We merely try to help the client reduce the frequency, duration, and severity of damage that occurs every time an episode occurs, so the recovery system needs to be onside and supportive of the person, if not the aberrant provocative and dangerous behavior. Often, we work to prevent a slip from becoming a slide into previous patterns. The result is that the supportive system is caught in a delicate situation of standing by and being firm but not rejecting when these incidents occur.

Sometimes we even find grounds for congratulating a client for regaining control after a slip.

Thankfully in Carrie's case, she had the long-suffering support of myself, her now fiancé George, her children, her church congregation, and other people. She had an amazing capacity to attract caring individuals to her side despite her frequent dramatic self-destructive episodes. She was indeed an engaging drama-queen. George was in love with her and her positive potential, so after a year of courtship, they got married. The wedding itself was difficult and complicated owing to Carrie's intermittent feud with her birth mother. Her father had been absent from her life after abandoning the family many years previously. Still, despite intense therapy sessions to resolve her issues with her mother, there were all kinds of potential disruptions threatening to occur at the wedding. Thankfully, none of them materialized.

One interesting theme was Carrie's profound dislike and disdain for police officers. She felt that her ex-husband had turned all of them into informants and evidence gatherers in the community and the educational system to prove her as a crazy and unfit mother. She became paranoid at the sight of any policeman or cruiser, and it took the best of my abilities as her therapist to allow her vigilance while diminishing her sense of persistent threat. It did not help that her ex-husband reinforced her paranoia with his attempts at destroying her name in the community. Even worse, it did not help that Carrie compounded this negative image with her erratic behavior. For example, on one of her angry drinking episodes, she took the keys to her new husband George's car and drove directly to the nearest police station and smashed it into a police cruiser. Of course no one, including Carrie, was hurt. She would never consciously harm anyone directly, but property damage was another thing. Both vehicles had bent fenders. Carrie was charged with reckless and impaired driving and lost her license for a year, so George and other friends had to drive her around, which resulted in her getting even more attention and involvement of other people for that time.

I guess you can figure it out by now: Carrie thrived on attention, and the way to attract attention was to generate chaos but absolve herself from the idea of instigation or even unconscious authorship of the crises in which she accidentally found herself almost every second week. She would often come into our session with favorable reports of generalized progress towards her treatment goals, While genuine, these reports were often followed with the apologetic words "and then something happened." It was as if the fates were conspiring against her in an incident either preceded by or followed by emotional upset and some impulsive act to reduce her distress while getting herself into more trouble with other people: her current husband, her ex, the educational or legal system, her children, her AA sponsors (she went through four of them quitting on her), and several other friends in her rotating support network. Being the kind, rather disorganized, but well-meaning person she was, I guess it was conveniently easy for her support group to dismiss her denial of personal responsibility whenever "something happened." It seemed as if she was the victim of fate, but upon closer examination, she was often the indirect author of her fate by negligence and denial of early-warning signals, inconsistent indulgent parenting of her children, and taking any contretemps as a personal slight and attack on her integrity. Eventually in our therapy sessions, Carrie came to accept more authorship in her personal narratives.

I am slightly embarrassed to say that it took many years of therapy for Carrie to turn her ship around. Nevertheless, as the years went on, she gradually overcame anorexia nervosa. She stopped using pot and other street drugs. She got married to long-suffering and patient George, who found a way to live with her occasionally outrageous mood swings and impulsive behavior. She came to have less frequent and severe binges with alcohol. She never abstained altogether but developed a better way to occasionally use alcohol, this time in a more measured way, at least most of the time. Her occasional slips did not develop into her former slides. Carrie also abandoned masochistic rituals like self-cutting and suicidal ideation. She regained the trust of her family physician when she renounced abuse of prescribed medication. Moreover, she even stopped smoking cigarettes, one of her last addictions. She was finally getting on an even keel in navigating her life through treacherous channels.

However, there was one important issue that threatened her new marriage: the remaining problem of vaginismus that persisted after her previous sexual abuse. In earlier sessions we used EMDR and other forms of desensitization to nullify the trauma on remembering the horrid scenes in which her ex-husband had raped her with his pistol. Nevertheless, Carrie still had a reflex reaction of clenching and tightening in the vaginal muscles whenever she tried to insert any object. She could not even tolerate the tip of her baby finger without going into painful spasms. Of course, tampons of any sort were out of the question and had been for years. One method of physical desensitization is to expose the body part to the smallest amount of an allergen or irritant, so small that it does not trigger a defensive reaction such as a histamine response, or in Carrie's case, a muscle spasm. So the object needed to be very small, soft, and compressible to become smaller if squeezed. Thankfully, most hardware and paint stores sell small tapered cellulose sponges for detailed painting of small objects or tight corners. The tips look like small sharpened pencils, soft but firm enough so that they maintain their shape. We could have used dental rubber tips instead, but these sponges were slightly larger and softer. Carrie's homework was to insert one of these small sponges, withstand any mild spasms until they stopped, then continue to keep the sponge inside the vagina for gradually increasing periods of time. She started with ten minutes a day. Despite the mild discomfort of a foreign object in her body, she was gradually able to extend the period of time of insertion, graduating after several weeks to use larger sizes of these tapered sponges. The spasms became less frequent or severe and their duration curtailed to less than fifteen seconds per incident. She was thankful that the sponges were soft enough to compress at those times.

Concurrent in these weeks of homework, Carrie was encouraged to be able to briefly insert fingers, starting with the smallest and eventually even her thumb. Given her strict Roman Catholic upbringing, she had to reverse a lot of negative prohibitions against touching herself this way. After two months she could begin to allow George to gently use his fingers as well, inserting and remaining motionless for a few minutes. The same sequence applied with Carrie doing the guiding of insertion of George's penis, in various phases of erection, at first virtually still, then gradually introducing motion, resulting in eventual full vaginal intercourse with Carrie controlling the action, and finally varying positions and initiative by both Carrie and George. This entire sequence was delicate and sensitive for the couple, and it took months, but it worked to their mutual relief and satisfaction. Patience and caring love prevailed over a legacy of trauma and fear.

Meanwhile, Carrie's oldest daughter had a brief encounter with bulimia nervosa and body dysmorphia issues but did not want to follow in her mother's footsteps. After some crucial therapy sessions, she was able to set her own course of personal identity. She went on to find a nice fellow, and they got married. Interestingly, he also had issues with his ex-wife but went beyond them to forge a new way of being with his new bride.

In the latter years of Carrie's therapy, she was definitely more self-responsible. Gone was the "and then, something happened" personal disclaimer that characterized our previous sessions. Nevertheless, misadventures continued to happen with remarkable consistency. I reframed her life at that time to say she still had an addiction: an addiction to drama. If she did not have a drama at least once every two weeks she would go into crisis with the idea that she was normal, defying all of her dysfunctional life scripts and ideas about herself and her deservedness of unhappiness. After several weeks of this reframing of her adventures as an addiction to drama, a unique event happened: nothing happened! It was strange for Carrie to realize that drama was expendable, no longer necessary. She came to know that she could have all the care and attention she needed from others without having to create or magnify life events to solicit a rescuing posture from her support system. She came to realize that they loved her despite her dramas, rather than because of them: a breakthrough insight. This shift could only occur if she stopped her dramas long enough to establish a break in the pattern.

As weeks and months went by with only minor general problems of living, Carrie adapted to the state of normalcy. She admitted that she did somewhat miss all the attention she used to get as a drama queen, but the peace of a normal life more than compensated for it. Her marriage was now stable and happy. Her oldest daughter had by now married a nice fellow and still maintained regular contact with her. Her younger daughter still had academic challenges going through junior high school, but was no longer involved with behavioral and emotional disturbances. By now Carrie had overcome virtually all her addictions, including cigarette smoking. Now I told her she had only one addiction remaining: we would work on her overcoming her addiction to psychotherapy. We began stretching out the time between sessions to bi-weekly, then to monthly, then to half-yearly. While Carrie had some initial resistance to this schedule of fading therapy contact, after a while she adapted easily, and filled her busy life with other connections and commitments in her community. In her case I decided to follow Dr. Milton Erickson's advice to leave a remnant, so I kept her case open, available on an as-needed basis. After two years of non-contact she was doing fine at the time of my follow-up phone call. That was over five years ago. So that was my closure on the longest lasting case in my career (8 years). Never again will I take on a dual-diagnosis multiple addiction borderline personality disordered case on a pro bono basis. Still, I am grateful for the lessons it provided, and for my unswerving dedication to her eventual recovery. I will always remember Carrie fondly, but with a sigh of relief and a smile of satisfaction.

Part Six:

ACCEPTANCE AND COMMITMENT THERAPY

This form of therapy integrates well within my solution-oriented counselling model (www.solutionorientedcounselling. ca). It is based on the concepts of mindfulness, detaching from thought and emotions, merely observing them and letting them go in the flow of the eternal NOW.

Acceptance and Commitment Therapy departs from the usual therapeutic stance of reducing client anxiety symptoms. It normalizes anxiety as a natural consequence of living in today's fast-moving world. The client is encouraged to reach for a life of greater value by embracing and accepting uncertainty and conflict rather than avoiding it. The result is often quite liberating, and at times, even spiritual. The process is about facing our fears, accepting them, and metaphorically going through the eye of an emotional hurricane and finding peace beyond it. Martial artists call this the eye of the tiger. This therapy requires client motivation and trust in the therapist, the client, and the process itself.

CHAPTER 38

Overcoming Major Fear By Decatastrophizing

Throughout my career I have helped people overcome fears and anxiety. Overcoming fear is largely the task undertaken by those whose occupation involves exposure to risk of severe injury or even death, such as soldiers posted to Afghanistan. Typically, if the client has been exposed to severe injury or threat of death, EMDR and other formats of desensitization and cognitive restructuring using CBT are the treatments of choice. This formula also applies to athletes in severe risk sports, such as high speed downhill and grand slalom skiers, lugers, and bobsledders. One other important strategy for these situations, especially if there is no previous experience in severe injury or lethal potential, is decatastrophising. This treatment regime is also helpful in cases of irrational fear, as seen in anxiety disorders and phobias, such as flying phobias.

To give you an idea as to how this treatment is done, let's take the example of a luger on Canada's National Team competing at the world and Olympic levels. Sometimes in the starting blocks it is possible for a competitor to have a brief but paralyzing flash of fear of crashing. This moment can lead to excessive muscle tension and other focusing problems that can inhibit chances of a successful high speed run, where milliseconds are the difference between medalling or being out of contention for rating at the world level. As many athletes experience this problem, at least momentarily, we typically we do this treatment in the post-season or the off season.

We start by asking the athlete," What is the worst thing that could happen if you crash on a run?" The answer invariably, is that he or she might die. Remember that some athletes have actually died in luge crashes, just like some passengers have died in airplane crashes, even though both are low probability events. We then ask our client, "How would that be a tragedy?" We then guide our client through a process of thinking the unthinkable and even imagine attending their own funeral. We might even explore their spiritual and religious beliefs, including that of an afterlife where they may be able to observe the world from a place beyond. When they arrive at that stage of imaging, they find that they have a surprising feeling of peace and serenity, disidentifying with their previous fear, and observing it from a distance. We are teaching them mindfulness about their own emotions, and detachment from what moments ago seemed insurmountable and unbearable.

Usually at that point our client realizes that death would perhaps not be the worst outcome. It might be surviving the crash, but being rendered quadriplegic, unable to control bodily functions from the neck down. We then guide them through their fears of dependency and having others look after them. Even with the modern advances of computer-assisted neurotechnology, a life with limited functioning is usually quite a frightening prospect for anyone, especially a world level athlete. Once they successfully negotiate coming to terms with this fear, we again ask a variant of the same question, "If you survived a crash, and weren't paralyzed, what's the next worst thing that could happen?" Usually, it is that they would have a career-ending injury that would permanently knock them out of competing in their sport. "And how would that be a tragedy?" At this point we have the athlete deal with their ego over-identification with their sport performance. This intervention is not just helpful in overcoming fear but also in the tendency of athletes to hold on too hard, to over-try and over-control, rather than competing in a more relaxed and confident manner. We have the athlete expand their scope of personal worthiness in many aspects of their being, not merely the roles they play in life. Finally, we ask them again, "If all these terrible things didn't happen, what's the next worst outcome you would have to deal with?" At this point they acknowledge the higher probability event that they could sustain an injury that could end their season or put them behind for several weeks or months against their able-bodied competition who are also continuing to improve while our client is rehabilitating. They fear "losing their edge" and never quite getting it back. At first we have them face that possible outcome, and accept it and come to terms with it. Then we invoke all the stories of other athletes in their sport and other sports who have made stronger comebacks after setbacks and injuries. By this point in the process, our athlete client is now fully prepared to deal with brief flashes of fear of crashing. Typically, as they review and practice our decatastrophising procedure in the early competitive season, they are no longer strongly bothered by such fears. It is not that the fear has been removed, because appropriate caution is still there, but it is no longer a paralyzing or tightening sensation. They say to themselves, "That's okay, I've already thought that through completely last June," and then they can relegate those doubts to the sidelines of consciousness, allowing them to focus on the task at hand.

The process of decatastrophising allows us the advantages of going beyond ego attachment of our identity to our performance of a role. When taken to the level of contemplation of death, it affords us the opportunity to connect with our clients on a more spiritual level, opening up issues of engagement, meaning, and life purpose. It takes us to a position of detachment, or more accurately, disidentification, with what we have come to know of ourselves, seeing our issues from a meta-position of courage and acceptance. This therapeutic procedure, in and of itself, does not guarantee these results. It merely opens up these patterns of possibility while helping our clients overcome their immediate and ultimate fears so that they are free to function effectively.

CHAPTER 39

Now, Cut That Out!

IN AN EARLIER CHAPTER I described the use of a strategy called decatastrophizing for helping people overcome rational fear, such as injury in high-risk extreme sports or occupations. The same technique can also be used effectively for overcoming irrational fears and phobias about lower-probability events that can still elicit very strong anxiety responses, such as fear of flying, or even phobias about spiders or mice, in which my client has had no previous negative experience that might result in such a strong reaction of anxiety. Nevertheless, the symptoms of activated arousal and alarm can be very distressing, such as trembling, rapid heart rate, flooding of panic thoughts, freezing or temporary paralysis, and a morbid dread that something terrible is about to occur.

Just to refresh your memory, in this strategy the client is guided by the therapist to confront the unthinkable, for example, dying in an airplane crash. We know that our client will experience fear and horror in the process, and we will be there to help them get through it. In the spirit of Acceptance and Commitment Therapy, we will help them get through the obstacle of fear to attain the greater goal of freedom. Obviously, we cannot begin this type of imaginal exposure until the client has a strong investment of trust in the therapeutic alliance.

We are teaching them mindfulness about their own emotions and detachment from what moments ago seemed insurmountable and unbearable. At each phase of decatastrophizing, we invite the client through a process of experiencing the unthinkable horror, only to find that after the process there arises a sense of peaceful acceptance. After we go through the worst situations, we work in reverse order into milder negative scenes involving embarrassment or minor discomfort, until finally the whole phobia is resolved.

One prominent example of this was a young married professional architect called Richard. At age 34, this father of two young children was married to a 30 year-old dental assistant, Maureen. In the past year, seemingly out of nowhere, he developed a strong fear of handling pointed or sharp objects for fear of accidentally cutting himself or others. There were no previous incidents that would account for this fear, other than a brief incident two years previous when Maureen had cut her arm preparing food in the kitchen. Richard had taken her in to the emergency department of a local hospital for stitching, and she made a speedy recovery. Richard also had a relatively benign family history with no evidence of abuse or trauma or anything resembling the kind of severe fear he now faced on a frequent daily basis. Nevertheless, his functioning was so impaired that he even had anxiety using ordinary kitchen knives, although he was careful to hide this from his children so that they would not develop a similar phobia. His fear mostly took the form of obsessive rumination about the danger around sharp objects, in case an accident might happen out of clumsiness or poor or forceful handling by someone else, but more likely, by himself. It also seemed that such anxiety was most intense when at home, whereas it abated quite a bit while at work, even at lunchtimes while handling table utensils.

I considered several treatment strategies, including various forms of graduated exposure such as systematic desensitization or EMDR. However, as we went further in the first interview, it became clearer that Richard was mostly afraid of his own impulsiveness and jerky handling of knives.

It almost seemed like more of an obsession than a true phobia. My questions about his relationship with his wife seemed to offer no leads, and there seemed to be no anxiety about their marriage. She and their family doctor were the only people who knew about Richard's disorder, but no one could account for its origin or how to treat it. I outlined several treatment options that could be used and asked him to consider his preference for treating his condition as we ended our first session.

By the second session a week later his symptoms had worsened. The couple were landscaping the walk around the side of their house and in the back yard, and Richard was in charge of cutting the sod and removing it to make room for a concrete pathway. He became increasingly avoidant of using the sod-cutting knife. He became agitated about wanting to get the job done, but too embarrassed to ask for someone else's help such as a neighbour or one of the other workmen doing landscaping in the back yard. With his permission, we decided to proceed with a decatastrophizing approach.

I asked him what was the worst possible event that could happen if he handled the sod knife. I was prepared for him saying he would kill himself. Instead he said that he was afraid that he would cut off his penis! Immediately, I asked him to close his eyes and visualize how that would happen. He had no problem creating the scenario. He would wait until no one was around on that side of the house. Then he would pick up the knife and start cutting. At this point he was wincing with imagined pain and horror, but I interrupted him to roll back the sequence to make sure he prepared adequately. I asked him to imagine he also had a towel and a plastic bag with him before he went out to the side of the house. So we back-tracked the video, inserted the correction, and moved it ahead to the cutting scene. This time Richard was actually able to complete the action all the way to entirely cutting off his penis. I asked him what was happening next. He was stuck at the freeze-frame, holding his cut-off member, watching blood spurt from his crotch, seemingly not knowing what to do next.

I suggested that he imagine using his towel to catch the blood, then pulling up his pants, and stuffing the penis in the plastic bag he had brought along. At this point I became a bit more directive in the imagery script and suggested he go into the kitchen, wash the penis in cold water, call his wife to come to him in the kitchen, and tell her what happened. Richard imagined that she would recoil in horror and fear, asking him why he would do such a crazy thing. He was unable to answer, again frozen with the fear now amplified by both of them. I had him imagine he would say to her, "I don't know why. I can't explain it. An impulse just came over me! But now we need to get to a hospital fast!" This script seemed okay. Now that both he and his wife were in action mode, it was easier to progress through the sequence of going through the emergency department, getting emergency surgery to reattach the penis and reconnect the blood vessels and nerve endings, all thankfully done under anaesthetic. Richard was able to go through these parts of the imagery sequence with very little anxiety. At this point we fast forwarded through the healing and recovery phase two months later when Richard and his wife were relieved that all sexual function was fully restored in his now-healed penis, and their sexual relations could return to normal. Such a scenario is quite plausible. There are ample protocols of accidental and even deliberate penal dismemberment restored adequately through surgery, especially with a clean organ reattached quite soon after the accident. Richard must have known that as well, and he reassured me that he had read articles or heard of such cases.

Together in imagery Richard and I had co-constructed and progressed through the entire process and converted every "what if" paralyzing scene into an "if, then" action sequence. By symbolically living through the scenario of facing his worst fear, we had broken through the worst of his fear of knives. I now asked Richard to imagine handling the sod knife confidently. He was able to do that with no anxiety or discomfort. We then proceeded quickly to check out the handling of other knives and sharp objects. The phobia had entirely disappeared. That was a good outcome for merely one session lasting 90 minutes. Richard felt exhausted but quite confident he had overcome his fear of knives, so we set up a follow-up session after a month, just to be sure.

In that third session, Richard told me that fear of knives had not returned. No other significant issues had emerged except one: with the symptom cleared it became more obvious to him that he resented and never fully forgave his wife for an extramarital affair she had five years ago. He had not disclosed this to me in our original assessment, nor did I specifically probe about his marital relationship beyond some preliminary questions which Richard handled rather easily with no anxiety. Well, it turns out that as the phobia became resolved, some unprocessed grief and resentment about the affair re-emerged. He and his wife talked about it further, reaffirmed their love for each other going forward, and the resentful feelings totally went away. Richard now felt complete in his psychotherapy. We arranged that he could contact me for further sessions in case his resentment or anxious feelings reappeared. Six months later in a telephone follow-up he said he was doing fine, so we mutually closed his case successfully.

As an epilogue, I am curious about resentment towards a spouse as a possible underlying issue in a fear of knives. Long ago I was trained as a psychodynamic therapist. In Freudian

Theory, it would make perfect sense that a fear of knives would be an unconscious way of guarding against acting out the impulse to hurt or even possibly kill another person. This dynamic would be repressed and unavailable to consciousness. According to theory, the therapist ought not to remove the symptom without uprooting and resolving the unconscious conflict through a long and thorough psychoanalysis featuring insight and subsequent resolution. If the case were not handled in this way, symptom substitution would occur, with the client no farther ahead in finding a cure for his neurosis. With the advent of research in the 1970s in support of Cognitive Behavior Therapy, it became clear that the predicted phenomenon of symptom substitution generally did not occur when a presenting problem was treated and eradicated. Thus psychoanalytic theory was largely discredited and held to be a relatively inefficient way to help clients attain their therapeutic objectives.

Nevertheless, a part of my psychodynamic training remains with me, although not at the forefront of my consciousness when treating most clients. I do recall a case that happened early in my career where a young woman had a profound fear of knives and other sharp objects. She loved her husband dearly, but her fear of sharp objects seemed to be much stronger in her new marital home. We used systematic desensitization, with a predictable successful treatment in about a dozen sessions. However, when she returned for a six-month follow-up session, some new information emerged. During the time she was in treatment with me, she never voiced any doubts about her marriage; perhaps she had no reason to have them. But something was uneasy; she just couldn't put her finger on it. Well, it turned out that her husband had been having an affair, and she discovered it. At first he denied it, but when confronted with her evidence, he confessed. Coming from her religious and moral background, she refused to forgive his mistake, and her parents supported her in going for immediate separation and eventual divorce. There were no children yet, so the decision was quick and firm. They had married young and impulsively after a short courtship, so for her it was just a mistake. She felt relieved and complete, with very little grief or remorse.

As frequently happens in an undiscovered affair, there can be subtle behaviors such as turning away from a spouse, which are unconsciously noted and recorded as a vague sense of unease, a note just slightly off-key. In the absence of a theme to make sense of that vague anxiety, sometimes it can attach itself to a sudden acute phobia, seemingly with no trauma or etiology to explain it. In the spirit of a detective, a psychodynamic therapist might help the client look for the skeleton in the closet, but often this insight-oriented approach merely delays rather than assists the action of effective treatment.

Nevertheless, in future whenever I treat my next knife phobia, I might just explore a little further the possible symbolic meaning or function of the symptom before launching into a radical treatment such as decatastrophizing. Then again, given how well these two cases went, perhaps I might just go ahead and treat them the same way. I just don't know.

Part Seven:

MINDFULNESS PRACTICES

Mindfulness is by now a well-accepted principle of awareness and perspective in the popular literature, and certainly in most progressive forms of psychotherapy. This way of approaching life incorporates the ideas of Zen, Buddhism, and Taoism, but it is not a religion in the traditional sense. As with Acceptance and Commitment Therapy, mindfulness encourages actively embracing reality as it is, optimizing personal effectiveness by detaching from the edicts of the ego and outdated narratives of the past.

Mindfulness is partly a paradigm of detachment and observation of thoughts and emotions, placing them on leaves floating down a stream and around the bend drifting out of sight. Mindfulness is also a daily practice, often involving daily meditation and connection with nature. Like physical fitness, it is not attained by merely wishing for it. It is earned through a commitment to regular behavioral practice. (Ed. Note: This section is more essays on mindfulness than client stories.)

CHAPTER 40

Starting A Practice Of Daily Meditation

WHEN I GRADUATED with a doctorate in clinical psychology I had a very busy lifestyle, crammed with many events, and virtually no margin of spare time in between them. I seldom made time in my busy life for nature, although I still yearned for it. I went fishing when I could and still took time to watch birds and animals whenever they crossed my urban forest paths. However, I took no time for formal meditation. I could not stay still and think of nothing for two 20-minute sessions per day, the recommended dose. Who has time for that in our modern world?

As I went further in the direction of Mindfulness as a more central principle guiding my counselling practice, I kept hearing about the idea that anyone who teaches these ideas should "walk the talk." To lead with integrity, you need to practice what you preach, and be prepared to model what you advocate for your clients. Although I often made time for walks in nature and other forms of informal meditation, and felt relatively balanced in terms of frequent breaks to relax, I still could not actually claim to have a daily practice of formal meditation. I was mildly embarrassed about this fact, and gradually I was almost feeling guilty that I lacked the commitment to go that extra step of daily meditation. My two major roadblocks were that I doubted that I could find the time required, and I lacked the confidence that I could meditate properly and correctly in a formal practice or structure.

My client Mork. Then I counselled Mork, a highly stressed businessman who was very successful but quite unhappy. His crammed lifestyle led to family bitterness, marital distress, and a sense of angry entitlement that nearly destroyed his family. Through therapy we navigated through the worst times of his healing and helped him move beyond success into significance in coaching toward happiness in an engaged and meaningful life. Almost everything was going well except for one crucial ingredient: lack of a meditative practice. By now I was teaching my clients various ways of Zen practices and yogic breathing. Mork was learning these techniques but was applying them occasionally and sporadically. I still had resisted dedicating time for a daily practice, postponing the commitment to "one of these days I suppose I should get started."

The real irony of this situation is that I had been doing sport psychology for years with national and international medalists who complained of the same problem: lack of time to practice mental rehearsal to imprint the ideal performance state and other imagery and identity-building skills. I would tell them to use one sustained 20 minute practice session per day and then work the rest of the practice into the myriad little opportunities of delay and waiting in an average day. For example, any time you are in a checkout line at a store or gridlock in commuting traffic, you could get lost in your MP3 music, and that would be okay too, but you could also use that time to tune into your sports imagery and improve your performance in the next competition. I guess you would have to forfeit reading the gossip magazines at the checkout counter or several minutes of mindless channel surfing or texting on your cellphone, all in support of better sport performance. However, it seems different when you are not training for a specific life event.

Creating Space for Daily Meditation. Finding time to merely meditate daily seems harder, at least for me and many other people. The dedication required does not correspond to the benefits, at least not at first. That is, meditation sessions may or may not provide relief from stress and a feeling of well-being right at that moment of practice. Many people become discouraged when they do not get instant results. Trying to make it happen makes it worse, because, properly done, meditation has no object, no result, except the abandonment of expectation itself, letting go of attachment to desire. That is one of the Zen paradoxes of the practice of meditation. But like every other good health practice, regular repetition eventually yields a general feeling of peaceful abiding with life, compassion, acceptance, and gratitude, all favorable to happiness. This paradox is better revealed in a story:

There is a saying that there is a gift that is bestowed on the seeker, but not in the act of seeking. There was a woman who went to a corner store every day to buy a lotto ticket. She never won any prizes, but she remained optimistic every day. One morning, while she was on her way to the store, she looked down and saw an abandoned ticket on the ground. She picked it up and brought it to the store. The clerk put it into the computer slot. It turned out that it was the winning ticket for the lottery, so she won an enormous prize. Leaving aside the issue of who must have lost that ticket, the purpose of the story is that if the woman did not have that daily practice, she would not have seen the winning ticket. Once again, a huge part of winning in life is showing up with an attitude of openness and relaxed optimism.

Despite knowing these stories and principles, I still had not made the dedication to a daily meditative practice. The constraint that prevented me from commitment was the idea that I had to do deep belly yogic breathing and maintain my concentration during the whole 20 minutes of the meditation session. That requirement was way beyond my ability, so I never tried for more than several days before quitting.

However, around the time I was treating Mork I was also reading Tibetan Sakyong Miphram's (2003) book "Turning the Mind into an Ally". According to his recommended method, there was no special breathing required. You could breathe quickly or slowly, shallowly or deeply; it didn't matter. All you needed to do was pay attention to the process of breathing in every breath. How many breaths for how many minutes? Once again, there were no minimal requirements. You could count to 21 breaths to begin. What about intrusive thoughts? Just let them come and go and return to attunement to the process of breathing. And what if you lose count? Well, you could go back to the beginning. I dreaded that punishment, so I came up with my own rule: I would continue counting each breath, and if I lost count, I would return to the last remembered count, not the beginning. If I was interrupted by the intrusion of someone else, I could resume the count from the point of pausing. Now that was something that I could achieve.

I also liked the idea of 108 breaths, the number that corresponds to the number of beads on a Buddhist rosary. Since I do not have a pure focus while meditating, I usually go for 112-124 breaths to be safe that I complete my daily quota. This process usually takes 4-7 minutes, depending on how quickly I breathe. Okay, now I had a way of daily meditating that was workable, so the question now was: what was the trigger to start the commitment? Like most of us, I did not want to make a commitment I would later fail to keep, so I started small.

The Therapeutic Challenge. Let's go back to the case of Mork I was referring to earlier. I knew that Mork would not likely complete the last phases of his full recovery unless he started a practice of daily meditation. However, one of my guidelines for counselling is that I would not ask of my client something that I would not ask of myself in similar circumstances. So I posed to Mork something that would bind us both, a therapeutic challenge. I committed to only 3 consecutive months in which I would meditate daily. I invited my client Mork to match me in this commitment, for each of us to do a minimum of 108 breaths of daily meditation and to observe whatever results might happen.

In our monthly follow-up sessions, Mork was mildly embarrassed to report that he had done frequent but by no means daily meditation sessions. However, he did notice that he was considerably more relaxed and more agreeable in his business negotiations. His family had noticed that he was not as irritable, and that he seemed more patient and compassionate. I was able to report that I felt good about keeping my commitment to a daily meditative practice. Apart from that there were few noticeable differences from before, other than a greater abiding peacefulness and even more cheeriness than before. I found meditation to be most useful when I was hungry or bored, like when I had just placed an order in a restaurant, or waiting for someone else to arrive for a meeting, or getting ready to go out. At that point my meditation habit was fully developed, so I resolved to carry on the practice for another three months, then a year. It has now been over four years, and I like the discipline of daily meditation. Meanwhile, Mork is happier than before, but he still has not mastered the commitment to daily practice, preferring instead to "fit it in" on a frequent basis. That is all I can ask of him. It has been years since we ended his therapy, although I do see him once every year or two for what he calls his psychological tune-up, wherein he updates me about personal, family, and business matters. Those sessions are a joy for both of us, and we still create time and space for those connections, like two old friends sharing their experiences.

So it took a therapeutic challenge to launch my commitment into developing a lifelong habit. It also needed the revelation that it can be done, that I can do it, that it can be continued when interrupted by life events, and that I don't have to go back and start over at the beginning. I now can let my thoughts come and go, merely observing them, then returning to resume the meditation focus. With that dedication, finding the time each day to do it is easy now, and life itself seems to be more calm and less hurried.

CHAPTER 41

CREATING SPACE

Mu-Shin. From over 40 years of deep involvement in the martial arts, I have come to know how important it is to create a space for learning to occur. All martial arts sessions begin with a ritual to set us apart from the world outside and resume a path of discovery of inner potential. Mu-Shin or Empty-mindedness is attained by a period of brief meditation at the beginning and end of every session. On the command "Mokusou" (pronounced "mock so") of the sensei or teacher, for about 2 minutes all participants close their eyes, focus on their breathing, and clear extraneous thoughts to narrow their attention to the learning theme of the session. The same ritual at the closing of the class creates a moment of quiet reflection so that the lesson can be absorbed at the unconscious body-awareness level of brain imprinting.

Beginner's Mind. However, often this ritual is not sufficient to overcome previously acquired mindsets or paradigms of how we think the world should be. Another idea about creating mental space and freshness comes from the rituals of judo, specifically the concept of "beginner's mind." Clearing presuppositions and assumptions about the world and the nature of reality, the 10th degree black belt once again wears the white, or beginner's belt. This act of humility indicates the wisdom of beginning again with an open mind. You cannot learn Zen when your mind is filled with your own opinions, attitudes, and habits of thought. The true student, as well as the enlightened teacher or sensei or sifu, aspires to the ideal "Hear like an echo, reflect like a pond." Here is one story illustrating this concept:

> Once there was an impatient American wealthy industrialist who came to Japan to learn the inner peace that arises from Zen philosophy. Repeatedly, he tried to gain the audience of the Zen master, only to be rebuffed. Eventually he was received by the Master, who insisted that they engage in the ritual Tea Ceremony reserved for such meetings of esteemed people. While the Master whisked the tea and rotated the brims of the ceremonial cups, then started pouring the tea, the visitor was almost scalded by the very hot tea overflowing from his cup onto his lap. Jumping up to his feet, the would-be Zen student said, "What are you doing?"
>
> The Master said: "You have come all these miles to learn about Zen. You are so full of your own ideas. Your cup of ideas is full! There is no room for fresh learning. Come back when you have emptied your cup. Then your lessons can begin."

Of course, creating space is more than merely clearing your mind so that new ideas and perspectives can emerge. It is also the skill of managing time and resources. For most of us, there seem to be more urgent priorities: making a living, commuting, taking the children to their many activities, and all the urgent demands of modern living. We are frequently over-rushed in today's society by the idea that we should live a productive and efficiently conducted lifestyle. Even recreational moments are scheduled narrowly in between the demands of modern living. Now it's time to consider how to make some space...But how? From where? Every moment is booked to the minute, with little or no margin for error, traffic gridlock, or the unexpected. Not only do we have to contend with external factors, but we are often delayed by a last minute marital conflict, or one of the children melting down, followed by the familiar apology "We are running a little late; we'll be there when we can."

The Time Management Seminar. Obviously we would like to escape to a lower stress lifestyle and to create more space for the enjoyment of life. And that reminds me of another story. I would like to attribute this to Stephen Covey, because he and his co-authors have conducted workshops and written extensively about personal effectiveness and time-energy management. However, perhaps it was not Covey. I can't find the reference, and maybe it was someone else that first conducted this exercise. But now it almost has the status of a universal lesson, an urban legend. It goes like this:

Life Rocks. Many executives and managers attended a workshop in time management. The instructor brought in a large clear glass cylinder and some other materials. At first he put into the cylinder some large rocks, filling them to the top rim of the cylinder. He asked the audience "Is it full yet?" Many people nodded their heads as if saying yes. Then he said "Well, let's see." Then he retrieved a pitcher of small pebbles, and poured them into the cylinder, tapping it occasionally to allow the pebbles to work their way around the rocks, until the pebbles reached the brim. "Is it full now?" Many of the participants just began to smile, whereupon he took out a pitcher of sand, and again filled the glass cylinder to the brim. "Is it full now?" He chuckled as many in the audience said yes. Again he said "Well, let's see." At this point he brought out a jug of water, and filled the cylinder to the brim. Finally, he asked "Is it full now?" and the audience were laughing as they proclaimed that it finally was full. Next the instructor asked "So what's the lesson in this demonstration?" Up shot a hand, and the person exclaimed "That's easy! If we plan carefully and work it out our schedules perfectly, we can meet all our objectives." The instructor said "Not quite, you're missing the point. If I had put the pebbles and other stuff in first, how could I have possibly fit in the rocks? The rocks are the most important values in your life: your health, your partner, your family, your fun. If you don't make a space for them first, then your life will be consumed by trying to answer other people's agendas, rather than the important values in your life."

Nothing. That instructor implied, but did not state, that one of the most important rocks was several hours per week of designated empty space and time. We need empty space to allow for impulses and random factors to colour our emotional lives. Sometimes the greatest moments of fun and enjoyment come from spaces where there are no agendas, no objectives.

When we were raising a young family, Saturdays were primarily dedicated to life with the children, often with me and my son and daughter. Obviously, when it came to skiing and other activities involving travel or organization, we would have to plan in advance or miss out. But some of our nicest memories arose from Saturday mornings in which I would ask, "What are we going to do today?" and we would all answer the chorus, "Nothing!!" with gales of laughter. The answer was pure recreation: we would do what we wanted, for as long as we wanted, and then do something different next. Consensus was easy to obtain. All of the available choices were easy and usually very inexpensive activities, like going skating or walking, playing video games, or even watching a nature show on TV. We usually did not know ahead of time what the activity would be, but it would wind up being enjoyable. The key was not to schedule anything into that time slot without family consensus, usually made up on whim and weather, or whether, depending on our moods and energy.

Creating Space for Date Night. One of Dr. John Gottman's most cherished discoveries in studying couples over the decades was the institution of five magic hours per week. Couples who were the most loving towards each other seemed to find time for contact rituals in departing and re-establishing contact and checking in with each other on a daily basis. Furthermore they found a way to make "date night" occur every week. Date night is an afternoon or evening interlude of 2-4 hours that the couple spend together and celebrate their relationship as companions and perhaps lovers. The couple are restricted from talking about raising the kids, household finances, relationships with in-laws, in other words, potentially conflictual problems. Instead, they just get to know each other with some freshness. Date night does not have to be expensive at all. In fact, a library date can be quite enjoyable. The couple spend an early evening in the library looking around at books and magazines. Then they meet together after an hour or so and share what they found interesting and exciting. In this way, they renew the fascination and interest in differences and shared passions that they had in earlier years.

Creating Space on Vacation. Another example of making space in couples and friends is the planning of vacations. Some people have every day planned: where they are going to be, what they are going to see and experience, what they will be eating and where, and their accommodation. The advantage is that there are usually no surprises and perhaps no disappointments. But often there is little room for random events or sudden opportunities to do unexpected things, and often these can be the most delightful moments of a vacation. Most families resolve the dilemma by planning one or two days and leaving the rest to chance, depending on the weather. By creating space they are allowing openness to respond to opportunities as they open up. As we know, good luck is often the intersection of preparation and opportunity.

Shinrin-yoku. Perhaps the best example of creating space is the establishment of a daily meditative practice. This does not have to be as big and daunting as it may seem. As a child I would spend hours in woodlands and ravines studying birds and animals. Many years later, it turns out that forest walks are a very popular form of meditation in Japan. Shinrin-yoku, or 'forest bathing', is a Japanese mainstream practice of preventative medicine with research-proven health benefits lowering stress, building immunity levels and general health. The manner in which I did it, i.e., slow and deliberate, is ideal for observing nature without disturbing it, and quieting the nature of the observer as well. As the Japanese saying goes "Everybody should spend at least 20 minutes a day in nature, but if you are in a hurry, better take an hour."

Creating space is a central principle of peaceful and enjoyable living. See what you can do to build this value into your life. As the jazz musicians say "God exists in the space between the notes."

CHAPTER 42

THE PRINCIPLE OF INEVITABILITY

THIS PHILOSOPHICAL principle of living is: It is not that it MUST happen. It is that it WILL happen. That is, we do not insist that good fortune will happen, but we are optimistic and prepared so that when an opening does occur, we are fully ready to take action to optimize it. This posture of living combines a Zen awareness and acceptance that nothing is certain, that life cannot be controlled, only managed, and that it is fun to anticipate life, but not depend on it. Let me give you some examples of how this principle might apply.

Whenever I drive to a busy place like a Farmers' Market, Zoo, park, or municipal attraction, I typically go right to the very front of the line and look for a parking stall to clear right as I arrive. Now, I hedge my bets slightly by arriving about an hour after the event or gathering begins, but it seems to work extraordinarily well in any community event that is ongoing. However, in the rare occasion when I do not get a great parking spot, I am not dismayed that I have to go way back to the end of the line watching people park in some of the intermediate spots I had driven by. After all, I took the risk and almost always it paid off, so I don't mind if sometimes I am worse off.

Great, you say, that works for ongoing events. What about stage shows and concerts? Well, surprisingly, the principle of inevitability can work in a similar way. Sometimes I decide on a whim to attend a show or concert that has been sold out for months. Perhaps I was uncertain about future events or weather, but I had decided that I would not buy the initial ticket offerings. So now it's a Tuesday night, and I call my friend John to see whether he's interested in seeing Jackson Browne performing in tonight's concert. He knows how the drill goes, so he accepts my offer. We arrive an hour early when the ticket office opens. The cashier says, as usual, this concert has been sold out for months, so there are no seats available to purchase. I calmly reply that in the event that house tickets are returned, can I be first in line to buy them? She agrees, so John and I go briefly to a nearby venue to enjoy a glass of wine while we wait. We return twelve minutes before curtain and purchase two seats in the second row orchestra, close to the best seats in the house, and enjoy the concert. How could I be certain that such good luck would happen?

Actually I was not certain, but I was reasonably confident that someone in that city would have a sudden illness or time conflict such that they would turn in their free tickets, given them by a sponsor or promoter, so that they would still be available for last-minute sale. But by far the most important transaction was that I was prepared to enjoy an evening downtown with my buddy John in the event that we were not lucky getting tickets. Our Plan B would have been almost as enjoyable as watching the concert. In the event that John had turned down my earlier invitation for a night out, I would have taken some reading material, per-haps even some technical journals that I seldom read, and glanced at them while people watching for almost an hour before buying a ticket or heading home. I still would have had an enjoyable evening.

I am not telling stories about parking spots or concerts to improve your luck in these ventures. These are merely everyday examples of a posture toward lucid living, a way of greeting the many patterns of possibility that can await us if we arrive prepared and open, while having a way of peaceful abiding with a different outcome if the primary event does not materialize. No disappointment need be crushing if we trust ourselves and our resiliency and take enjoyment in even the simplest of things. What does this have to do with psychotherapy and counselling? You already know many people who have different life paradigms that trap them in victim narratives. The principle of inevitability is merely one of several strategies to liberate them to a perspective of measured optimism in living in the spirit of mindfulness.

The principle of inevitability also applies in sport psychology. We train our athletes and our teams to anticipate opportunities for turnovers and lucky breaks; we regularly have drills such as tip-ups and pass interception drills. We also train recovery from error drills in gymnastics and figure skating, so that if an element is missed early in a routine it can be integrated later in the program. These practices do not guarantee good luck; rather they train athletes to anticipate and recognize opportunities to act quickly and decisively when the breaks come, knowing that they likely will come from time to time in any given competition. Again the mantra is not that they must come but that they likely will come, and we will be ready for them.

Beyond sport psychology, there is a purpose for the principle of inevitability: it is the posture of the solution-oriented therapist or counsellor in greeting his or her client. Now, it is true that not everything is solvable. Nevertheless, the optimal stance of the therapist is that of openness to possibilities for solution, with the quiet confidence that viable solutions will emerge as a function of our collaboration utilizing supports and clients' developing skillsets. It is important to note that the attitude of confidence that a solution will emerge does not arise from the skill of the therapist, but rather the trust in the potential of the therapeutic relationship that could develop in their collaboration together. Perhaps a story might help to exemplify this principle in action.

Tara is a bright precocious 8-year-old girl suffering from Obsessive Compulsive Disorder (OCD). As you know from reading several other chapters, I seem to do well treating people suffering from this disorder, but I have never treated a client as young as Tara. Other than gymnasts, figure skaters, and dancers, I seldom treat children this young. However, Tara's mother was enthusiastic about my model and results helping a teenage OCD daughter of one of her friends. Often in the case of younger clients, I try to have at least one parent in counselling sessions to support their child's recovery.

The world of a child is largely the world of imagination, and I could tell from our first session that Tara was outstanding in this regard. After letting her mother answer for her in her initial shyness, she gradually warmed up to the interview process, telling me about her fears of illness contamination and themes involving death. Her high- functioning parents and her sister were mystified about how Tara developed such intense anxiety around these themes. No one among family or friends had suffered severe illness or death with any connection to contamination. The whole pattern started with reading "The Book of Awesome" in which the author began the preamble with many personal setbacks, including a dear friend dying of an infectious disease. Tara panicked and would not touch the book for fear of being contaminated and dying. Even when her mother contacted the author, and the author wrote Tara an email reassuring her that she was safe, Tara escalated and now would avoid touching most books and many other objects. For example, Tara was obsessed with the smallpox outbreak that nearly wiped out entire tribes of indigenous peoples, so now she avoided touching or even being near books describing the epidemic or even being in rooms where native art is prevalent. Over a period of several months her anxiety and avoidance had spread in her mind like an internal meme epidemic. Her parents and other helping professionals were at a loss about how to help her to reverse her condition.

Fairly early in the first interview, I approached Tara with the conviction that she would find a way to get better. After all, it was the runaway of her imagination that had generated her fears and made up her rules, which on some level she knew were irrational, but nevertheless compelling. Because she had made up the rules in her world, she could also undo the spells she had created. I now had the job of convincing her that my confidence in her was well-placed, in that she had such powers.

One of my first interventions was to show her a demonstration I use to show how imagery guides our behavior. I call it "The Ring on a String." Basically, you take about 20" of thread and put it through a ring and join the thread ends together between the thumb and the index finger of your writing hand to make a pendulum. You sit forward so that your feet are on the floor, your elbow is now on your knee, you steady the ring with your other hand, then remove that hand. Then you imagine that the ring will swing from side-to-side. Don't try to stop the motion; just allow it to grow larger and larger. Then I have the client imagine that the ring will begin to swing in a circle. After the circle is established, I have the client imagine that the ring will swing in a straight line towards and away from the chest. Most people are amazed at how the ring swings almost by itself in the imagined direction. This demo is an introduction to mystery and the magic of the mind. It demonstrates the role of alternate neural pathways which we can call "your unconscious mind." My main intent with Tara was to arouse her curiosity with fun, to engage her in collaboration about the power of imagery and imagination in constructing our subjective world. The ring on the string is an example of doing therapy as "deadly serious fun." From here we went on to explore

Tara's imaginal world of characters, superpowers, and spells. I talked about "Mr. Trailer," an imaginary friend I had as a four-year-old who could do anything better than my parents' friends. It was my way of joining adult conversations in a dramatic way, although at times it drove my mother to exasperation.

And so it was that Tara and I had a great exchange about the power of a child's imagination in reshaping the world of adults. I asked her how she would begin to use her powers and challenge herself to overcome her anxieties. She seemed at a loss, so I suggested she begin by touching a book on my bookshelf. That challenge seemed to be too big to handle, but she thought she would begin by touching some of the "cleaner less-contaminated" books in her parents' library. Perhaps in the next session she might try touching one of my books.

Curious about all the positive changes in that week, Tara's family came in for the next session, including her father and her younger sister. We went through that session in a fairly lighthearted way, commending Tara for facing and overcoming many of her fears and avoidance rituals. She beamed with satisfaction about the amazing progress she made that first week, and her family rejoiced about her accomplishments. As predicted in my challenge, she was able to touch several books in my bookshelves. To keep the momentum going, we devised a homework assignment where her father would be taking her to the civic library where she would touch many books touched multiple times by a large number of unknown people who had all kinds of germs.

By session three Tara had narrowed her field of avoidance down to fear of death and disease, and books and other trigger situations associated more closely with death. After her library excursion with her father, she could touch a wide variety of public books. She still harboured a fear of native artifacts, associating them with the death of many natives from smallpox. With some coaxing from me she was able to touch all the native paintings and carvings in my office. After that accomplishment, I thought that her mother might be able to set up a visit to a hospice where all the patients were dying from terminal illness. Her assignment was to be able to touch them and hug them and understand them better.

By session four Tara had accomplished almost all of her recovery goals, according to Tara and her mother. They still had not arranged the hospice visit homework assignment, but Tara sounded confident that she would be able to handle it. As she was almost recovered and school was about to begin after summer break, we arranged for a follow-up session three weeks later. Meanwhile, Tara said she was now ready to touch the original source of her anxiety, "The Book of Awesome" on the family bookshelf. I assured her mother not to give in to Tara's residual avoidances, but rather give her some time out to figure out her own solutions whenever overwhelmed with anxiety. This intervention would take care of Tara's occasional avoiding tidying up and putting away toys and cleaning up messes she made because she claimed she was too anxious to do it.

Several weeks later, Tara and her mother came for their follow-up session. Tara was able to overcome her reluctances and get more organized for her school term. A follow-up call several months later confirmed that Tara was doing well in her school work, and anxiety was minimal.

CHAPTER 43

Beyond Competition: Sport And Spirituality

(Ed. Note: This was published as an article in *Impact Magazine*)

WE NEED TO COMPETE, to get the juices flowing, and go beyond competition to keep the spirit flowing.

In previous articles in this series, Dr. Jerry Rose and I focused on psychological factors involved in short-term injury (Sept. '98) and long-term injury (July '99). We noted that mental attitude and imagery can have a profound effect on the healing to health process. We also cautioned about the need to develop stress management coping strategies preventively throughout your sports career, to increase your resilience to setbacks, and improve your enjoyment of living. We even hinted at the concept of injury as a portal for an inner journey of meaning. In this article, we extend those ideas to shape the extension of sport as a metaphor for life and branch into a life beyond competition, on a journey to explore inner space.

This idea is not as abstract as it sounds. There are practical benefits for approaching your sport through these lenses. You are going to spend from 4 to 16 hours a week for most of your life in your main sport, so this article is about improving the depth of your enjoyment and your overall return on the time you invest.

The central idea is that we are all essentially on a path inward, to return where we started as a child, in a state of unity with something greater than ourselves, but now, as a more experienced and differentiated adult.

A child begins with the premise, the felt certainty, that (s) he is not only the centre of the universe, but the very universe itself. Everything is an extension of the self. By age two we begin to realize that we are separate from, and dependent upon, all other beings. In order to have our needs met we need to negotiate with others. We learn patterns and rules that generally reward social behavior. We also learn how to play by the rules in games and sports as we progress in mastery of the skills involved. Beyond the practice of basic skills, we desire to measure our progress. That is where competition enters as a powerful factor in our definition of mastery and identity.

At the junior and senior levels of sport, we rely quite heavily on external role models, rule structures, and external guideposts of excellence and achievement. We need competition, and comparison with others both current and past, to gauge our success and development in sport and life. That is, we begin to live in a world where we are measuring our worth as a competitor against everybody in our age/weight/ability category. These comparative standards are ruthless, but they are clear. For every placement in the medals, the top 10, the top 100, there are hundreds or thousands more who never make it to that level, and millions more who never even tried. For many of us at the senior competitive level, we want to make it in history, to have our one moment in time. Perhaps more realistically for most of us, maybe to go as far as our talents and training can take us.

At some point, all athletes need to consider the decision to transition from the senior level to the masters level. A crucial crisis of identity, meaning, and mortality occurs at this juncture. The standards are still clear and external: number of seconds, height climbed, goals scored, speed, power exerted per second, etc. What happens, of course, is the shift between competing with the best in the world, to the best in your age category.

The signposts of excellence and mastery are now becoming more internal. From best in the class or group, you are gradually shifting to personal best as the standard, and eventually, personal best under these particular circumstances on a particular day in a particular match. You are now progressing to a comparative, rather than an ultimate, standard. You are beginning to deal with issues of limitation and handicapping. Enjoyment is being redefined in the dawning awareness of resignation, and for the first time, of surrender to mortality. In other words, acceptance is a step on the path of transcendence. Acceptance involves the skill of surrender. Surrender is not passive. It is embracing life as it is, not as you would like it to be.

Ultimately, you question what is truly meaningful in life; what is your decision path? A path that has a balance of physical and mental aspects of focused awareness in living seems like a promising approach to restoring overall health and wellness. This principle applies to the athlete recovering from and preventing injury, to the masters level competitor, and to the athlete in a state of attitude beyond competition. At this stage of awareness, you are now starting to catch up with yourself and your ultimate destiny, beyond competition into the uncharted regions of personal depth, tranquility, and quiet personal power.

Factors such as progression and skill mastery still motivate, perhaps more than ever, but the factor of enjoyment and satisfaction are now becoming most important. Process is beginning to be more important than product. You are returning to the level of enjoyment you may have had as a child, the pure joy of rhythm and flow.

The process of flow is paramount. It is the optimum state of enjoyment for which you continue the practice of the sport.

You become one with the spirit of the sport, or at least, at those spectacular moments of flow you feel as if you and the sport are one. You have blended into the sport, losing your ego, but having an expanded sense of your peace and oneness with the sport. You have moved into the zone beyond competition. You and your opponent are in skills opposed, in spirit united. You have moved beyond competition into ultimate flow, the experience of total blend with unity at last. Thus you progress in sport to the level of a total child, where your identity and that of the universe are a seamless whole.

Now you have moved into the zone of flow, beyond the external structure of competition. Now the journey is internal. The question is: where are the signposts now? The internal journey is subjective and spiritual. You will need to find your own signposts. Here are just a selected few:

- How do you assess your true potential for technical excellence now and in the future?

- How will you know you are making progress to your ultimate goals?

- How do you regard your competitors, as embarrassing threats, or friendly adversaries?

- How are they teaching you about life and its ultimate enjoyment?

- What do you need to do on my next step to fulfillment and completion, to transcendence?

We all live for these moments of transcendence. We know intuitively that they cannot be extended beyond their natural time. We wish to replicate them by creating the same circumstances. After repeated experience, however, we learn that it is not the circumstance, it is the attitude we take to the event that determines a major part of the experience.

When we look beyond competition and into the spirituality of sport, we experience these states of ecstasy more deeply and more often.

It is for this experience, the pathway to inner excellence, that we continue in sport. In the inner journey, the pathway is more difficult because the way is uncharted and the signposts are unmarked. Often you do not have a sense of progress, lost in a zone of process. This is the zone of spirituality in sport. It is total flow, total ecstasy.

Beyond the individual experience of ecstasy is communion, the notion of the collective, the validation of teamwork in the participation of excellence. Does this mean that the spiritual experience of sport is greater in team sport experiences? Perhaps, but that's another article. For now, know that there is no greater experience than that of the unity of the Flow experience. This experience is beyond competition, the blending of sport and spirituality.

CHAPTER 44

MARTIAL ARTS METAPHORS: LESSONS FOR LIVING

(by Frank D. Young Ph.D., R. Psych. 4th dan judo)

THIS ARTICLE PROPOSES that metaphors of personal integrity and systemic harmony derived from the Martial Arts can be utilized to promote personal growth, peace, and a philosophical basis for living a full life. Before we begin this venture, let me point out that you do not need to be a martial artist to attain these insights or use these metaphors. Many of these ideas are common to all fields of human excellence and consciousness development. Nevertheless, there are extra philosophical colorings that derive from the personal and spiritual struggles that emanate from a combative model of conflict into confluence.

While these insights or lessons are not exclusive to martial arts experience, they are common to serious practitioners of these arts with 5 or more dedicated years of experience in diligent physical practice and contemplative thought. It is possible to be a good fighter in the martial arts and avoid these lessons, but this limited technique-and-conquer mind-set is rare among the masters that go beyond the 2nd dan level. To the masters of the art await the treasures of consciousness and philosophy that make the practice of the art a meditation of daily living. But before we begin our journey together into this realm, perhaps we should best define our terms:

OPERATIONAL DEFINITIONS

1. **MARTIAL ARTS** are skills of self-defence using primarily unarmed or minimally armed (weapon range less than 2 metres) strategies and skills. We are focusing primarily on those derived from Japan, China, and The Orient for their practical effectiveness and especially for their spiritual foundations.

2. **METAPHOR** is an indirect stating of a concept or principle using a story or image that compels the imagination of the listener into reframing a life situation.

Martial arts experience and practice lead to meditative and focusing states in which metaphors for the reframing of daily living are compellingly attractive and adaptive. Following our outline, let's see how this unfolds.

A. CREATING A CONTEXT OF OPEN-MINDED LEARNING

1. **Clearing the Mind.** All martial arts sessions begin with a ritual to set us apart from the world outside and resume a path of discovery of inner potential. Mu-Shin or Empty-mindedness is attained by a period of brief meditation at the beginning and end of every session. For about 2 minutes, all participants close their eyes, focus on their breathing, and clear extraneous thoughts to narrow their attention to the learning theme of the session.

2. **Beginner's Mind.** Clearing presuppositions and assumptions about the world and the nature of reality, the 10th degree black belt once again wears the white, or beginner's belt. This act of humility indicates the wisdom of beginning again with an open mind. You cannot learn Zen when your mind is filled with your

own opinions, attitudes, and habits of thought. The true student, as well as the enlightened teacher or sensei or sifu, aspires to the ideal "Hear like an echo, see like a mirror."

There are several stories that come to mind to express the Beginner's Mind concept.

The first has to do with an impatient American wealthy industrialist who came to Japan to learn the inner peace that arises from Zen philosophy. Repeatedly, he tried to gain the audience of the Zen master, only to be rebuffed. Eventually he was received by the Master, who insisted that they engage in the ritual Tea Ceremony reserved for such meetings of esteemed people. While the Master whisked the tea and rotated the brims of the ceremonial cups, then started pouring the tea, the visitor was almost scalded by the very hot tea overflowing from his cup onto his lap. Jumping up to his feet, the would-be Zen student said "What are you doing?"

The Master said: "You have come all these miles to learn about Zen. You are so full of your own ideas. Your cup of ideas is full! There is no room for fresh learning. Come back when you have emptied your cup. Then your lessons can begin!"

The second story describes the situation of a proud young fellow who arrived at a Zen monastery with a very beautifully carved ornate bowl that had been designed by his ancestors. The chief monk looked at this masterpiece of art and said, "Very pretty, but do you really truly want to become a Zen monk, renouncing attachment to desire?" The student repeatedly protested that he wanted to learn Zen more than anything else in the world. After several exchanges of the student's declaration of intent, the Master took a hammer and shattered the bowl, with the words "Very well then. Here is some glue. Glue the pieces back together. Then you will be ready to be a monk, with a proper and humble beggar's bowl. Now you can begin the work of enlightenment!" The preferred posture for learning is not that of ego or vanity; rather it is open, balanced, peaceful, and receptive.

If you think that these stories exist only in the world of Zen monasteries, consider this more contemporary scene. Have you ever washed your car in the spring when the snow is melting on the road? Notice that as you drive your spotlessly clean car down the road, you delicately avoid puddles of slush, and avoid the splashes of oncoming traffic. The painstaking care that you exercise almost always takes away from the joy of driving, until finally you get splashed. Then the spell of perfectionism and cleanliness is finally broken, the struggle is now resolved, and you resume the enjoyment of driving normally.

The lessons are clear. Let it go. Clear your plate. Stop trying to hold it together with the bonds of control. Create a quiet and curious space for learning. As the jazz musician said, "God exists in the space between the notes."

3. **Structure and Clarity of Roles.** Teacher–student, leader-follower, are useful roles in the learning process, and can be reversed as the student progresses beyond the master. The martial arts are hierarchically organized to facilitate the acceptance of the roles that enable the learning process, and to clarify role shifts as they occur or are requested.

4. **Social Contract of Mutual Respect.** Bowing Rituals prevail in most acts of engagement in the martial arts. When we enter the dojo or exercise hall, we always bow to announce our respect for an authority of shared knowledge and wisdom greater than our own. This practice arises from the architecture of temples where the roofs and doors were so low that they forced all

people who entered to lower their heads, an act of humility and respect to a higher order than individual greatness and ego.

Bowing to your opponent also occurs before and after each practice engagement with that partner. As you bow, in effect you are saying to your partner, "If you ever wanted the perfect time to hit me with a cheap shot, now is the time because my head is bowed forward and vulnerable. But if we both come out of the bow without incident, we are making a contract of mutual respect, honor, and integrity. As mutual participants we are in skill opposed, in spirit united. Your body is respected as an extension of mine as we endeavor to master but not destroy. We are connected in a united ecosystem of passion and philosophy. Although we are engaged in a win-lose paradigm, the underlying social contract is win-win. We bow to a higher order of ethics in our shared love of the martial arts, and we bow to each other as its mutual adherents.

B. NARROWING THE FOCUS TO WHAT IS RELEVANT

1. **Exact Focus allows us to break through obstacles** to penetrate the illusory barriers of life to realize opportunity and vision. Precise focus allows us to care about ourselves and our living systems while we mould and transform external and internal realities. The greatest test is breaking through our own fears. Much of this discipline is counter-intuitive, in that we need to approach and embrace our fears in order to manage them. We create the art of the impossible, enter The Eye of the Tiger, the centre of our worst fears, to discover an astounding zone of peace where we least expected it. That is, when we focus entirely on the

Eternal Now there is no past to regret, nor is there future to fear. Our mind is entirely one with our actions. The present moment is our provisional reality, the only relevant reality in our flow, and we use this platform as if it were the only reality at all. Also, we learn how to absorb a hit without cowering or flinching, until finally we realize we are liberated from the paralysis of fear. We can still feel fear, but we can respond assertively, rather than react under fear's influence, when faced with a challenging situation.

2. **Ki or Chi is a sense of Guiding Internal Spirit that overrides all considerations.** This spirit is both fierce and compassionate. Its ultimate expression is the mystical "Moment of Truth" when your body operates totally unconsciously with lightening speed to produce a beautiful moment of Pure Flow, an ecstatic time of awe and spiritual rapture. Ki and its development are assisted by rituals and acts that focus subjective reality.

   Dissociation from ordinary reality. Obstacles such as pain, fear, limitations, doubts, are left behind by the setting of context through ritual and extraordinary focusing experiences. The Sanshin or Breathing Kata and the "Kiai" power-shout that represents the **meeting of the spirits** exemplify powerful techniques to block out external reality and narrow focus into the here-and-now of our present context and our purpose within it.

C. OTHER FOCUSING ASPECTS OF THE MARTIAL ARTS

1. **Affirmation of the Positive.** Similar to the Yes-set Induction in hypnosis, we focus on the technique of the impossible, such as putting a straw through a potato in one stroke. This demonstration is a layman's version

of the breaking of boards or smashing through ice seen in theatrical demonstrations of the power of focus. At a more philosophical level, in life we can use what I call the **Principle of Inevitability** to affirm an outcome that we envision, but we do not insist that it **must** happen, merely that it **will** happen. Thus we keep the required intensity and focus, without the attendant fuss and bluster that distract ourselves and others from our mission.

2. **Repetition and the Boredom Barrier.** The highly meditative alpha and theta states are induced by the sheer weight of millions of repetitions of basic movements until they are totally instinctive. Meanwhile the learning process itself induces altered states of consciousness and quasi-mystical states by virtue of its requirement of mind-numbing repetition of a kinetic action mantra. That is, the analytic thinking associated with beta rapid brainwaves is blocked, forcing the induction of hypnotic alpha and even theta deep trance states.

3. **Kinetic Meditation of Connectedness.** Like other forms of dance and rhythmic motion, the Martial Arts engage a sense of aesthetics of balance in motion. As this motion is in response with real and imagined opponents, the meditation extends beyond ego and includes a profound sense of connectedness with ourselves, our opponents, our group, our community, nature, and the universe.

D. BUSHIDO: THE WARRIOR'S CODE

1. **The Suffix "-do" is an ethos that is a blueprint for a philosophy of life for its practitioners.** The practices of judo, aikido, bushido etc., have the suffix –do to

indicate a way of being. This way of thinking and its corresponding codes of morality and action gradually acquire a guiding and automatic "life of their own" that, at least in theory if not in practice, guide every breath we take. From a constructivist solution-focused model, the world is appreciated calmly from a perspective of opening patterns of possibility.

2. **The Martial Arts are indeed arts.** There is adherence to pure form or method. All action is based on a substrate of applied biomechanics. That is, if the technique is practically ineffective, it is not worth learning. Thus, in many martial arts there is frequent emphasis on Kata or prearranged forms of practice, so that the building blocks of classical method can be thoroughly mastered and understood. As in art and music, technical method leads to strategic linkage and synthesis, and finally artistic expression. Only then can elaboration, improvisation, adaptation, and the creation of personal style be effective. Still, "No one may enter the hall of mastery without the key of pure form." This guideline means that classical form or method must still be the platform underlying the surface of personal style and creative flair.

3. **Mindfulness** and every-moment-Zen awareness are essential to the vision and perspective of the Martial Arts. Earlier we outlined the mantra-like repetition of practice to go beyond the limitations of the analytic mind. However, even in these many repetitions, we remain aware of our movement and our surroundings, especially the interaction feedback loops between ourselves and our opponents, so that we are still alertly present and observing ourselves and our surroundings in the spirit of calm reflection and appreciation.

4. **Conflict Into Confluence.** Many of the Martial Arts emphasize flexibility, pliability, gentleness, and harmony in dealing with both internal and external field forces or seemingly conflicting trends. The martial arts of Aikido (the way of harmony) and Judo (the way of gentleness or flexibility) particularly utilize this principle of moving with field forces that are impinging upon us.

   Force that could harm us is not merely neutralized. When we actively join its energy with our own, we amplify that power in confluence to create startlingly powerful outcomes. The image of the empty paper cup demonstrates this principle. Although the cup itself is light and frail, when you push it around with your finger, it gives way and moves out of the way so that it is not crushed. When two fingers push at it from opposite sides, it spins out of the middle, allowing the two fingers to meet each other with the cup standing by on the outside of the conflict, rather than being crushed by it. Thus the paper cup models **formal integrity with spatial flexibility,** a key dimension of the flexible martial arts.

5. **Patience, Discipline, and Persistence** arise from a doctrine of Acceptance. Acceptance is a global concept of humility in regarding our limitations as well as our strengths, and acceptance of life as it is, rather than as we would like it to insist that it should be. This spirit can apply in situations that are unfair, or where strong power differentials make it seem that our efforts will not prevail. Yet this form of acceptance is far from passive, and actions arising from it are often powerful in the expression of personal spiritual integrity. **Acceptance is the surrender of attachment to desire while maintaining personal purpose.**

There are stories of patient but persistent change produced by an attitude of quiet firmness and its accompanying spirit of fierce courage.

One such story involved the general of a conquering army insisting total allegiance of all the citizens to the new occupation political regime. Most of the citizens complied, except one silent monk meditating under a tree. The general dismounted from his horse, and with all his armor and weaponry, towered over the little monk. He bellowed in a loud and angry voice, "Do you know who I am? Do you realize that I could decide at will to raise **my** sword and cut off **your** head, without blinking my eye?"

In a steady and quiet regard of compassion, the monk nodded slowly and replied, "And do you know who I am? Do you realize that I could have you decide at will to raise your sword and cut off **my** head without blinking **my** eye?"

The courage of this monk, choosing an opportunity of acceptance and spiritual integrity, and even a potential coaching or teaching moment with this arrogant general, exercised a spirit of detachment in the practice of life. That is, even at the risk of potential death, this monk chose to follow a path of mutual enlightenment by asserting his compassion and acceptance of the situation, rather than collapse under the weight of its power differential. Here, truly, is an example of courage in acceptance. Socrates said "Practice dying." In the Martial Arts, we indeed do this symbolically many times in each training session, thus participating in an experience of acceptance, rebirth, and symbolic immortality of spirit.

6. **Understanding is only a step toward Realization.** Understanding acknowledges that a principle in theory could apply in reality, maybe for somebody else, but not necessarily in my life. Realization is the convincing belief based on evidence in application that this principle can and **does apply effectively in my life.** Once this realization has occurred, the possibility of peace, joy, and enlightenment become more attainable and practical.

7. **The Circle of Life becomes a Spiral.** Linear time becomes a circular recursive concept, as all lines of opposition are transformed into circles that reflect upon each other. Let me expand that sentence. Instead of the notion that time is a linear sequence of events, consider that time is a circle that orbits over itself in a spiral. Thus, when we think we are back to square 1, we are actually experiencing square 101. We are not quite replicating an experience we have had before; we are in fact elaborating that experience with our revisiting its circumstances and our developing skills. Thus our life view reflects a systemic idea of a reality that folds upon itself. This insight can lead to adaptive ways of functioning in post-modern constructions of social and global life connectedness. Other applications derived from this philosophy are that underneath the maya or illusion of separateness is the implicate order of unity in a holographic universe. In a hologram, each instance reflects a microcosm of the whole it represents. As such, each of our individual actions at a moment in time can represent and shape the experience of our evolution as a species. This phenomenon can be represented by the "Butterfly Effect" in which the beating of the wings of a butterfly can amplify in resonance

so that a powerful wind blows somewhere else in the world. There are many examples in physics and other spheres of life where strange attractors and other examples of congruencies or resonances combine and amplify their effects in demonstrations of quantum or chaos theory. These lessons are also inherent in the mutual or group practice of the Martial Arts as we experience and combine synergy of action. Furthermore, in this practice, the adherents often go beyond the illusion of the individual ego as the emergent self of Flow becomes a vessel of expression of this unity.

E. APPLICATIONS IN GUIDING OTHERS TO A MORE COMPLETE LIFE

Many of the spiritual understandings derived from the experience and practice of the Martial Arts can be powerful metaphors for the reframing of life stories and the incorporation of frameworks that encourage peace and transcendence of life adversities. There are many ways to refer to the collective wisdom of the warrior archetype, whether or not you or your client or friend has had any direct exposure to the Martial Arts. Here are some suggested applications:

1. Learn and explore the application of these lessons **with those who have experienced the Martial Arts.** Obviously, the lessons of the Martial Arts extend beyond the dojo and become a way of life and a guiding philosophy for its practitioners. Even if you yourself do not share this background, you can discuss these principles and wonder with your client whether they have valid application in reframing their life narrative story. You can have them go back into the trance of their martial art as a naturalistic utilization of a well-rehearsed

induction, and then have them feel these principles applying in trance and beyond.

2. **With those with no Martial Arts experience, use vicarious identification with the Inner Warrior archetype.** Since many media such as television and movies render depictions of these actions and principles, you could have a client with no direct experience imagine what it might be like to be a Warrior, and get in touch with their Inner Warrior, instead of identifying their Inner Worrier.

3. **Cultivate in your own mind an appreciation of the utility of conflict.** Many counselors or personal coaches wish to avoid metaphors that invoke the concept of conflict. Particularly, many feminists would rather bypass the traps of conflict and use metaphors of joining and collaboration. However, such metaphors of incorporation and joining can be integrated in a model that has the dynamic of conflict. Researchers in stress management have talked about the need for some sense of opposition or struggle or the challenge of positive stress in order for growth and resiliency to be developed. Researchers in creativity, flow, and happiness have also cited the need to simulate or generate some kind of challenge dynamic to generate flow states.

4. **Encourage the model of Conflict into Confluence.** In imagery fantasy and simulation, have your clients imagine their opponent's objective, then use their opponents force in congruency with your client's signature strengths to generate a win-win whereby their opponents now become their allies, and they come to understand some of the benefit and even benevolence in their former adversary. At a bare minimum,

they come to have some empathy, compassion, and acceptance of their former foe. A corporate example is a technology firm that drops its lawsuit for copyright infringement on an encroaching competitor by making that competitor company into a licensed manufacturer of a similar product, a mutual win for both companies.

5. **Forgiveness is largely self-forgiveness; acceptance is largely self-acceptance; trust is ultimately self-trust.** As your client comes to see that much of the misery of life is generated by attachment to desire, have your client or friend forgive themselves for falling into the illusion that we are all separate, and then promote metaphors of cooperation and integration of shadows and opposite parts of the self. Rejoice with your clients as they grow in integration and transpersonal ways of seeing humanity and their role in the evolution of our collective consciousness.

Summary. I am proposing that metaphors of personal integrity and systemic harmony derived from the Martial Arts can be utilized to promote personal growth, peace, and a philosophical basis for living a full life. The outline begins with the creation of a context of clearing the mind to make space for learning and insight. We also observe roles and rituals of conduct to create a social learning contract of mutual respect and integrity. Focus and spirit allow us to break through life obstacles and internal barriers to create new realities. Affirmations of the positive and kinetic meditations about connectedness use the principle of inevitability to bring forth the fulfillment of our goals. Mindfulness, discipline and persistence are essential to the warrior's code of honor and way of living. Formal integrity is fortified by postural and spatial flexibility. Conflict is blended into the confluence of aligned forces. Patience and compassion arise from acceptance. Acceptance is the surrender of attachment to desire while maintaining personal purpose. Living this way through applying these principles allows us to experience the circle of life as a spiral of spiritual connectedness with the evolving mind of the universe.

By combining conflict into confluence martial arts metaphors can form a philosophical code for living a life promoting both passion and peace.

Part Eight:

Other Professional Stories And Issues

This section has to do with my clinical method, some essays about underlying theory, and a few stories about issues in supervision. Until more recently I have been a clinical supervisor and trainer of therapists from diverse professional backgrounds and qualifications. Sometimes it has been challenging to match my supervisory style to the background of my trainee or supervisee, but these constraints actually made the work more interesting and fun.

Beyond the issues of supervision are general topics that derive from research on what makes therapy work. For example, the theory of sequential parsimony (do the least invasive intervention first before attempting more intrusive or complicated strategies) is utilized in the Front-Side-Backdoor Model and the essay on the design and delivery of therapeutic metaphors. Other miscellaneous ideas complete this section.

CHAPTER 45

DEALING WITH THERAPEUTIC FAILURE

MOST OF THE TIME, I like to talk about success in psychotherapy and the factors that promote it. Still, there is a lot to be learned from failure as well. In this chapter I am not talking about miserable sessions. Often those sessions involve marriages that arrive at your office dead on arrival, rendering your role little more than a pall-bearer. In those situations, you have scarcely more you can do than assist the couple in separation counselling, so that they have some ground rules of communication and problem-solving with minimal collateral damage to each other and their children. But often they are so burdened with destructive anger that even this offer of minimal help is futile. While these sessions are disheartening, I do not think of them as failures. The odds were entirely stacked against all of us from the outset. No, when I talk about genuine therapeutic failure, it is situations where I gave it my all, and so did my client, but the outcome was no positive movement toward resolution of the presenting problem.

One case that comes to mind is Winston, a young single man in his 20s who was referred by Workers Compensation for phantom limb pain a year after losing his right arm in a factory accident. Apparently, a part of his industrial uniform got caught in some machinery, dragging in and mangling his arm before either he or a work-mate could access the emergency stop-button. A year later and after several programs in a pain clinic there was no improvement in his severe phantom limb pain. His upper arm stub had fully healed at the point where the amputation had occurred. He was learning how to write with his left hand and poke a keyboard to do some communication and computer work, but still his life was quite functionally impaired. However, he had his occupational therapy to deal with that and other life adjustments. He said he just needed help to reduce the incessant aching of his right hand and forearm that were no longer there. He was taking medication to dull the pain, but due to habituation, this was diminishing in its effectiveness. Perhaps hypnosis might work; that was his hope. I had experienced previous successes in helping people "dial down their pain" with hypnosis.

Using an eye-fixation induction, Winston showed the classic signs of being in a mild to moderate depth of trance. We used the metaphor of dialing down his pain, but he could perceive no reduction of pain using this method. I attempted other methods of dissociation but to little avail. I also trained him to induce a trance in himself so that he could practice on his own during the following week. He practiced for at least 20 minutes per day that week, but still with no results. We did another session of hypnosis in the following week, but nothing happened. At that point he thanked me for trying, but we decided to quit at that point because there were no encouraging results.

Sometimes you give it all you've got and you know your client is doing likewise, but your best just is not good enough to match the demands of the task at hand, or perhaps the skills of the therapist are inadequate. So much is unknown. For example, many years ago, we were just getting a name for Tourette's Syndrome after I tried every technique I could think of to try to ameliorate the jerky involuntary movements in my client's neck and face. That therapy did not succeed either. But now, years later, we are learning more about organic neurological conditions and how to treat them. Norman Doidge in the book *The Brain that Changes Itself,* talks about neuroplasticity and rechanneling brain connections so that new responses can replace old ones. For phantom limb pain, the preferred treatment is to have the client observe their functional arm through a special mirror arrangement that makes it look like the client is seeing and experiencing their severed limb once more, and this remembered functioning allows the client to let go of pain sensations in the brain. As time goes on, we will be learning about more specific techniques to help people with neurological syndromes.

But meanwhile, I still had to deal with the reality of occasional therapeutic failures. Early in my career as a psychologist, I took these cases almost as personal defeats, as I expected success in any case I was qualified to treat. However, in my early forties, I came to adopt a different posture in psychotherapy. I decided to have God as my co-pilot. Now, I'm not what you would describe as a religious person, but I posit the existence of God as a philosophical convenience. That is, I prefer the notion that there is a God, even for dyslexic people, only they call him Dog. But even if you dismiss the existence of God, consider that in every human encounter, you leave room for fate to play its hand. That is, you do the best you can, your clients do the best that they can, you let go of the notion of control and you let the sequence play through, whatever conclusion happens. At the end you accept the verdict, learn what you can, and move on. This shift in philosophical stance has allowed me a greater sense of peace and calm. I don't take myself as seriously, and my clients and I are freer to have more fun.

And so we can learn from failure.

CHAPTER 46

WHEN EMDR STALLS

WHEN I THINK ABOUT counselling and psychotherapy, often I am interested in what I call "the Mind of the Therapist," or how the therapist and client make a decision about what strategy to use and when to switch and what to use next. I have conducted several workshops with trainees and experienced clinicians addressing this fascinating issue. Of course, when therapy is failing after a fair and consistent trial of your first approach, you need to change. By failing, I mean that your client is worse off or there is no forward movement towards change in a positive direction. But what if therapy is stalled? By that I mean that your client is improving, but the rate of change is so slow that both you and your client are losing motivation to keep going with that approach. Let me give you a case example of this process and its resolution, but first some background about EMDR.

About twenty years ago I was one of the first professionals in my area to be trained in a somewhat new technique called Eye Movement Desensitization and Reprocessing, or EMDR. (If you want to learn more about how it works, go to emdr. com). Over the years I have used it frequently in many cases, especially treating trauma and in particular post traumatic stress disorder (PTSD). I rarely use it as my only modality but instead combine it with several other strategies and techniques in helping people who have experienced sustained or severe trauma in their lives.

Actually, EMDR can be applied in many situations of triggered extreme emotion, including anger or irrational fear such as experienced in phobias. Of course, there are many other ways of treating these conditions, such as Cognitive Behavior Therapy, Acceptance and Commitment Therapy, Mindfulness Based Stress Reduction. As a psychologist in private practice, I want to help my clients effectively in the shortest time and the least intrusive method possible. So with specific phobias EMDR is often my first treatment of choice, also using what is called a cognitive interweave to help the client reframe a difficult situation in a less threatening way. But when these techniques are still not working, I shift to other types of desensitization that are slower but likely more effective, or even another strategy altogether.

In this case I am rearranging some of the specifics to protect confidentiality. Jim was a middle-aged sergeant in the military who directed a small but tight group of technicians at a military base. He was proud of the work they did in maintaining armored vehicles with years of experience working together. As with many members of the military, the principle of loyalty and support of your unit or working group is one of the central values of a leader. In Jim's case, the triggering event was a decision about promotion of his unit. He and his division were about to be promoted and their role expanded. Instead, when the time for decision came, the commanding officer of the base passed over Jim, instead promoting a person who was close to the base commander from a previous posting. This candidate had less seniority and considerably less relevant experience than Jim. Within several weeks after this event, Jim experienced severe panic attacks and was diagnosed with a generalized anxiety disorder; his doctor put him on stress leave and he was subsequently referred to me.

The referral letter noted a significant immediate stress response when in the presence of his commanding officer, and to a lesser extent the base commander, feeling an overwhelming need to leave the area. Symptoms of anxiety and panic included racing heartbeat, shortness of breath, acute chest pain, and shaking. The base social worker and the base medical doctor both thought that EMDR would likely help him overcome this recent but debilitating condition for which he now was on medical leave for more than three months. At home his symptoms had widened to almost a generalized stress disorder, with beginning signs of agoraphobia.

In his first session, Jim said he felt overwhelmed with the world and had a dread of leaving his home to go anywhere in public, even to shop for groceries. He complained of almost constant chest pain, despite a normal EKG and healthy heart functioning. In his childhood Jim considered himself "the black sheep of the family," a middle child who had anger management problems when he was smaller than other kids and got picked on. Gradually after lots of schoolyard scrapping he became better at defending himself, but he still didn't like school very much, skipped classes, and dropped out, eventually completing his grade 12 as an adult student. He liked life in the military and had no problems until April when the base commander "fired me for doing my job right." He apparently was the gatekeeper in his section and people started to become frustrated with his playing by the rules instead of cutting corners and doing personal favors. He was transferred to another section where his new workmates were okay, but they were "all a bunch of 'yes men'" who had no spirit or backbone. He felt this transfer was a demotion of duties. Furthermore, his immediate commanding officer did not support him in resisting this change, saying "No one else follows the rules, so why not you?" For Jim this betrayal was like "my C.O. gave into the school bully." Jim was so angry he wanted to throttle both his superior and the base commander, but instead removed himself from the situation. Very soon he developed a strong fear of any contact with the base commander, or even returning to work. He was now on beta blockers and taking Ativan when his anxiety became overwhelming.

One possible approach to this situation would be to use the affect bridge, returning to address childhood experiences of being bullied. However, my general approach is more solution oriented, dealing with problems in the here-and-now, and only going back to the there-and-then if the client leads me there in EMDR scenes. And seeing that my referral sources were specifically requesting EMDR as the preferred treatment, we decided to start with the current feared situations. Typically I start with scenes that are in the mid-level of disturbance, eventually going for the most severe scenes later after my client feels some confidence and success with the method. When I started Jim with a moderate scene, he quickly accelerated into a panic attack with considerable chest pain. We took a break from the EMDR scene, and I quickly taught Jim 2-4 breathing. (Technically, respiratory therapists call this hypnocapnic breathing, where the intent is to stop the hyperventilation syndrome by changing the ratio from too much oxygen to a better balance of carbon dioxide in the client's blood stream). But never mind the technical stuff; this technique is highly effective in stopping the weird physical sensations that happen in a panic attack. Two-four breathing starts by getting your client to count out loud steadily and at a moderately slow pace, 1-2-3-4, unfolding fingers as he exhales. Next, inhale on a count of 1-2, repeating this sequence several times. It is vitally important to have your client exhale evenly, rather than expelling all his air on the first exhales. Like a singer, make sure you don't run out of breath before you finish the last note. Usually, your client will find the 2-4 count easy to master. Next you progress to the more challenging 2-6 count, and finally to the masterful 2-8 count. This level is actually not difficult for most us (try it now!). However, for most of our panic attacks clients, this simple intervention is almost magical in its instant settling of the physical aspects of a panic attack. Of course, you need to instruct the client on the cognitive aspects, what he says about the meaning of these events and their potential threat to his life and his sanity. You know how to do that.

Returning to our case, Jim was amazed at how quickly he was able to settle down with this technique. We went through another set of EMDR on the intermediate scene, this time with no panic or pain, but still a moderate feeling of other tension and subjective anxiety discomfort. He agreed to practice on his own at home using both upper corners of his room as anchor points for his eye sweep.

In the next session, Jim reported only slight success in bringing his anxiety down when reviewing the scene in his home practice, although at no time did the panic return. We worked on handling scenes at the base and scenes where Jim might encounter Mr. X (as he called him) at a store in the community. We mentally rehearsed how he would deal with these scenes by merely carrying on with his own agenda and duties. However, despite repeated exposures of the same scenes, Jim was barely able to diminish tension in his shoulders and considerable chest pain, still at the level of 6 out of a scale of 10. At that point I decided to do something different. With his permission, I borrowed an old technique from Gestalt therapy still used today in Emotionally Focused Therapy (EFT). I had Jim place his chest pain and tension in a nearby empty chair in my office. Jim was given the task of interviewing his pain, trying to find out its meaning and purpose in his life. At various points, he switched places and became quite animated as he and his pain continued their heated discussion.

Finally the hoped-for resolution occurred. Jim continued to be angry and disgusted with the base commander and even angrier at his commanding officer, Mr. X, for not supporting Jim when Jim was threatened with the demoting transfer. Such a betrayal in order to be a yes-man to the wishes of the base commander was to Jim an outrageous example of cowardice, not supporting the men Mr. X. led. Jim's anger and its transformation into a strong anxiety reaction was its way of proving that he was different from Mr. X. Jim was intensely loyal to those in his unit. In a soldier's code courage and loyalty are highly cherished values, so his symptoms were almost like a red badge of courage. As he said "I have always backed up my people when they are right. I've never hung anyone out to dry. I am fiercely protective of my people. They are like family to me." With my coaxing and coaching gradually the part of Jim that ran the symptom, what we call the Somatic Self, made a pact with Jim's Executive Self, that they would work together to find acceptable ways for Jim to remain loyal to his unit without having to sacrifice his health or career.

After the empty-chair role play I told some motivating stories about embracing acceptance, even in circumstances that were terribly unfair. I self-disclosed two situations where several staff were being harassed by a mentally deranged department head. Five of his key staff resigned in one year, finally exposing the director's irrationality, such that he was assigned to medical leave, eventually being forced to resign. I also told some Zen stories featuring the embracing of acceptance. Other examples included the incarceration of Nelson Mandela for many years and the ordeals of Viktor Frankl in the Nazi prison camps. Even Jesus found a way of saying "My kingdom is not of this world." Acceptance and compassion found their way of personal triumph in the spiritual life of the oppressed. Jim listened intently to these stories, and his Somatic Self had a way of embracing these reframes such that his anger and fear melted away right before our eyes. As we returned to several EMDR scenes, there now was no fear, just a quiet feeling of transcendence of all the conflicts. The chest and neck pains were now gone.

In the following week Jim was able to return to work symptom-free, but he still felt a dislike for working at the base, even though it required very minimal and distant contact with Mr. X and the base commander. Rather than carrying on his crusade for justice, he applied for a transfer to a military base in another city, returning to a previous posting where he was well known and respected. His family were also supportive of this plan, and within several months the move was complete. Even before this time, Jim felt no need to come to sessions for any further treatment because as far as he was concerned, all was successfully resolved. In a follow-up session just before moving to the other city and base, Jim came back to say all was well, thanking me for the help. Although he thought the EMDR was okay, he felt the turning point in therapy was the work we did in the empty-chair format, paving the way for acceptance, compassion, transcendence, and finally a sense of personal mastery in managing his emotions. I felt good about how we were able to turn this dilemma around in six sessions. The shift we made was only one of several we could have done, but the main point is that when we identified that therapy was stalled, we shifted smoothly to a more effective alternative approach when required.

CHAPTER 47

Taking The Fast Lane

I WAS WORKING in a mental health clinic in London, Ontario, when I saw George, a 25-year-old orderly in a general hospital who had a profound fear of driving. He could drive locally within the city, even on 4-lane arterial roads, but not on major highways where the traffic was heavier and the speeds faster. To a beginner Cognitive Behaviour Therapist, as I was earlier in my career, this seemed like an easy and straightforward case using systematic desensitization for a specific phobia. So I proceeded with my client to induce a sense of relaxation, then presented in imagery the fear-inducing scenes, gradually stripping away their anxiety–provoking qualities, and proceeding to more daring scenes. Within two sessions, my client was ready to handle an in vivo session of actual driving on a fast highway. In our area, the equivalent of driving a U.S. Interstate was a major highway across southwestern Ontario, called highway 401, linking Windsor, Ontario to Quebec City. This expressway is known for its traffic and frequency of big trucks, an intimidating route for a timid driver.

In session three George drove me around is his car. We went on local city roads, then larger arterial roads, then short stretches of the 401, and finally a ten-kilometre section of the highway. He was able to handle all assignments skilfully and surprisingly calmly, including passing big long 18-wheeler trucks. He was excited and triumphant to have cleared his phobia in an amazingly short time.

When we returned to my office to debrief the driving session, his enthusiasm had now surprisingly transformed into a higher level of anxiety. On further exploration, it emerged that George was not only happy, but gay. That is, although he had a secret homosexual relationship, he had not yet "come out" to friends and family about his erotic preference. He was shocked and taken aback about how easy and quick this therapy had been, but his success had now stripped away his excuse for not dealing with this underlying problem of keeping his erotic preference a secret unknown to anyone except his boyfriend. In the following sessions we used the Gestalt empty chair technique to resolve and integrate his conflicted attitudes and feelings about being gay. We then proceeded to explore the advantages and disadvantages of "coming out," eventually preparing him with role-plays to prepare him for the various reactions of significant others in his life, especially his family. With this level of preparation in my office, he found his actual experiences of disclosure to be relatively mild in anxiety, and definitely much more supportive than he had imagined it would be.

What I learned from my sessions with George was that clients can present with a surface problem, but actually it is a test or trial run for the effectiveness of therapy and the establishment of trust in the therapeutic relationship. Only when these conditions are met will the client be forthcoming with an issue that is far more sensitive and personal or secretive. My headlong rush to take the fast lane to a "quick cure" almost lead me to end the therapy rather than be sensitive to other cues from my client that our work was only beginning. This underlying issue was not disclosed in our assessment interview and may not have come to the surface except for our success in overcoming the driving phobia. Now, when I help people with a phobia, I usually make pre-emptive remarks predicting that sometimes as one problem is resolved, perhaps the time may be right for dealing with other issues. Usually the client is satisfied to end therapy as a success, but sometimes there is a second or hidden issue that can emerge when the time is right and the confidence of efficacy is established.

ASK NO QUESTIONS

FOR THOSE OF YOU who are not family therapists, you might not know that the main verbal tool of this profession is THE QUESTION. Family therapists typically ask many questions. Most of the time, these questions are **not** to provide answers to the therapist so that (s)he can make the correct determination of what path to follow toward resolution of the presenting problem. Instead, it is far more likely that questions serve the purpose of inviting the client to see a situation differently. For example, questions can elicit relationship shifts in a family system by asking about which members of a family would be affected by a proposed change, and in what way. For a full review of the type and intent of questions in family therapy, I would like to refer you to the classic article by Dr. Karl Tomm (1988) Interventive Interviewing: Part III. Intending to ask lineal, circular, strategic, or reflexive questions? See Family Process 27 (1) March 1988, pp. 1-15. Questions are the main tools of the trade in family therapy, and training settings emphasize questions more than any other interventions. However, there are some situations where questions can actually impede the process of therapy.

When I was working as a team leader and senior clinical psychologist in a mental health clinic in a Calgary community hospital, I trained psychology interns and practicum students preparing to be psychotherapists. One of these interns, Juliette, was especially bright and adept in her use of therapeutic skills. I was observing an intake assessment session with a depressed client. As the interview progressed, the client became more depressed in content and tone. Juliette was doing an excellent assessment, but the client was not responding favorably. As that session ended, I recommended that we observe the first ten minutes of the second session carefully. If there were no reports of improvement by the client, I had an idea that perhaps Juliette could employ after the break early in the session.

In the second session, this female client seemed worse than before. Her energy was low, and I could barely hear her through the microphone in the interviewing room. She reported no improvements in her situation or her attitudes about it, and she was not hopeful about any of the ideas that were seeded or proposed in the assessment session. Nevertheless, it seemed to me that she really needed to talk about her plight and have someone listen supportively. About ten minutes into the session I called for a five-minute break to consult with Juliette.

In the break I conveyed the idea that perhaps if Juliette stayed solely with empathic reflection and emotional support for her client, that perhaps that would be enough to turn the corner on the case. Juliette agreed that it would be worth a try. I took the intervention one step further. As a training exercise, for her own growth as a therapist, I asked Juliette to conduct the rest of the interview **without asking one question!** If she followed this assignment properly, she was not even allowed indirect questions, such as "I wonder if ..." My intern was dumbfounded. As almost all of her previous training had been exclusively in family therapy, she had never done or observed a session without questions. She thought she would be totally helpless without her tools. I challenged her to merely be with her client emotionally, and calmly but caringly just listen and reflect her client's emotions, even her perceived hopelessness. Juliette seemed overwhelmed by the constraints and requirements of this intervention, but agreed to carry it out faithfully. She went back into the interviewing room, and began her posture of active listening. The pace of their talking was slower. The therapist allowed more time for her client to experience reflective silence, sobbing, sighing, and breathing through her sorrow. As the interview progressed, the cloud of depression seemed to be lifting. Juliette's client started to brighten her outlook, see many possibilities where she could make positive shifts in her circumstances, being more effective in taking charge of some of the aspects that were within her control. As her client changed, Juliette herself became more relaxed and confident doing less and merely being there emotionally, witnessing and validating the changes she was observing. The session ended well, and the client thanked her therapist for a wonderful and helpful talk.

In the post-session debriefing, my intern was amazed at the transformation she had just observed. Her client had shifted markedly, whereas Juliette was relatively quiet during much of the session, slowly nodding her head, reflecting a few statements and themes, and generally approving and validating. As the session progressed she observed that she was far from helpless in the skills of supporting her client, and actually enjoyed playing a less active role in the process. We both were keen to see the next session the following week. I asked Juliette to maintain her active listening stance and again refrain from the use of questions. She still felt she would need to discipline her urge to ask, but complied with the assignment again.

When the time arrived, the client looked fresher and much more relaxed and confident. She had made some good adjustments in her work situation, resolving a conflict with an office-mate. She decided to taper off one discordant friendship and strengthen several others that were a better fit for her gathering sense of optimism. The changes were not dramatic but encouragingly solid. The depression had lifted markedly, and the session ended well. Two weeks later the client came in with an attitude of confidence and self-efficacy. She felt she had resolved her emotional upsets and was now able to move forward on her own. These changes had continued through a follow-up session a month later. In that interview I lifted the ban on questions, but by then Juliette had just a moderate desire to use questions, confident that her client knew what to examine and how to view her life situation. In that session, Juliette and her client mutually agreed to close her case file as a success.

It was noteworthy that I never prescribed that restraint for my intern again in all her other cases. In most therapy cases, we can proceed with our greatest interviewing strengths. However, sometimes we need to think and act outside the box to get the job done. In her recollections of her training experience with me, she emphasized that the greatest learning moment of her internship training was when I issued the restraint: "Ask no questions."

CHAPTER 49

Forty Years Of Overcoming Fears

OFTEN CLIENTS ASK ME, "How do I overcome my fear of ...?" Fears can be realistic and based on trauma, such as an alpine downhill skier who crashed on a high-speed downhill race and wants to go back to competition but fears falling. Another example is a flight attendant who broke her back in an airliner in heavy turbulence and now wants to resume her career but is still afraid of flying. Fears can also be irrational, such as a phobia about spiders or mice despite never being bitten or injured by these little creatures. Fears can also be generalized, such as several pervasive anxiety disorders where strong anxiety or fear symptoms are felt in the absence of any known triggers or specific situation.

Over the years of my career in treating these disorders I have employed a number of very useful approaches, guided by research on best practices and the progress of my clients. I usually follow the principle of sequential parsimony, that means the least intrusive way first. In the therapeutic alliance, I offer my clients a menu of strategies, and let them choose which ones they like best.

Long ago (1930-1960) fears were thought to be overcome by insight-oriented psychodynamic psychotherapy, on the basis of talking about underlying unconscious internal conflicts that solved the reason "why" these fears existed. Despite some limited success, many fears and phobias persisted after months and sometimes years of therapy.

In the 1960's outcome research demonstrated that Cognitive Behavior Therapy (CBT) was effective with many forms of depression and anxiety. The central technique was called systematic desensitization. This process was based on the neurological operation of reciprocal inhibition, meaning that the nervous system cannot be in a relaxed (parasympathetic) and anxious (sympathetic) state at the same time. It was a simple idea: just induce a relaxed state in your clients, then have them imagine or view still pictures of the feared object or situation starting from easiest (e.g., a comic cartoon figure of a mouse) and graduating to the most difficult or graphic (a large realistic looking mouse). If your client had a fear response during treatment, you would just go back to an earlier scene in the hierarchy and come back to where you left off. This treatment was wonderful in that it provided calmness and comfort in the process of facing fears. Subsequent research in that decade and the 1970s showed that the method was somewhat effective but not necessarily because of the protocol. You didn't have to follow the hierarchy of scenes. By that time the process of systematic desensitization using still pictures seemed to be less effective than it was in the early days of CBT.

It was around this time of the late 70's that I devised and began to use a strategy I called "The Expanding Video Format of Desensitization." The acceptance of this format was largely due to advances in video technology. People in the general population were now able to view two television programs simultaneously by watching the main program on the full screen while observing a second program in a small window in the corner of the main screen. You could now zoom in on that frame and expand it so that it almost completely overlapped the main screen. Another media technology advance was the arrival of IMAX theatres where wrap-around screens and sound production created the illusion of really being there in the projected scene.

I used these concepts by having my client imagine they were in a relaxing locale like a beach on a south sea island. Then I would have them look at a small video screen such as that of a four- inch screen video player showing a black-and-white cartoon of a feared situation. As the cartoon progressed there would be greater contrast and color and the use of animated figures that became more human-like. More advanced videos would feature people similar to those in my clients' world, perhaps even seeing themselves in the foreground. Gradually the camera angle would shift over my client's head and shoulders, and finally the camera would be shooting the scene through the client's eyes. As my client could tolerate that on the small screen, I would have them image that these same motion videos were played on a larger screen, then an even larger screen, and finally on an IMAX screen that was so large you could hardly see the surrounding beach anymore to the right and left of the full-screen image.

As popular entertainment technology advanced in the 1990s, I more often used the idea of relaxing at home watching a video of a beach on the wide screen and picture-in picture on the small screen gradually becoming larger and more realistic as the client could tolerate it, finally becoming a huge home theatre video of the feared scenes. This strategy was quite effective but still often required several sessions to get through all the videos processed in the client's imagination.

In the early 1990's I went for training in a format called Eye Movement Desensitization and Reprocessing (see emdr. com for more about this). Although it was developed and designed to overcome Post Traumatic Stress Disorder, this strategy could be effectively applied to overcoming fear or any disorder that had a strong emotional component. To describe it briefly, the client has his eyes open with the therapist visible nearby. While imaging scenes of the traumatic event, the client is given the task of moving his eyes to follow the waving fingers of the therapist across his line of vision. The eye movement task can also include two flashing ends of a light bar or tapping his own fingers to his thighs in rapid succession. The key element is bilateral brain stimulation disrupting the neural integrity of the original scenes. In a later part of this sequence, client and therapist make a new verbal phrase or caption so that when the flashback occurs in the future, a positive reframe will be attached to it. This is the cognitive element, called reprocessing.

There are at least two strong elements that distinguish EMDR from other forms of desensitization. The first is that **the client keeps his eyes open and can see the therapist throughout the process.** This anchors reassurance about the present therapeutic relationship while reviewing traumatic scenes from the past. The second and most interesting aspect is that **the client is not induced into a calm state while these scenes are reviewed.** In fact, the client is invited to allow negative and strong emotions to happen during this process so that they can be accessed fully and allow for new neural connections to form in response to the images.

More recent research in the 21st century is confirming that allowing the client to experience negative emotions such as fear and anger while facing disturbing scenes is a more effective process for overcoming fear than the older and more comfortable forms of desensitization. Other recent developments in psychotherapy emphasize Mindfulness and living in the Now, even though you may be experiencing fear based on the past. Acceptance and Commitment Therapy encourages reaching through your fears to a life that is more authentic and actively reflects your true values and freedom from your past. These approaches might use mantras such as "feel your fear and do it anyways" or "I am not what happened to me. I am who I choose to become."

What is common to virtually all of these approaches is that, in some way or time, the client will need to get beyond denial and avoidance and actually face what they fear, whether in imagined rehearsal and/or real life. We call this real-life graduated exposure "in vivo" desensitization. As part of that training at some point the client will need to assess whether they have overcome a fear by putting it to a real-life test or sequence of tests.

For example, what about the downhill skier that got seriously injured in a high-speed crash? We began with systematic desensitization of still pictures, graduating to videos of the actual event as the event cameras saw it. From there we encouraged her to imagine the crash as she would have seen it from her own perspective, adding the sound of wind-roar in her helmet, skis scaping the ice, then crashing, rolling and skidding, and hitting the restraining fence.

After imaginal practice in my office we began to help her overcome fear of falling by learning judo break-falls on my office floor. Next, we went to snow-covered nearby hills where she would fall and roll and skid on the downhill slope. Then we graduated to slow-speed bail-out falls with skis on at low speed, and finally controlled falls at medium speed. At this point she was now fully recovered from reconstructive surgery and was able to rejoin training with the national team and carry on with a successful alpine ski career.

The next illustrative case is that of the injured flight attendant. After she recovered from her broken back, we began CBT psychotherapy. We used various forms of imaginal desensitization including the "expanding video screen" format in sessions in my office. I also engaged her husband to take her on rough country roads where she would be jostled and pitched around while blind-folded. When she graduated from this phase we went to a local municipal airport, where we hired a flight instructor to take us up in a small Cessna for a flight of increasing (but safe) uncertainty and simulated turbulence and g-forces. In these two flights my client was in the co-pilot's seat while I was coaching her from the rear seat diagonal to her. These two in vivo sessions were sufficient for her to regain confidence in aircraft turbulence; she went on to resume her flight attendant career.

"Haven't you forgotten something?" In another case of flight phobia, the client did not have a history of physical injury or severe trauma, but merely experienced some difficulties with turbulence and some sudden losses in altitude on a previous flight, perhaps as unsettling as a roller coaster ride. This was enough to precipitate a significant disabling phobia, another example that the incident itself does not have to be severe to result in a great deal of subsequent fear. Robert was a plant designer and engineer, highly valued by his oil company for designing oil processing plants. Now he could no longer fly to Dallas and Houston, landlocked in Calgary by his flight phobia.

We began in my typical fashion of cues to recognize early warning signs of panic attacks. At this point he was to switch our well-practiced routines of 2-6 breathing, 4-square breathing, deep belly breathing, and progressive muscle relaxation to bring down his activation level when he sensed he was drifting into the zone of fear and its anticipation. Next, we went through the standard protocol of desensitization of all the scenes involving flying, including shaving at home in the morning of his flight, progressing through the various phases before boarding and during the various phases of the flight itself, including dealing with episodes of turbulence. These sessions in my office went well, preparing Robert for our two flights in a light Cessna aircraft at the local flying school. He was able to handle these flight exercises and variations well. So now he was able to commit to the real test of his overcoming the fear of flying.

I persuaded Robert to book a flight for both of us to fly from Calgary to Edmonton return, (40 minutes one-way), turning that commuter flight around after a half-hour stopover in Edmonton. Robert was somewhat nervous that morning in all the preliminary procedures of boarding and flying that we had rehearsed so well. During the flight itself, after he settled his nerves he became mildly distracted as he had me look down on several of the processing plants that he had designed. I was truly in awe of his engineering expertise. Soon he seemed quite calm and confident as we approached our landing in Edmonton. We deplaned and went uneventfully into the main lobby of Edmonton Airport. I complimented Robert on how well he had used our strategies and techniques during the flight to actually make it an enjoyable experience for both of us.

Now our return flight to Calgary was announced and we proceeded to security clearance. As you know, this is the area in which security people check your carry-on luggage and scan your body for possible hidden explosives and potential weapons. Of course, I was watching Robert to see how he was handling this phase of preparation for our return flight. Robert was looking flatly and absent-mindedly into the flight departure lounge as he was being whisked by the security officer. Once we got through security and into the departure lounge, Robert looked very relaxed and confident. I asked him "Haven't you forgotten something?" He answered blankly "Huh? What do you mean?" I said, "Don't you remember that you used to be afraid of flying?' He said, "Wow! I actually forgot that I had that problem!" So I asked him to pretend that, at least for the part of our return flight, he would try to remember what it was like to be phobic so that we could over-practice his coping strategies as an exercise in relapse prevention. He agreed to do this, although we both knew it was almost unnecessary. After all, when you forget that you ever even had that problem, it's a good sign that the problem has been resolved.

Perhaps a footnote is in order here. In order to test whether a client has progressed in overcoming his fear, we as therapists often prescribe that the client enter his feared situations to assess his progress. In that sense we are invoking the paradox of prescribing the symptom, asking clients to re-experience fear and perhaps learn how to cope with fear situations applying our rehearsed strategies.

Switching modalities. After many years of helping people over their fears with several approaches and strategies, a question arises: what do you do now? The answer is that I lay out several different ways we might approach potential paths to solution and let the clients choose. This is especially applicable for clients presenting with trauma. Giving those clients choices in therapy counteracts the taking away of choice in their traumatization. If they choose the most avoidant one, I accept their decision, even though that process might be lengthier and possibly costlier. I often suggest EMDR first, as significant results may be obtained in a shorter time. However, I can remember one case of an anxious war veteran with obvious PTSD symptoms who was referred to me for EMDR treatment. He was very worried that I would ask him to re-experience his war traumas. In fact, this prospect was a major factor in his anxiety in our first session. I instantly told him we did not have to use EMDR. I would help him with his current living difficulties and conflicts. Hugely relieved and reassured, we settled into a relaxed relationship of therapy that helped him resolve his current issues, and the previous nightmares and flashbacks faded into insignificance.

That's news to me. Finally, there is one further case that can illustrate the principle of sequential parsimony (the easiest and least intrusive intervention first). There was a prominent female television newscaster who suddenly and unexplainably developed stage fright when reading the evening news. No confounding factors could account for this sudden development, but she urgently needed help to regain her status as local news anchor. It was significant that her temporary assignment as field interviewer was relatively safe, in that there could be several retakes and edits before that segment would be broadcast, so mistakes would not be exposed, whereas with live news there are no re-takes. She was terrified, although her previous mistakes were actually quite minor but noticeable among some of her viewers. When I offered her several treatment alternatives, she opted for EMDR as the fastest track back to her job. This seemed okay, and within three sessions she was back to her position of live news anchor. However, she returned a few weeks later to report that although she was capable in her role, her anxiety still remained high.

This time I offered her the slower but more thorough route of my expanding-screen video desensitization format. Over several sessions, we collaborated to design an effective scenario. Thankfully, my previous experience with television production made it easier to imagine that she, her cameraman, director and producer were on a sand beach in Maui. The teleprompter was in the foreground; at times it blotted out the rest of the beach-sand studio as she read the news in a dedicated and animated way. Whenever she became self-conscious, the sand and the waves and palms would soothe her so that she could return confidently to the teleprompter. She would then be absorbed in the presentation in the news she was reading and presenting to her audience. I resumed watching her with pleasure in the confident way she did the evening news.

CHAPTER 50

Four Questions To End A Session

HOW CAN YOU END a therapy session with the greatest likelihood of engagement, follow-through, and enjoyment? For most of my career, I would end a session with the usual scheduling of the next session with a brief exchange of comments and a goodbye and well-wish for the coming week.

About ten years ago, several years of research about successful outcome factors in therapy began to accumulate trends that emerged as significant across various types and models of psychotherapy. Barry Duncan, Scott Miller, and other researchers found that most of the factors that predicted successful outcome in therapy were associated with the strength of the therapeutic alliance between therapist and client. They also found that the very fact that process and outcomes were being measured had a positive effect.

They then advocated that therapists track client ratings of the therapeutic alliance and progress in terms of outcomes with brief questionnaires that the client would fill in after every session. Quite a few of my colleagues implemented this practice and said that tracking these client ratings improved the strength of the therapeutic relationship. Also, the questionnaires and rating scales have the aspect of seeming to be one step removed from the therapist, even though the therapist later read them. Perhaps if their clients had problems with assertion, they could write on paper what they found difficult to say directly to their therapist. On the other hand, if their relationship was strong and good, you would think that any thought could be voiced during the session. Meanwhile, client files were thickened by all the paper of these rating scales. I also know from my experience with psychometrics and tests that people in general find filling in forms to be a hassle, especially if they yield essentially the same information week after week, so I was reluctant to impose this extra burden in my office. So I came up with another plan to extract the equivalent information. I ask four questions at the end of virtually every session as part of our session closure procedure.

1. DID YOUR GET WHAT YOU CAME FOR TODAY? This question implies that the client has some sort of objective for each session. Obviously, many clients do not, especially in more loosely structured, client-centred conversational approaches where the relationship itself is the key therapeutic ingredient. This factor is even more important in my solution-oriented approach, where I encourage my clients to have an objective for every session, like every physical work-out. It is also okay to have no objective but to engage that open space and take partial responsibility for our co-creation in that session. I call that strategy "creating space," a playground where creativity can emerge, with the genius of the unconscious mind taking centre stage. Sometimes it is delightfully surprising to discover the insights that arise from a seemingly oblique or lateral series of ramblings that emerge as a coherent theme to our conversation.

2. HOW DO YOU KNOW? This question directs the client to observable benefits derived from the session. It invites the client to ratify the value of the session, and thus

indirectly, the therapy itself. It also leads the client to be mindful of whatever wisdom emerges from our work together. It helps prepare the client for the next question, the one about transfer of training into real life.

3. WHAT ARE YOUR TAKE-AWAYS FROM THIS SESSION? SUPPOSING THIS WAS THE LAST AND ONLY SESSION WITH ME AND WE NEVER SAW EACH OTHER AGAIN. HOW WOULD YOU USE WHAT WE TALKED ABOUT AND EXPERIENCED TOGETHER AS A GUIDE FOR YOUR LIFE GOING FORWARD? This question is designed to help the client move into application mode in the coming week or weeks, or even a lifetime. It extends therapy into the everyday world of the client. It motivates commitment towards therapeutic action. Sometimes when the client might have forgotten a key point or possible homework task, I can supply the suggestion "Well, one takeaway you might want to consider is..." That prompt is usually sufficient to get back on track.

4. WHAT WAS YOUR FAVORITE MOMENT OF THIS SESSION? There are several reasons for this question. The origin derives from Positive Psychology's "The Blessings Exercise," which is a positive practice that generates greater happiness and resistance to stress. Research has proven the benefit of cataloguing 5 positive moments every day. A positive moment could be my doing something kind for you, you doing something nice for me, or even observing third parties treating each other kindly. Examples are holding a door open for somebody or letting them into a traffic lane. After noting these kind acts during the day, you then celebrate them by repeating them back to a family member

or roommate that night. If no one is present in your household, you review the 5 blessings mentally or even say a prayer of thanksgiving and gratitude for having witnessed these nice moments. This habit of celebration of the positive also works by attuning your mind to moments of kindness that you might have otherwise missed in our busy world.

At times it can be ironic that a seemingly small intervention can have pivotal impact on the outcome of a case. That last "favorite moment" question really caught the interest of Maria. She was the 44-year-old mother of three children in an unhappy marriage with Allesandro, a successful entrepreneur relentlessly chasing his career dreams and seeming to have little time or enthusiasm for family life. Maria came to individual therapy hoping to save the marriage and the family, stating that her husband wanted nothing to do with psychologists or therapy. After her fourth session with me she decided to take her children back to her home neighborhood in Mexico for the summer. She invited Allesandro to join her, but he was reluctant. He was too busy in his enterprises here to consider that. At that point Maria was totally fed up and left to be closer to her family and friends. This move could be a prelude to a marital separation. She would consider her options based on what developed during the summer. She told me she would return to therapy in September if she decided to continue with married life here.

After no contact from her by November I decided to do a follow-up telephone call. Maria said she had been meaning to call, but first wanted to see if all the positive changes were continuing in their marriage in the months since moving back here. She reported that all was going well and that she had no further need of therapy. Naturally, I was quite curious to hear about these positive changes. She then told me about how Allesandro had come down to join her and the kids, but the first weeks were tense, and he was bored and restless as usual. She was aloof towards him and really involved with the children. It was their same old pattern.

However, Maria did one small thing. She and the children implemented the Blessings Exercise. Every evening at dinner Maria and the children would review the five blessings they had observed during the day. Allesandro was dismissive and refused to join in this "stupid" ritual. After several weeks he decided to join in; instantly Maria and the children were captivated by his positive stories. He then decided to fully participate in the family ritual. Respect, inclusion, and affection began to flow more freely in the family. Allsandro became calmer and happier to be an involved father, which in turn rekindled Maria's love for him. Upon their return to Canada Allesandro turned down several contracts such that he now had more time to be involved with Maria and family life. Thus the one small thing that she did set the stage for redefining their marriage. The seed for this one small thing was the "favorite moment" end-of-session question.

It has now been at least 4 years since beginning to implement these questions at the end of sessions. I can't say with certainty that outcomes have improved significantly: they seem to be as good as ever. However, I can say that both my clients and I are much more in tune with the therapeutic alliance, and the feedback of client satisfaction is positive for all of us.

The first three questions have definitely improved client memory of what happened in the session and commitment to apply it in their daily lives. The practice has shaped and improved the concept that therapy is a task-oriented conversation most of the time, so it has helped direct our efforts more efficiently towards desired outcomes. But the last question is by far the most interesting and yields the most valuable and sometimes surprising information.

The first time I ask the question, the client is usually puzzled and unprepared. After I explain to them that this question will actually help them enjoy the process of therapy even more, they begin to track better. Since I frequently employ humor and irony in the metaphors, stories, and examples I use, I sometimes think that the client favorite moment was when they laughed in a funny moment of the session. Humour also tends to lower the client tension level, at least momentarily, so often it is not tagged by the client as a favorite moment. Rather, my clients usually say the favorite moment was at a pivotal or crucial insight, an "aha" moment when the pictures of the puzzle suddenly fell into place and a clear pattern emerged. Another frequent favorite moment was the instant when they felt most truly heard, validated, and supported. All four of the last questions in a session are helpful in refocusing the client and strengthening the therapeutic alliance with perceptions that are often rich with meaning.

CHAPTER 51

What About Follow Up?

IN MANY OF THE chapters you have read, I reference the routine practice of follow-up sessions or telephone calls to see how my client eventually made out months after therapy has ended. It is an almost automatic habit related to my professional commitment to my client's enduring welfare and a testimony to thoroughness and closure. Perhaps even more, it satisfies my sense of curiosity. Even if the feedback is that the positive changes in therapy have faded over time, that information helps me learn and improve my knowledge and skills in a feedback-informed therapy.

There is one added advantage: I want to close cases that I have seen partly because I am winding down my professional practice. While highly unlikely, it is possible that any open case can also be an open liability if my client experiences or inflicts serious harm on himself or others. This liability can extend even if the case were closed up to ten years previously, so registered psychologists need to maintain and guarantee the secure maintenance of records for that time. Documented closure and follow-up procedures are yet another way to demonstrate due diligence and client care.

However, some have argued that follow-up enquiries can inadvertently suggest to the client that therapy is ongoing and never complete. I maintain that personal growth itself is never complete, but episodes of mental illness and personal incapacity can remain behind us as we move on. Of course, new problems can emerge or even activate old maladaptive reflexes, so occasionally a "psychological tune-up" consultation or even the resumption of therapy can be helpful. This possibility remains open.

It should be noted that in the solution-oriented brief therapy approach that I do, sometimes effective therapy can occur in merely a few sessions, and often even in a one-session consultation. My former colleague Dr. Arnie Slive, now based in Austin Texas, has written about and supervised a whole movement of brief therapy delivery called "walk-in clinics" that have proven to be effective in one-session consultations. Also, considerable research has shown that the modal number of psychotherapy sessions in North America is one and that some of those single sessions can be transformative. In fact, many people learn and change quickly from the very moment they come to the decision that they need external help. Dr. Steve DeShazer in his Milwaukee Wisconsin Clinic would even begin his first session with a client by asking "What's happened better since you decided to come to therapy?" This query is a great platform on which to build a potential solution focus.

Often therapists who do not routinely follow-up are left with uncertainty about the effectiveness of their sessions and the ultimate outcome of their clients. This could include clients who choose to end their therapy prior to the completion of the agreed-upon contract. Sometimes therapists think that circumstances in their clients' lives have changed, or that there was insufficient engagement, or a change in client motivation for change. Especially in the era of client-as-customer, it may be the case that "we just didn't click." This type of outcome is hard for the therapist to face, as I sometimes experience in my reluctance to do a follow-up cold call on a former client that I have not seen for months. However, I overcome occasional avoidance and often I am unexpectantly rewarded with the report of a very good outcome. When habits of follow-up are neglected, or when the therapist has just lost contact numbers and traces of former clients, the therapist is met with uncertainty and perhaps negative doubts. You have read this in a previous chapter called "A Terrible Session." That reminds me of another story that happened a while back.

Sean was a likeable 19-year-old university student in second year Biology. He was friendly and soft-spoken, but I soon realized from his rambling and lateral-thinking account that he was stoned on some substance. He readily admitted that he was a daily and heavy user of marijuana but felt helplessly entrapped by the high it provided. When we discussed his addiction I learned that he had never tried to stop using consistently for an extended time. I told him that unlike heroine, cocaine, and some other hard drugs, the withdrawal symptoms were very mild. Because THC is fat-soluble, you remain mildly stoned for up to six weeks since your last usage, so abstaining is actually a gentle decline in dosage to zero as you persist in your course of abstinence.

Sean acknowledged that such a move would be manageable, but the bigger problem was that his entire social system was a group of stoner students who somehow earned enough university grades to get by. However, we both acknowledged that even in conversation Sean could barely hang enough words together to maintain a coherent conversation, let alone a complex thought sequence. He was headed for failure if he did not change his addiction. But how could he maintain his happy life without his circle of friends? At this opening of a coachable moment I boldly decided to do a Front-Door intervention. I made a direct suggestion! I told him to get rid of his friends and start to develop friendships with serious and goal-oriented students.

This brash move, especially in a first session with a client, is often likely to fail. Predictably it did. Sean instantly broke into an angry rage and told me that was the stupidest and most insensitive thing I could ever say. He could not betray his most loyal friends and go on without them and survive without the highs and stress management that grass gave him. This was my mistake in motivational interviewing. I jumped beyond the readiness of my client for change. Still, somehow I felt it was right and the appropriate thing to do, never knowing if he would return to treatment and properly sort out how to make a commitment to change. Perhaps he might even enlist some of his friends as a support group for abstinence, similar to an earlier chapter in this book. However, we never had that chance; Sean stormed out of my office. I never saw him again. I felt badly for quite a while about my mistake. I was too avoidant to even try to follow-up. Maybe it's just as well.

Three years later I received a brief letter. It was from Sean, announcing he had just convocated with his Honours Degree in Biology with excellent marks and likely an entry to continue on to his master's degree. He said that he remained furious about our session for days afterward, then reconsidered what we had said. He let go of virtually all of his former friendships and started hanging out with serious and goal-oriented students who also knew how to have fun and share good times without the necessity of getting high. He conveyed his thanks for our session together as a turning point in this life. I felt relieved and gratified. Then I began the discipline of regularly following-up on my clients, despite occasional reluctances. I have felt better ever since.

CHAPTER 52

A Delicate Supervision Situation

DARLENE WAS A crisis worker in the emergency department of our community hospital. She was a registered nurse and regarded as highly competent in her role. Moreover, she was personable and pleasant and a dedicated hard-worker.

However, the historical context forced her to transfer into a position in our mental health services unit. At that point in time there were severe budget cutbacks in health services in the province of Alberta. Due to union regulations, whenever there were mass layoffs, jobs were shuffled according to records of seniority, not by merit or suitability. This notorious process was called "bumping." It resulted in many junior health professionals being laid off, while others with greater seniority were given the choice of taking a lateral position or having to resign. This choice was hardly a reasonable option for a young single mother raising two children on her nurse's salary, so Darlene accepted the transfer to become a mental health therapist. I was her new clinical supervisor in a multidisciplinary team.

Now you may think that the skills of a crisis worker are highly transferable and applicable in a mental health therapy role. Certainly the aspects of quick engagement and assessment of a client situation and referral to relevant community resources are vital to crisis work. Moreover, crisis intervention can occur in up to six sessions before the client has to be referred on to a different service. There are even single-session walk-in clinic models of rapid therapeutic consultation such as those designed and promoted worldwide by my friend and colleague Dr. Arnie Slive.

However, there is a large majority of cases in which the presenting problems are complex and chronic in nature, so that a quick fix is not adequate to resolve the situation. An understanding of complicated mental health problems and the dynamics of family systems in which they are often embedded goes beyond basic training as a nurse. Darlene was cooperative and eager to upgrade and broaden her skillsets to meet the demands of her new position.

Thankfully our hospital also provided courses and supervised training in practicums and internships in the Family Therapy Training Program, an internationally well-regarded institute. Thus, we were able to offer Darlene extra courses and training opportunities through our institute. She responded with high motivation and optimism as she began the process of upgrading. I was her clinical supervisor and mentor.

We engaged in a contract of eight months duration, at which point we would evaluate whether she had attained enough skill to fulfill her new role. If not, she would have to forfeit her position and return to the Crisis Unit, leaving a vacancy whereby we could legally rehire our former staff member who had been bumped. The entire team had mixed feelings about losing our former staff member and having to train a replacement. On the other hand, we wanted to do everything possible to give Darlene the best chance to succeed.

Partway through the process the strain of coursework on top of her regular duties and caseload were starting to show. Darlene was becoming more fatigued and anxious that she could not handle these additional demands while returning home to raise her children in a single family with some support from family and friends. Although I tried to give her as much coaching as I could, she was overwhelmed by the difficulty and complexity of the course material and the sheer volume of study required. By now we were all cheering for her, but still she needed to handle the course material, and her clinical caseload required skills she had not yet mastered. It was sometimes a difficult challenge to work with cases that were more chronic and recidivist, and at times she was becoming frustrated dealing with them.

By the six-month mark, Darlene made the decision to withdraw from her post in mental health services. She was grateful for all the new learnings and help she had received from us, but relieved to return to her former and familiar position. I felt a little sad that she could not make the grade, but also a little relieved that the process was over. And so it is in life that sometimes we give a situation the best we can under the circumstances, and sometimes our best isn't enough. But at least we gave it what we could, so we can look at the experience with a feeling of acceptance.

One aspect of this situation is crucial for wise decision-making. Every job needs to have its own benchmark: a measurable criterion of quality, a threshold of adequacy to accomplish the task at hand. A benchmark also entails a reasonable measure of volume, such as the number of hours required, the volume of effort and the expense of materials involved to produce the outcome. Successful managers and supervisors know these metrics and make them clear to employees and team members throughout the process of a team project, with monitoring and guidance along the way. If these measures remain fair, everyone involved can feel okay about the process regardless of the outcome. For example, my son Mark has hired several friends to fill I.T. positions in his computer department in a medium-sized company. He has had to let most of them go when they did not quite measure up to the benchmark criteria in a learning time of several months. Mark was fair throughout the process, and these people remain friends with Mark to this day. Be true and fair in the application of a benchmark, and everyone involved can come to a position of acceptance and gratitude about the learning experience.

CHAPTER 53

THE "INEXPERIENCED" SUPERVISOR

BEFORE COMING TO WORK in Calgary, I had been in supervisory capacities in terms of both graduate students and staff in virtually all of my previous 10 years as a psychologist, and several years before graduation in various other jobs. In fact, I felt relatively seasoned as a supervisor by the time I was appointed Senior Clinical Psychologist and a Clinical Supervisor at the Holy Cross Hospital in Calgary in 1982. The position involved more supervision of a multidisciplinary staff of psychology, social work, and nursing graduate students, and interns. My arrival also coincided with a time of political upheaval, as the mental health unit shifted from line management to an interesting but controversial model of matrix management that disrupted many traditional patterns of supervision. My role was to implement and champion the new system. Despite some initial reservations about me and the new system, the staff and students generally adapted quite well to the system and my supervision style.

There was a lot of hiring of new staff as well. One of the new mental health workers, Patrick, (not his actual name) provided me with one of the most awkward and challenging experiences of my supervisory career. Patrick came to us highly recommended by his former employer, a well-respected family therapy supervisor at another hospital. Nevertheless, his work statistics in the first 4 months after arrival in our unit revealed a surprising number of no-shows, drop-outs, and cancellations for a therapist in a public clinic. Moreover, in screenings of cases for team consultation, his interviewing style seemed to be quite obtuse, pedantic, and condescending towards his clients. As his first supervisor at the Holy Cross Hospital, I also needed to intervene in mediating an unusually high number of client complaints about him as well as rather frequent clinical crises that would occur on his caseload. I tried to be as supportive and solution-focused as I could, but the data seemed to indicate that he was a rather ineffective therapist at best, and at times seemed to be lacking in basic areas such as empathy and genuineness. However, whenever I tried to guide him and offer suggestions, he would bristle with hostility and defensiveness. He would complain that I did not know "the Milan model" from which he operated, although I had previous experience with this model, and his explanations of what he was doing in therapy were frequently not consistent with the precepts of the model. I tried every approach I could think of to gently but firmly reshape his clinical style, all to no avail. He merely got more defensive and oppositional, claiming that I was an "inexperienced" supervisor, that none of his previous supervisors had ever criticized his work, and that I definitely did not know how to effectively lead him in any way. I asked for his input in helping me learn more effective ways to supervise him (essentially, that I should overlook his statistics and problems with clients and let him carry on in his own way). We would try that for a while, but the same problems would resurface.

In discussing these difficulties in supervising Patrick, my Team Director attempted to be supportive of me. However, he also wanted me to continue to find some way to effectively motivate and channel Patrick, who seemed to have an unblemished career and clinical record as a therapist up to that point. Pat continued to be oppositional and resisted my input, while I continued to search for the magic key that would allow us to work together as a team. In collaborating on his 6-month and 9-month performance appraisals, I noted these ongoing problem areas. Patrick was incensed that these negatives were in the evaluations and that the recommendations included more rigorous attention to record-keeping and some form of remediation for his shortcomings as a therapist.

He launched a union grievance, using the technicality that a performance appraisal was being used in a disciplinary manner. At this point, our management team was being briefed by a senior hospital administrator, and all of us in the management matrix were being encouraged to document critical incidents carefully and thoroughly. From this administrator I received a crucial note of support: that it was Pat's problem to learn how to adapt to me and receive supervision, rather than my problem to try to find a way to be effective with him. The monkey really jumped off my back when she told me how to handle the next incident in which he was insolent and defiant. I was instructed to tell him the words: "Patrick, are you aware of the seriousness of what you have just done? Take the rest of the day off to think about it and we will discuss it tomorrow morning at 9:00 am with your Nursing Unit Supervisor. This meeting is now over and you are dismissed." Now I was ready and prepared for our next confrontation. However, within a month, the decision was made to rotate all the supervisors and shift the memberships of the supervisory groups. Now Patrick would come under the direct supervision of my immediate superior, the Team Director.

Pat tried harder to be diplomatic and receptive to Arnie's style, partly to show that the previous situation was my problem. However, within 2 months the same patterns emerged in Pat's cases supervised by Arnie. Although Patrick never got to the same point of insolence with Arnie (we think he was coached to be careful by his union as well), the situation between them was steadily deteriorating. Meanwhile, in preparing for the grievance action, we also learned that some of Pat's previous supervisors at his previous hospital had noticed similar problems with record keeping and client dropouts, but no one had confronted the situation and tried to enforce remedial action.

As the date of the grievance hearing was approaching, Patrick was becoming more depressed and moody. He was having difficulties working with the union staff, who were attempting to document his case, and it looked as if his grievance would fall apart on inadequate grounds. At one point he was making veiled references to suicide to his co-workers, that his career was being ruined and he was thoroughly discredited. The atmosphere of tension was high among the clinic staff, waiting for the verdict. As the grievance was filed against Arnie (as Unit Director) and the nursing unit supervisor, I was by this time more of a witness than a participant in the hearing that followed. As predicted, the grievance was found to be unsubstantiated, with Patrick at times contradicting his own testimony in the hearing. We mainly felt sad in watching him discredit himself. Within several days he tendered his resignation, and soon after left Calgary altogether. It was an unfortunate situation, but staff morale improved noticeably once the situation was resolved and they could witness that incompetent therapists would not be allowed to practice indefinitely in defiance of supervision.

Looking back on the situation, I suppose in one sense Patrick was right about our situation. In my tolerating his verbal abuse and insults, and in attempting to try everything possible to rectify the situation, I was actually proving his contention that I was an "inexperienced supervisor." I had never before contended with a defiant and argumentative supervisee. I did not have the initial administrative support to be firm with him to stop the situation from dragging on and eventually escalating. I did not know that I could use the magic words: "Are you aware of the seriousness of what you have just done?" But then, I was inexperienced at the time.

CHAPTER 54

Front-Door, Side-Door, and Back-Door Approaches To Your Client's Problem-solution: A Simple Model for Pragamatic and Ethical Intervention

Frank D Young Ph.D., C. Psych.

(Ed. Note: this article was originally published in The *Journal of Strategic and Systemic Therapies) 1981, 1, 1, 16-27*) when these therapies were still in their early stages of development in contrast to more orthodox insight-oriented therapies of that time. This chapter is a condensed version of the original publication.)

The Awareness Ethic: Throughout my graduate training as a clinical psychologist, assessment and analysis were supposed to precede genuine insight and awareness which in turn would lead to therapeutic change. Regardless of whether it was psychoanalysis, transactional analysis, group dynamics, client-centered therapy, Gestalt therapy, family therapy, or cognitive behaviour therapy, the basic role of the therapist was that of scientist-educator and/or awareness-facilitator. That is, we were supposed to assist the client to arrive at an insight which would then result in change (with varying amounts of modelled or overt skills instruction). Even when the focus began to shift from content to process, from intrapsychic to interpersonal, from linear to circular, enhancement of client awareness was still typically deemed the cardinal goal of therapy on which success or failure ultimately hinged.

However, the realities of my early clinical practice as a psychologist in an outpatient clinic demonstrated both the advantages and limitations of this basic premise. Several times I was perplexed by intelligent, well-informed and insightful people who nevertheless seemed immune to the traditional interventions of other well-respected therapists before me, and sometimes my best efforts met with the same demise. Fortunately, a number of creative experiences with several clients resulted in significant changes when techniques of inverse logic or paradox were applied. Only then did I begin to research the literature and realize that a new body of knowledge was rapidly growing that later came to be labelled strategic and systemic therapies.

However I still had some difficulty reconciling an approach in which the process of change bypassed my client's conscious awareness. At least three basic issues would have to be addressed: the ethics of informed consent, the pragmatics of dependency, and criteria for changing strategy in mid-treatment.

The issues of consent, dependency, and strategy change generate so many complex and interlocking questions that it is difficult to discern any patterns or guidelines. For several years my answers to these issues lay in individual case decisions according to their respective merits. Gradually, however, a number of configurations emerged with increasing consistency, but no organizing principles arose to assemble the sections of the developing blueprint. Then suddenly a metaphor provided both the foundation and the framework to integrate the clinical practice of strategic therapy. I refer to this model as "the locksmith analogy" although sometimes the metaphor does not correspond as isomorphically as I would like. As with all representations, it is only an approximate symbol for the experience it represents. Nevertheless, this idea can serve as a handy reference for decisions in dealing with clients in therapy.

The Locksmith Model: In this schema your client (or client system) is like a man who is locked out of his own house and calls you, the locksmith, to reopen it so that he can use it again. The client seeks your professional services because he has a problem for which all his previous attempts to locate adequate solutions have failed. Your best pragmatic assumption is that all problems, when properly formulated, are solvable. Perhaps your client has lost the ability to formulate flexibly. Whatever the difficulty, your client has lost access to his locked-up resources, and it is your job to enable or restore such access. As a locksmith you have a large selection of keys and devices that fit the doors and frameworks of similar problems of other people who have been locked out of their houses. However, before attempting to enter your client's house at all you want to make sure that you have secured his/her permission to work effectively. Contracting is a very important part of ethical strategic therapy because you will be doing a number of things both within and outside the client's awareness, and you need his blanket endorsement to use your greatest potency throughout therapy. You are hired as an agent to facilitate change as effectively, as efficiently, and as elegantly as you can, i.e. maximum change with minimal disturbance to the client system. Once the client openly declares that he wants you to open up his house, you ask him, "Suppose I can't do it by trying to unlock the front door, suppose I have to go around the side door or maybe even take the back door off the frame; is that okay? If none of my keys work, do I have your permission to get into your house whatever way I can, like even going through a window?" When the client has fully considered the consequences of change, and has agreed to proceed, you now have the freedom you need to do the job.

The Front Door: First you go to the front door, and you notice that it is locked, bolted and barred both inside and out.

Since the front window is boarded up it is impossible to see the dimly lit interior. Obviously front door approaches will not work here. By front door, I mean straight-forward cognitive or awareness-oriented approaches, like education, reason, advice, support, empathic reflection, direct instructions, communication, confrontation, reality therapy, cognitive behaviour therapy, etc. All the standard keys of friends, relatives, authorities, or other agencies have not worked. Perhaps the client can now talk more glibly about his problem and the reasons why he has it, but it still remains unsolved. At this point the therapist is well advised to change his line of approach away from the client's typical patterns of thinking, feeling, and behaving.

The Side Door: Having briefly checked the formidable front door, the locksmith now goes around to the side door. He may find it easy to open or perhaps unlock altogether. By side door I mean metaphorical approaches (Gordon, 1978) in which affective or attitudinal components of the problem situation are adjusted or realigned by implication from other areas of living or other symbolic syntheses. The techniques of guided fantasy, empty chair, anecdotes, and analysis of the transference are examples. Another side door tactic is to give the client direct instructions and guidance for positive change in an area of functioning which is peripheral but isomorphic to the central but highly defended problem area. The result is often a compelling reframing of the problem to lay the basis for its resolution. Although most therapists have their favourite examples of this principle, perhaps none are more elegant than the classic cases of Dr. Milton H. Erickson. For instance, Erickson might begin to shift the underlying affect and attitudes of a couple towards their sexual problems by talking to them about the prospect of having dinner together, emphasizing the pleasant possibilities in sharing individual tastes and preferences. Similarly, Erickson motivated a previously withdrawn and chronically inactive schizophrenic who called himself Jesus by saying "I understand you have had experience as a carpenter?" and then involving him in building a bookcase (Haley, 1973, pp. 27-28).

In using the side door approaches the therapist circumvents the prism of the dominant hemisphere so that change can occur "spontaneously" and can then perhaps later be ratified or integrated into the scope of linear awareness (Watzlawick, 1978).

A further example of the side door principle occurs in family systems where the disturbed behaviour of a child is the presenting problem. By utilizing the client system's definition of the identified patient and making the parents totally responsible for controlling him with firmly and consistently applied rules, the behaviour modification therapist is actually resolving the underlying but central problem of the denied marital conflict. Thus when a presenting problem is a foil for a crucial but masked problem, it is probably most effective to deal with the presenting problem as if it were the major concern, and simultaneously resolve the masked problem by inference or structural realignment in the process of the system. Thus dressing, cooking, and serving to the client his own red herring can be the culinary delight of both the client and the therapist using the side door approach.

Side door or metaphorical reframing methods are often gentler for both client and therapist because they imply a movement towards change, the ostensible goal of the therapy contract. However, some client systems are so rigid in their homeostatic mechanisms that even side door approaches fail. Metaphorical demands for change no matter how remote or implicit often elicit the counter-contract or hidden agenda to resist change and change agents. At this point the therapist will likely try what are here referred to as back door approaches.

The Back Door: In the illustration the back door is represented as a screen door which you can often enter easily without straining yourself. In this group of strategies are restraint procedures, symptom prescription, relapse prescription, exaggeration rituals, etc. Virtually all of these therapeutic recipes have the strong flavour of paradox heavily seasoned with positive connotation. Often there is also a light sprinkling of judicious skepticism regarding the probability, desirability, or permanence of change. The back door approach is designed to decommission homeostatic devices by insisting that they continue under the auspices of the therapist's control. The client system is thus caught in a therapeutic paradox regarding the issue of change. As discussed thoroughly by previous authors (Bateson, 1978; Haley, 1963, 1973; Selvini, Palazzoli et al., 1978; Watzlawick et al., 1967, 1974) the client can only resist such therapist bids for metacontrol by compliance with the directive or rebellion into health. Back door approaches thus often feature the "I command you to defy me" variant of the "be spontaneous" paradox (Watzlawick et al., 1974).

It should be noted that back door approaches require considerable skill and cognitive flexibility on the part of the therapist. Since the directive to continue or exaggerate the symptom appears to be contrary to the context of therapy, the therapist must convey congruently and convincingly the rationale of his intervention. As with side door manoeuvres, careful attention is often given to wording, metaphors, gestures, and timing to incorporate both the history and current structure of the client system.

Opening the Front Door from Inside: To return to the locksmith analogy, there hopefully will come a time when you gain access to your client's problem. Through the side door or back door the problem has been redefined as solvable with the tools you use and the existing or trainable resources of the client. At that point you have another decision to make regarding integrating the client's cognitive awareness of the problem solving process. You would like to facilitate future flexibility in his skill repertoire both within and especially beyond therapy. On the other hand you may jeopardize the whole extent and permanence of the change thus far achieved if you disclose the process. Clearly what you would like to do is open the client's front door and let him in, and yourself for that matter, in subsequent sessions. But careful timing is required or again you will be locked out and have to go around the side or back again. Thus it is likely no accident that strategic therapy is often said to occur in stages as the therapist tests the consolidation of change and the client's ability to integrate it in awareness.

For the point of opening the front door from inside, special precautions may need to be taken to ensure the continuing effect of your back door entry to the problem-solution. For example, after a symptom prescription the client resists by spontaneous cure and what used to be a problem suddenly is inexplicably resolved; a crucial change occurred. When this happens in my client, the behaviour therapist part of me wants to reinforce and consolidate that change. However, if I openly declare that I am delighted with this change, then the client becomes aware that I was in favour of that movement when I first prescribed the paradox. But the behaviourist in me will not be quelled. My eyes light up like a pinball machine and he knows that I'm happy; I can't disguise it. At this point, I generally do a twist of attribution. "Last week I told you to exaggerate your problem and now you're telling me you've made all these changes! I congratulate you for coming up with a creative solution like that, but I also am quite curious about how you were able to make these changes so soon. I must caution you that your solution may be short-lived as so often is the case for rapid change. So let's schedule another session in case you really need more therapy." This blend of confused admiration and skepticism usually satisfies the conditions for enduring change. Whenever positive change results from a paradoxical procedure, if you give reinforcement it must be accompanied by a disqualifying statement to keep the therapeutic bind in effect throughout the rest of treatment.

When to Abandon the Front Door: Unless otherwise indicated, in my opinion it is preferable that front door approaches be used throughout therapy for their enhancement of problem-solving process learning. However, there are several criteria that qualify a case as more amenable to side and back door approaches as the preferred strategy. The first criterion is whether there is a **previous history of failures** by competent therapists using your front door approach. If not, then generally speaking you use the front door approach until another criterion applies. If there were therapy failures, what is your estimation of the competence of the previous therapists? It is possible that the client has not received good treatment yet; if so, proceed through the front door, but be prepared to switch quickly if you encounter obstacles. Another possibility is that previous therapists were not generally incompetent, but merely that they used approaches that are not especially effective in dealing with that category of problems. For example, suppose the problem is a phobia or compulsion or something you know can easily be handled with cognitive behaviour therapy. Previous unsuccessful psychoanalytic or client-centered therapy in this case is irrelevant; you can proceed using behaviour therapy at least until you encounter another criterion for switching. However, if the problem has remained impervious to the helpful and skilled attempts of other therapists or agencies, the collusion of the client system in resisting change is the central point of therapy. This is a clear indication that back door strategies will be most effective in dealing with the problem.

The second criterion is evidence of **interpersonal gain and its simultaneous denial by the client.** An example of interpersonal gain is the use of the symptom such as pain or a highly anxious state that can excuse that person from typical household duties or responsibilities. If the manipulation is acknowledged by the client, then changes can be negotiated directly with the client and his interpersonal environment to solve the problem by rearranging the contingencies. It is the component of denial that signals the advisability of side and back door approaches.

The third criterion is the therapist's awareness of a **therapeutic impasse.** An impasse is likely occurring if there has been no change in the client in the last three sessions. That is usually indication to you that whatever you are doing with the client is presently ineffective. In the rubric of strategic therapy, it is assumed that if there is an impasse, then it is the therapist who must devise a solution. The client has already demonstrated the limitations of his own resources, whereas the therapist always has access to greater requisite variety. Even if his own ideas fail, the therapist can rely on the emotional and technical support of his colleagues or consultation group.

The fourth criterion is met when it is obvious to you that **a bind is in effect** such as the "be spontaneous paradox." Examples are "If you really loved me, I wouldn't have to tell you what I want. If I tell you that would spoil it all," and "I insist that you take charge of our marriage." Some of these binds can still apply despite the metacomment of the client trapped therein. As long as the contingencies are loaded in support of the paradox, its power can still remain in effect until the interpersonal matrix is restructured. Often the lever of counter-paradox realigns the contingencies by recombining split levels of operation in the system. **It is possible for meta-structure to work where metacomment alone might fail.** That is, sometimes a radical departure in behavior sequences can realign a system when mere metacomment was ineffectual. Interpersonal realignments can dissolve many communication binds.

Contracting: Having assessed what the problem is whether to use side or back doors, and what group of specific tools to employ, the therapist still lacks one crucial element: the contract. The locksmith needs permission to use his full range of skills and tools to get the job done. He does not ask the client for permission to do each routine in the process any more than your auto mechanic asks your permission each time he uses a different wrench to fix your car. He contracts for the goal, making you aware of the estimated costs involved and any anticipated difficulties or by-products of the process. Once these risks have been discussed and the goals agreed upon, then just like a surgeon, the therapist has informed consent to use his clinical judgment in the client's best interests. Wherever possible, however, it is advisable to be as explicit as you can regarding the specifics of the procedures you will be using with your client so that the ideal of full procedural information can be approximated.

Thus the issue of "manipulation" of the client only pertains when a contract regarding goals has not been reached with awareness and consent regarding perceived risks, or if the clinician deceives the client into a change which is antithetical to the goal context of their contract. Therapeutic manoeuvres outside the client's full cerebral awareness are therefore basically technical rather than ethical concerns in properly contracted strategic therapy.

As most forms of therapy include contracts, perhaps I should specify what elements I usually include in strategic therapy.

Towards the end of the first interview I return to the problem definition as stated by the client (system) in operational, specific, and therefore observable terms. I ask the client what is the desired ultimate goal, again in operationally defined terms ("How will you know when it's time to quit therapy? How will you measure the achievement of your goals?"). We set the contract to work together toward the goal provided; we assess that it is within the client's reasonable capacity given the limits of his resources and interpersonal ecology.

I then proceed with a mini-lecture that establishes the basis for multi-modal or strategic therapy at any further juncture of our work. I tell the client that the approach to be taken is the most parsimonious regarding the most likely function of the presenting problem.

I mention that the problem might be simply resolved with cognitive behavioural or basic communication skills. On the other hand, the problem could reflect unresolved issues from the client's past which might have to be addressed if the problem is not resolved using a "here and now" approach. Furthermore, sometimes problems involve other persons who might have to be included in treatment if working with the client or his nuclear family is not fruitful. Most clients prefer to shield their personal life from the archeology of the therapist's probes or the political scrutiny of relatives, friends, and employers; thus you usually secure their alliance in working as simply and quickly as possible.

However, this therapeutic alliance can generate its own counterproductive performance anxiety. This is decommissioned by two mild restraint conditions. First, I inform the client that she/he will likely be cured, but it may be unwise for us to do so because it could adversely affect the intimate others in his life. Therefore his assignment in the coming week is to discuss possible anticipated negative side effects of problem solution on other people and their relationships.

His list will be augmented by several stock consequences supplied by the therapist next week. This directive assures informed consent regarding outcomes and side effects, provides further diagnostic information about the roles and stated attitudes of significant others, and usually generates a wave of rapport between therapist and client ecosystems.

The second mild restraint in the contracting process occurs as an extension of the discussion of goals. After the terminal goals of treatment are set and mutually accepted, **proximate goals** for each target area are listed ("What amount of change on that index would let you know that you're making real progress towards your goal?"). Then I **assign the client to collect baseline data** on the problem during the coming week. The data is usually in the form of three columns for each incident of the problem, before (antecedent), during (behaviour), and afterwards (consequence). Besides providing more information, this homework reduces anxiety by refraining client cognitions and problem solving. Since recording is reactive, there is bound to be a reduction of frequency of incidents, already increasing therapist placebo potency in advance of the first official intervention. These effects are augmented by the directive to **"resist the overwhelming impulse to apply new awarenesses about solutions"** as this would "contaminate the data" and render therapy "ultimately more difficult." The client then has the option of co-operating with eagerness and frustrated creativity or rebelling into a spontaneous cure during the baseline week.

Finally, at the close of the contractual interview general topics are discussed such as client and therapist role and commitments, frequency, duration, spacing, and number of sessions in the contract (e.g. 6 sessions, biweekly, option to mutually renew if necessary after evaluation of results), fees (if applicable), etc. Mutual feedback about the process of the first interview is also exchanged after securing client commitment to the contract.

By that time, of course, a major step in strategic therapy has already taken place with the reframing of the assessment-contractual session and **the mild restraints of the first homework assignment**. The way is now ethically and pragmatically clear. The therapist can alter and vary subsequent strategies with all the flexibility required to assist the client in finding and using the required solution.

Conclusion: A metaphorical model was proposed to integrate an active strategic approach to therapy on the client awareness continuum. The therapist role can be described as locksmith to the client's problem, gaining or restoring access to resourceful solutions. Wherever and as soon as possible the locksmith opens the front door (full conscious awareness of the therapy process). Nevertheless, some solutions require access through the side door (metaphorical partial awareness) or back door (paradoxical minimal awareness) to break the locks and remove the bars. Even in these cases it is preferable for the therapist to open the front door from the inside to consolidate the client's cognitive learning of the problem-solving process. However, the therapist must exercise discretion to ensure that such awareness is not likely to erode or undo the problem-resolution achieved.

The ethics of informed consent were discussed with specific recommendations for contracting in strategic therapy to allow the optimal level of requisite variety for the therapist. Emphasis on mutually acceptable goals with full disclosure of possible side effects of change would be augmented by a general description of possible levels of intervention. Once client consent was secured, the therapist would then be compelled to use his clinical judgment on the level of awareness required to ensure solid therapeutic change in the client's immediate (curative) and ultimate (preventative) best interests. Thus issues of client dependency could also be assisted by clear contracting. Underlying the whole therapy process would be the therapist's implicit commitment to "full awareness wherever possible."

REFERENCES
1. BATESON, Gregory - The birth of a matrix or double bind and epistemology, in Berger, Milton, M., (E.D.) *Beyond the Double Bind: Communication and family systems, theories, and techniques with schizophrenics.* New York, Brunner/Mazel, 1978, PP. 39-65.
2. EFRON, Donald - *The Creative Symptom.* Unpublished manuscript, 1979.
3. HALEY, Jay - *Strategies of Psychotherapy* New York, Grime & Stratton, 1963.
   - *Uncommon Therapy.* New York, Norton & Company, 1973.
   - *Problem Solving Therapy.* San Francisco, Jossey-Bass, 1976.
4. SELVINI PALAZZOLI, Mara; BOSCOLO, Luigi; CECCHIN, Gianfranco; and PRATA, Guiliana - *Paradox and Counterparadox: A new model in the therapy of the family in schizophrenic transaction.* New York, London, Jason Aronson, 1978.
5. WATZLAWICK, Paul, BEAVIN, Janet, and JACKSON, Don D.
   - *Pragmatics of Human Communication: A study of interactional patterns, pathologies, and paradoxes.* New York, Norton & Company, 1967.
6. WATZLAWICK, Paul, WEAKLAND, John H. and FISCHE, Richard - *Change: Principles of problem formation and problem resolution.* New York, Norton & Company, 1974.
7. WATZLAWICK, Paul - *The Language of Change: Elements of therapeutic communication.* New York, Basic Books, 1978.

CHAPTER 55

What's A Meta For? Designing And Delivering Therapeutic Metaphors

(Ed. Note: this is an outline for a workshop presented at the annual conference of the Canadian Federation of Clinical Hypnosis, Banff, AB, 2004).

METAPHORS WILL BE discussed in terms of where and when to use them. Several formats will be presented with demonstrations and opportunity for skill training in small practice groups.

Part 1. Conceptual Basis of Metaphors in Therapy:

1. Definitions.

A metaphor could be defined as a grouping of symbols, often in words, that represent a concept. (Example: the description of the brain in the first paragraph of Ackerman (2004)).

A therapeutic metaphor is a coherent collection of verbal images that partially reflect a client dilemma, and indicate potential patterns of possibility for its resolution. (Example: islands of security emerge from a sea of chaos as the flood of anxiety recedes, a metaphor for solution focused management by exception).

Therapeutic issues or problems, even when pervasive, are often embedded in contexts so thoroughly that solutions are seemingly unavailable. By using metaphors and stories, the listener is led into a context of dissociation in which parallel processes may be considered and creative solutions may emerge. The key is having dissociation with optimal emerging similarity and coping modelling so that the client is encouraged to make the intuitive leap to resolution. The story or metaphor can also contain interspersal metaphors or images that are analogically marked for unconscious embedding.

2. The Locksmith Analogy. When a client presents a problem or therapeutic dilemma, often the client is bewildered, as if they had locked themselves out of their own house. After many self-initiated attempts to get back in to access their internal resources, they employ the services of a locksmith. The professional locksmith usually tests the unthinkable obvious first: he tries to open the front door (see Chapter 57). Like a computer consultant he checks first to see "Is the power turned on?" or "Is the equipment connected?" Many clients are so panicked by their predicament that they can't believe that they overlooked the obvious. A professional checks this hypothesis first, using the principle of sequential parsimony. That is, do what is least intrusive first. Sometimes, a relatively simple psycho-educational intervention is enough. Sometimes the fact that it is offered by an independent and supposedly expert perspective, the mere placebo of posture is adequate to resolve the dilemma.

Typically, this offering of the obvious is ineffective, but it needs to be tested. Usually, the client has tried the most sensible and linear solutions. Even then the therapist needs to assess "were they tried consistently and long enough to work?" As I often say "Pianos don't make good music. I know, because I tried one once."

When the straightforward is exhausted, the locksmith tries the side (metaphorical) door to help the client gain access. Often, all that is required is to listen empathically and offer guiding and strategic questions to open patterns of possibility. When clients feel that they have been thoroughly understood and validated, they can spontaneously expand their horizons in search of solutions. Listening and questioning may be sufficient. But often, even that is not enough.

This is because most solutions offered and tried have been seen through the lens of some kind of restraint, whether personal, familial, or cultural, that says "you cannot go beyond this barrier."

At this point the consultant is enlisted to help the client "think around corners." The side-door approach of metaphors allows escape into the context of dissociation. The therapist-consultant tells a story, or reflects on iconic symbols of culture or current events to illustrate a point indirectly. Measured indirection is the key. As the client listens and makes connections with patterns of possibility, new realities are grasped, new life narratives can evolve. At this point it is as if the locksmith has helped the client get into his house of resources through the side or even the back door.

Access has now been restored.

3. Escaping the Restraints of Context. Therapeutic issues or problems, even when pervasive, are often embedded in contexts so thoroughly that solutions are seemingly unavailable.

For example, the engines in some exotic super-cars fit so tightly in the engine bay that some repairs cannot be made unless you pull the engine itself out of the bay, make the repair, then fit it back in, a costly but necessary compromise. This solution sometimes applies in plumbing and other types of home repair. Many assemblies are made compact to save space but have to be partially unpacked to get the proper leverage or access to the core of the problem. When the problem has been solved, the entire subsystem is reassembled and put back into place.

4. Similar but Dissimilar. Metaphors utilize the principle of dissociation to allow the client to detach from the embedding context. The key feature is the balance referred to in Gregory Bateson's "The difference that makes the difference." It needs to be just close enough that the client intuits the connection to solution, and just far enough removed that the client's defense mechanisms can reject it by saying "well, this doesn't apply to me because the metaphor is insufficient to describe the subtleties of my situation." With this dismissal, the impact of the metaphor is free to circulate through the underground of the unconscious. If an apt metaphor applies to a client situation, it sinks into the validating world of the client's mind by degrees.

Thus, by using metaphors and stories, the listener is led into a context of dissociation in which parallel processes may be considered and creative solutions may emerge. One key is having dissociation with enough displacement to a magical world where dreams are fulfilled (instilling hope and optimism). Again, the balance is to have enough similarity to the client's context that the offered solution is, at least, conceivable. On the other hand, the metaphor must be removed enough that the client can duck the association being offered ("This does not apply to me; I am a musician, not a mechanic."). In other words metaphors are symbolic gestures offered by the therapist to the client for considerations of "goodness of fit." The client is the ultimate arbiter of the effectiveness of the metaphor. The therapist merely offers beautiful wood for the consideration of further carving and sculpturing by the client and therapist in their mutual creation of their therapeutic art.

5. Collecting and assembling motivating stories. A story or metaphor should include a context marker of an "as if" world, at least one step removed from the client's dilemma. The most obvious is a fairy tale beginning "once upon a time" or the more contemporary "that reminds me of a client I once had ..." Certainly it is easier for experienced therapists to accumulate therapeutic stories and symbols based on their own experience and wisdom throughout a career in helping people. Still, a beginning therapist can use research findings of "best practice" and use stories of case examples featured in articles and books. Another practice is to read current papers, magazines, news programs and popular literature. The metaphorical therapist can benefit from being informed and knowledgeable about current geopolitical issues. Thankfully, such research-based metaphors, stories, and analogies are not necessary, but are helpful. Traditional therapists can still rely on fairy tales, stories, metaphors from just about any era or point of view. The scope of potential sources is almost infinite. However, the craftsmanship of fit is preferably as precise as possible.

6. Utilization and Pacing of the Client's World. In the selection and delivery of an image or story that can captivate the imagination of a client we are often skating on thin ice. Our client knows this territory better than we do, so our metaphors will seem amateurish and inept. However, our outsider perspective of hypothetical scenarios will often score an unexpected hit, as our clients see a familiar situation through a new lens. Often these interventions are the most creative breakthroughs in seemingly impossible situations. Time permitting, there are several exercises that can promote training in customizing interventions to clients' language and cultural styles. Examples include: How would you tell this story to a musician, an engineer, a housewife, an accountant, an astronaut? And how would you use words in that metaphorical story that match your client's primary representation system, whether visual, auditory, or kinesthetic?

7. Using a Coping Model. Whenever a metaphor or story is offered, I prefer that the main model or protagonist is not masterful. That is, he or she does not solve the problem perfectly or easily. Here I include selective and rare self-disclosure by the therapist. Like us, our clients are merely mortal and imperfect. To optimize on this feature, and to increase our clients' identification with our model, we should emphasize that the story models make mistakes too, but eventually succeed. This infusion of doubt and drama allows the listening client to identify with the protagonist who eventually surmounts obstacles. Educationalists all know that a Coping Model (through difficulty to success) outperforms a Mastery Model (instant success) in terms of motivating students to master the skill to be learned. Perhaps a larger lesson, especially when dealing with adolescent clients, is that the drama is the essence of the story. Create a conflict scenario, and you engage the imagination of the listener.

8. The Delivery of the Metaphor: Notes about the process. The most important thought to maintain about metaphors is to realize that a direct statement should not be offered unless you have already thought about an indirect or metaphorical expression of this statement, prior to its delivery. If you cannot think of a metaphor or story, the intervention is often premature and likely ineffective. Stop and listen to your client, think carefully, and construct a story or metaphor designed to resonate with client world paradigms. Include an inventive and creative twist that might indicate patterns of possibility that side-step the mind-traps of the client's current thinking.

When you have found a metaphor or iconic symbol that might be helpful, consider when and how to introduce it into the flow of therapeutic conversation. Essentially you are looking for ideal "coachable moments" when the client is most receptive to change. One example is the pause that occurs when the client has just outlined a narrative resulting in confusion or a state of frustrated stuckness or hopelessness. After an empathic reflection, this is the moment of maximum impact to tell a story.

When you have secured the interest of your

client-listener, you might want to consider interspersal messages or images that are analogically marked
for unconscious embedding during the delivery of
the story. The story will be remembered, and the
messages will be imprinted.

Part 2. Demonstrations of Therapeutic Metaphors.

The presenter may elect to show a video example of
the integration of metaphors and utilization of client
symbols designed to promote a therapeutic outcome.
This DVD interview features a single-session intervention to resolve a systemic problem. In another
situation The Black Knight case will be presented as
at least one example of iconic imagery and its transformative power in guiding a strategy for multigenerational therapeutic integration of a conflicted family.

Part 3. Exercises In Designing and Delivering Metaphors (in triads)

Triad Warm-up. Participants generate quick examples of stories to illustrate a principle. For example,
generate a story to illustrate the principle of surrender and acceptance, that life cannot be controlled,
but it can be managed, that detachment to outcome
with love of process can be a helpful orientation.
Each person in the triad tells their favorite story to
address this principle.

Triad Client Dilemma and Therapist Metaphor.
In the second exercise, one person volunteers to be
the client. The client presents a summary of a stum-
bling point that seems to prevent growth or solutions
from emerging in a problem context.

The therapist can begin with a few empathic statements, and then say something like, "that reminds me of a story..." leading in to a metaphor that can be somewhat isomorphic with their situation. This phrase often is the beginning of a potential hypnotic induction. An alternative delivery can be used when the client is used to hypnotic interventions given in a naturalistic style. The therapist can start with conversational induction of 5 pacing and leading statements, then begin a story (anecdote, fairy tale, legend, etc.) in which the protagonist is mildly similar to the client. As the plot or story develops, it helps to have one or several obstacles that look like they will overwhelm the character, but eventually success and resolution prevail. By the end of the story, the character can evolve into being slightly more closely resembling the client, but different enough that space for separation and dignity is allowed. Finish the induction with several ego-strengthening statements, then reorient the client. Discuss the effect on the subject, and integrate the observations of the consultants.

With either delivery have the story go on for about 2-8 minutes. The client listens and then gives feedback about the effect of the story. Then the observer-consultant feeds back what she observed. Time permitting, roles in this exercise are circulated among the participants.

Larger group feedback from the triads will be given to the whole workshop assembly. Time will be given for final questions and answers. The end objective is to encourage participants to recognize opportunities to use metaphors, to construct and deliver them appropriately, and to enjoy the collaboration that results from their application in enhancing the therapeutic collaboration relationship.

Part Nine:

PERSONAL STORIES

This group of chapters might not meet the editors' cut. They are vignettes about my life and some lessons learned. I am a bit reluctant to share them in that several do not portray me or my circumstances in a very good light.

However, I sometimes use self-disclosure in motivating stories where I disclose the errors of my former ways of thinking. I am presenting a coping model, rather than a mastery model. After all, I am merely a fellow traveler on the way. I portray myself not as an expert, but a professional who knows something about "best practices" in how to approach quite a few problems in living. I am not a master, but rather a journeyman still developing his craft

The reason why I am considering including these stories in this book is that I have seen the sometimes radical shifts in the way clients viewed their life circumstances and choices after hearing a personal story that touched upon a crisis of meaning that they were facing. It is in this spirit that I offer these self-disclosing stories, and encourage therapists to use their own stories in a limited and tasteful way to encourage patterns of possibility.

CHAPTER 56

THE GIFT HE GAVE ME

AS MANY OF YOU may know, I often use Eye Movement Desensitization and Reprocessing (EMDR) as part of a treatment package when helping clients who are suffering from Post Traumatic Stress Disorder or some other severe emotionally upsetting scenes. If you are not familiar with this process, go to emdr.com for a full description of how it works.

As with all techniques, I describe in detail how EMDR can function effectively and what to expect in using it in our work together, so that I have informed consent to apply it in treatment. It is relatively easy to explain how desensitization occurs, but some people have greater difficulty understanding the Reprocessing part of EMDR. We can review the ideas from Cognitive Therapy, that how we talk to ourselves about our experience can greatly alter our emotions about that issue or event. However, usually the client needs a more moving and dramatic example of how this reframing of experience can make a huge difference going forward while remembering a past event. So I sometimes tell them an old story that is dear to me, although it has its shameful elements, but we all have those moments occasionally, don't we? It is a part of our roots, and our humanity.

In the late summer when I turned age fifteen, my father gave me an hour or two of driving instruction on our family car, a '57 Nash Rambler. It was a clunky but very reliable car, with a manual transmission that I jerkily learned to negotiate. But with its manual steering, it was hard to handle for a boy who matured late and was still barely 5'7". I nearly had a chance to feel competent, but my father suddenly discontinued the lessons. I can't remember why. Maybe he and I just got too busy with our respective lives, him teaching and coaching, me as a student and football player. However, we had a strong bond on weekends in that car, fishing on summer weekends and hunting in the fall. The Rambler was unique in that it had a bench back seat and a bench front seat that folded flat so that you could sleep in it. So Dad would sleep in the car, and I would sleep in a tent outside. We had many happy memories of shared times in our outdoor adventures together. On chilly hunting days in the fall, we would both sleep in the car together, with brief but insightful conversations about how we saw ourselves and our options in life. We lived in mid-town Toronto, and would travel up into the Cottage Country north of the city for our fishing and hunting, especially in a region called Haliburton, known for its many picturesque small lakes and lovely forests.

One weekend hunting trip that fall we had no luck all weekend. It was Sunday afternoon, time to head home for the two-and-a-half hour drive to Toronto before nightfall. Dad got lost on the confusing maze of dusty country roads going past cottages on various small lakes. Finally, we decided to ask for directions, so we stopped at one cottage that had several vehicles in the parking lot and blue smoke drifting lazily out the chimney. Dad was invited in to have a drink with a circle of men around a kitchen table with a case of beer. Dad told me to wait on the dock by the boathouse while he talked with them and asked for directions.

The view of the lake from the dock was beautiful, with the sunlight bringing out the bright yellow of the birches and the blazing red of the maples reflecting on the water with a deep blue sky in the background. It was a perfect autumn day. However, after being out there for about 20 minutes I came back to the cottage and knocked on the door, asking for my father.

He shouted from the kitchen that he would be out shortly. I went down to the dock again for quite a while. The sun was getting lower and I was worried that we would run out of daylight for the trip home. This time when I knocked at the door I insisted that I needed to see my father and that we needed to get going right away.

Dad came out smelling of beer and walking a little unsteadily towards the car. I asked him if he was fit to drive. He snapped back angrily that of course he was okay to drive. As he was driving, I noticed he was not negotiating the curves very well and almost driving off into the ditch on several occasions. I was scared and told him to stop and let me drive. This only made him angrier and more insistent on continuing to drive. Then I made a dramatic move. I yanked the keys out of the ignition! Rather quickly the car came to a stop in the middle of the gravel road. Both of us got out quickly. He demanded that I give him the keys. I refused. Then we engaged in a fist fight. Dad was 6'2" and heavier than me, so I was quite scared. Fortunately, because he was drunk and because it was a fist fight rather than a wrestling match, my quickness prevailed. I few quick punches to the midsection and the head, and he went down and gave up. He let me drive, and as I seemed to be handling the car okay, he quickly became my sleeping passenger. Somehow, I was able to find my way out of the maze of back-country roads and get onto the highway.

As the miles went by in the dusk I became more overwhelmed with emotional questions. How could a father be so cruel as to force his son to drive while he was barely able to handle a car? What if there were an accident, and here I was, an unlicensed driver? How could I handle driving at highway speeds and in the dark? Tears were streaming down my face as I worked through my anger and fear. After that internal shower passed, I became more relaxed and confident, although I found driving in the city traffic of Toronto a bit unnerving. The final challenge was going down our long narrow driveway between two buildings. Slowly and carefully I made it without a scratch. By this time Dad was reviving from his sleep and seemed sobered up and normal. We made no overt pact of secrecy, but we both knew that the whole family would be better off if nobody knew that I drove home. My mother and sister expressed concern that we were home so late. While we were unpacking Dad covered off that we had gotten lost for a while.

Nothing came of the whole incident. However, from that moment forward, my father regarded me with a new and hard-won respect. We still had occasional teenage verbal clashes, but no major disagreements as I matured and left home. We hardly even mentioned that trip ever again, perhaps once or twice when we were alone when I came back home for a brief visit. It remained our private understanding.

Many years later I left public practice in a mental health services unit of a civic hospital in Calgary, and was now doing a thriving private practice in the northwest segment of the city. My father had died at age 78 of an aneurism and its resulting complications. About two years later I became a founding member of a recently formed men's support group. All the members were psychotherapists, and one of our key objectives was to shelter our spouses from the stresses of our careers in mental health. In that regard we succeeded quite well, and we enjoyed sharing our thoughts and emotions as we negotiated the conflicts of marriage, family, career and personal fulfillment. As the group developed over the span of three years, we also arranged for several weekend male bonding experiences. As most of the group members were non-traditional males, team sports and other athletic activities that I proposed got voted down. However, we did several camp activities that in some way tested our courage and endurance, if not our good judgement. One of these was a native-style sweat lodge led by a Metis medicine man.

The whole process was quite interesting and elaborate, building a bonfire to superheat the rocks, doing a sweetgrass smudging ceremony honoring the four directions, and other native spiritual rituals. Later came the packing of the very hot rocks into the pit, then covering it with a ready-made animal-hide round tent, sealing most of the edges, and finally going into the hot darkness of the sweat lodge one-by-one, following each other. Prayers and chanting continued in the extreme heat. We learned how to pant shallowly as there was not much fresh air to share. It was a mark of honour to remain in the lodge rather than wimp-out. Each one of us remained as long as we could stand it, relenting to group pressure to tough it out, and finally breaking out into the fresh air in the fading light of dusk. Those of us that made it out earlier were invited in to do another even hotter round with some of the tough guys who stayed. Several of us declined. We had had enough of this macho ritual.

In the weeks following the sweat lodge weekend our group sessions greatly focused on the personal experience of each member, as well as how it had affected us as a group to go through this hazing together. We all shared a deeper bonding through surviving a mutual hardship. Perhaps because it was voluntarily self-inflicted, the experience felt somewhat artificial and contrived, but the emotions elicited were nonetheless quite real for all of us.

As you might imagine in a men's group, on several occasions a central topic was our relationships with our fathers. However, in the sessions following the sweat lodge, many emotional and heartfelt emotions poured out, as if the sweat had opened up the pores of our spiritual being. Many if not most of the guys reported a distant and somewhat rational and detached relationship with their fathers. Sometimes we use the expression "absent fathers, lost sons" in our work counselling men. These fathers were not necessarily physically absent, just that they were not fully emotionally engaged with their children for whatever reason, often career preoccupations and other distractions. With most of the men in this group, one major theme began to emerge. They never felt they had an adequate ritual of passage into adulthood in their teenage years and beyond. Mainly because of this shortfall, many of the men felt that they felt a compulsion to prove themselves, their worth and their courage in life, over and over again. Of course, there are many other reasons, both psychological and cultural, why people believe they have to prove their worth repeatedly. However, most of the men in our group were psychodynamic in their orientation, so the idea that this compulsion originated in the dynamics of their relationships with their fathers had a strong resonance with the group.

The more I heard these heartfelt stories after similar weekend activities with this theme, the more I became increasingly aware that my teenage experience had been different from most of the guys in the group. On that hunting trip many year's ago, my father had given me a special gift: my rite of transition into adulthood. So whenever I recall the events of that trip, my heart is warmed with the gift Dad gave me that day.

And that is what we refer to as reframing, and what EMDR therapist call the final R, cognitive Reprocessing or recalling a traumatic experience with a positive caption.

CHAPTER 57

LESSONS LEARNED IN LONDON

THIS IS A PERSONAL STORY. It happened in 1975, when I was training in judo in London, England, prior to the Montreal Olympics in 1976. In that era, Britain was one of the best places for English-speaking judoka to train and compete. It was close to the European continent, where most of the judo competitions outside of the Orient were held. For the first time in the history of judo, European players such as Holland's Anton Geesink, and Britain's David Starbrook and Brian Jacks were challenging Japan's superiority in this sport by winning medals in world championships and Olympics. Europe was becoming a major epicenter for the sport.

In the autumn of 1975, I made a rather bold career move. At that time I was working as a psychologist in a mental health clinic attached to a community hospital in London, Ontario. It was my first career placement after finishing my Ph.D. at the University of Windsor. This was a great job, with colleagues such as Arnie Slive Ph.D., and Dan Bogue M.S.W., all aspiring and brilliant young therapists breaking into the new fields of gestalt, CBT, strategic family therapy, and even hypnosis.

But I had another passion: judo. I was blossoming at the age of 28 as a light heavyweight competing mostly in eastern Canada and the Midwest United States. Although I was improving, I still had not developed enough skill to qualify for the Canadian team. Furthermore, I was deemed too old to send to tournaments overseas. The Ontario and Canadian teams were focusing on younger players who would have a longer potential career line as international athletes. I was on a siding, and the express trains were bypassing me. I had but one chance to make my Olympic dream a success: if I trained in Britain, and placed outstandingly well in European competitions, perhaps I could quality for a fight-off to make the Canadian Olympic judo team. It seemed like a long shot, but my only shot. There was another factor in my reasoning. My wife, Sue, really wanted badly for us to try to live and work in her native England. She was homesick, and thought it would be a great adventure for us to settle in London or perhaps another area of England. She made it clear she would not rest and relax until at least we gave it a try. As we seemed to have fertility problems in starting a family, and we both were relatively young, now would likely be the best time to move on this adventure.

In the years prior to any Olympic game, many employers in Canada and other countries might consider allowing an athlete contender to take an unpaid leave of absence to train. In 1975 this was more likely, as Canada would be hosting the 1976 Olympic Games. So I approached the administrative head of our mental health clinic, the senior staff psychiatrist, for a leave of absence. Without a moment of hesitation, he turned me down flatly. In an equally decisive move, I handed him my resignation. It was a moment of hollow triumph, but it felt good to abandon what was an excellent position to go for a great but uncertain adventure, a date with destiny. We then packed up and rented out our little home and set off for England.

Life in Britain was just as hard and uncertain as my fears would have it. At the beginning, we were optimistic. From my previous connections visiting and working out in London, we were able to rent a flat in a brownstone entirely rented by martial artists and owned by a judoka, so we had a central, although rather slummy, location in West London. Thankfully, within several weeks Sue was able to get a position as an executive assistant just before our savings ran out. Still her meagre salary was not enough to sustain us.

Meanwhile, I began training in earnest, following the circuit of the British National Judo Squad, a group of around thirty players that met each night in various groupings as they went from club to club around the greater London area. We trained hard and long six days a week. It was a gruelling schedule, but we were honour-bound not to miss a practice session or we would be called the slang equivalent of "sissy." At the end of the first month we assembled as a team plus extra workout partners for a two-day clinic at Crystal Palace, a sports complex south of London. It was gruelling training, and I now had a chance to match skills with the best judo players in England. One of the light-heavyweight contenders threw me extra hard; the result was that I separated my shoulder. This injury meant that I would need to ease off training for almost five weeks, setting back my hopes of contention to compete in Europe soon.

For over six weeks I had been pursuing leads for positions as a psychologist in England. None of them panned out. The policy of the British Health Service was to hire British only, and even a highly qualified Ph.D. from a Commonwealth country had less standing than a British candidate with merely a Bachelors degree. All my experience and credentials were useless in the eyes of my potential employers. The constant rejections were very disheartening. As our money ran out I tried other kinds of employment, anything to provide basic food and transportation. For a while I did furniture removal work, gingerly trying not to reinjure my shoulder. This work was long and hard, but barely paid enough for meals and bus fare for evening workouts that I was now resuming. Eventually, I felt as if I was grinding my body down, not giving it enough chance to recover between workouts. I pushed as hard as I could, but I was exhausted. I gave up the furniture moving job. I didn't seem to be qualified for much else.

Finally, through a temping agency, I accepted a job as a file clerk in an oil firm in downtown London. I was desperate to make this job a success, even though it too paid little. However, I had always prided myself on my ability to work hard and consistently, so I thought it would be easy to master the requirements of this job. It seemed easy enough. Take an armful of files from the in-box, and file them alphabetically in a bank of thirty or forty chest-high file cabinets. Remember, this was back in the days when England was not computerized, and all records were stored on paper. So I set about filing as quickly and efficiently as I could. I thought I would impress my employers with my work ethic, and perhaps get promoted to a better and more lucrative job. There were at least two flaws in this strategy. Our managers were not around to check our work, and individual initiative was unnoticed because the only metric to observe was a group effort of how many files were correctly placed over a daily shift.

My work-mates on the filing crew were all Australian ex-pats who lived in the district of Earl's Court, an enclave of London with a large Australian population. They were a jolly group of people, and I quite liked their fun-loving spirit. However, soon my work ethic alienated them. They criticized me for working twice as fast as them, saying that my productivity was making a disincentive for the office system, preventing my teammates from getting management to hire more of their Aussie friends to cope with the volume of work. I was horrified at their work-to-rule ethic, thinking that this was the very source of the low productivity attitude that typified the well-known "British disease," a unionized work ethic deliberately slow-paced to make more work for everyone. My teammates reminded me of our paltry wages, and that my work pace was crazy and unsustainable, and in essence, anti-social, ruining the situation for every-one. I ignored them and pressed on stubbornly in my lone crusade, but by the end of the second week I could not cope with their shunning rejection of me. This was the first time in my work history that I had alienated an entire work group. I was demoralized, and quit the Friday of my second week. I was depressed, but relieved to be out of there.

In the next month I continued to find brief periods of temporary jobs. I even tried to collect welfare, standing in lines for hours at a time to collect just enough to pay for two meals a week. I knew the meaning of humility and basic need. The worst time was in January 1976, still unemployed, Sue announced, to my joy and dismay, that we were preg-nant with our first child. I broke into tears of joy and help-lessness. Here we were, just barely surviving, and a child on the way. No, we weren't starving, although I was almost a weight division lower due to over- exercise and restricted nutrition. We still had a roof over our heads. I was still train-ing in judo, getting stronger, tougher, and more technically skilled each month.

I kept applying for psychology positions. Finally, my bad luck broke. I applied for and secured the position of chief psychologist for the Emmanuel Centre for Families and Children, the oldest family child and family clinic in the British Empire. When I saw its premises in Stepney Green near Whitechapel, in a run-down slum of east London, I knew it was old and run-down. I worked there for several months as the assistant director of the clinic and one of its chief clinicians. I provided a unique perspective in my family therapy cases, because I was an alien to their cockney culture, so as the foreign Canadian, I could say irreverent but poignant questions to confront cultural camouflage. For example, in couple sessions, I could say, "I don't under-stand what is going on here! In our culture, what you just said describing your wife would be quite demeaning and dismissive. Is that how you really feel about her?" I thus was able to talk about the unspeakable elephants in the room, the unwritten taboo subjects, because I was the uncultured "colonial." I used this to great advantage in resolving many intractable family dilemmas, especially those involving gender issues and multigenerational communication and loyalty conflicts in immigrant families.

However, in terms of my judo career, I suffered a profound setback. In an injury sustained in a vigorous workout, I sustained a medial collateral ligament tear in my left knee. Emergency services slapped a plaster cast on my left leg from my crotch to ankle. My Olympic dreams were now effectively shattered. My left leg muscle tissue atrophied, and there were many other functional difficulties as well being in such a cast in London's tight quarters. It took at least six weeks to have the cast removed and begin a physiotherapy rehabilitation. When I returned to judo, my primary objective was to avoid re-injury. My next objective was to survive the workout feeling better than I did at the beginning of the workout. Gradually, as I strengthened in recovery and strength, my objective was to vanquish some opponents. Finally, my objective was to win contests. Thankfully, I began to win some tournaments in England, although not the British Open, from which I was eliminated in the earlier rounds. In truth, although my skill had progressed greatly, I had to accept that I was not a world contender, and would never become a member of the Canadian Olympic team. Sue and I went over to watch the Montreal Olympics in 1976. Canada's team in judo was ambitious, but over-trained and basically dead on arrival. Still, I enjoyed watching the world level competition, and I could sense our healthy baby Mark jumping inside Sue's uterus whenever there was the sound of a loud break-fall at the side of the tournament mats.

After attending the Montreal Olympics we again flew back to England for me to resume my duties as Assistant Director of the Emmanuel Miller Centre for Families and Children in inner London. Still, the prospect of living in England and raising a child there seemed bleak compared to life in Canada, especially given that we had a baby on the way. With some regrets, I had to leave my placement in England, and felt bad about abandoning the staff of the clinic there. We decided to return home to our house in London, Ontario, and await the birth of Mark. Even with Sue now unemployed, and me collecting unemployment insurance, we were still better off financially than we were with both of us employed in England. When Mark finally arrived, I enjoyed several months of bonding with him daily in our new family. Eventually I found employment as a psychologist at a psychiatric hospital, and everything stabilized for a while in our lives as a young family.

In London I learned many lessons about perseverance in the face of adversity, and recovery from a situational depression. Another minor but important lesson was that I was beginning to know the difference between peak performance (a statistical anomaly) and optimal performance, (good performance that is sustainable). Remember my job as a file clerk? I sure do. I alienated my workmates by attempting to do a superhuman unsustainable pace by imposing a work ethic that was a poor fit for our social reality. I still occasionally do this in my own professional life, but I no longer make the mistake of imposing my unsustainable goals and performance standards on my teammates. I still work hard and well, but enjoyably.

CHAPTER 58

Saying Goodbye To Dad

NO MATTER HOW WE TRY to deny it, mortality still has a shock when it appears in our lives. We may try to dampen the shock, through the delay afforded by denial.

My moment came when I went trout fishing with my Dad, Fred, on the shore of the Spray Lakes in Kananaskis Country in the Rocky Mountains near Calgary, Alberta. My Dad was always a better trout fisherman than me. Thankfully, I was always better at bass and pickerel (Ontario language for walleye). But it was disturbing in this visit to the West that Dad had difficulty in balance and strength negotiating the steep banks of rock and scree (loose shale) getting to the shore where we made our casts. I could not believe how winded and awkward he was. I just chalked it up to a difference in altitude that exhausted him so quickly and thoroughly. I was mildly worried when he said "I'll just watch you fish," from a guy who almost always would say the fisherman's continuous refrain "just one more cast." Maybe I should have known then, but again, like me, Dad was never much to complain. That was our last time fishing together.

Two years later, on a Friday night I had a phone call from my sister, Sylvia, telling me that Dad was dying. He was in intensive care on a respirator in a Toronto hospital. At the time I was living in Calgary, Alberta, and preparing to drive off to Edmonton for a judo tournament. I was a National A referee, and it would be a dishonor to waive my responsibilities, or so I thought. My sister was incredulous. "Didn't you hear me? Dad is DYING!" she shrieked.

This time the message registered. I got on the next plane to Toronto. During the four-hour flight, it occurred to me that Dad might already be dead, that I might arrive too late. I did some mental reminiscing and pre-grieving as I remembered all the good times we had shared together. I remembered his touch; the way he would touch me on my left knee sometimes when we were driving and talking about life. And sometimes when we walked together he would put his hand briefly on my shoulder to mark his love for me. But now it was just a few memories on a late-night flight.

The next day, on the way to the hospital, I had learned that a few days before, Dad had been having stomach problems and had stopped eating. He had collapsed in weakness and pain. In emergency surgery they found a large embolism had developed that had constricted blood flow to his digestive system. The surgeons estimated that this problem had likely been going on for two years with only minor symptomatic pain. Dad, being rather stoic about pain, had likely been underreporting his increasing discomfort. Now, major sections of his bowel had to be removed, and he was struggling for his life in recovery from this major surgery.

When we arrived at the hospital, several family members were gathered around my father's bedside in the dimly lit intensive care room. There were tubes and wires and monitors seemingly everywhere, and a respirator regularly inflating his lungs. My mother and sister, and several of my nieces and nephews, being Roman Catholic and highly religious, were praying for my father and invoking God's help to bring him back from his coma. We were also aware that a dying person's sense of hearing was the last faculty to go, and that perhaps he could hear us, so collectively we begged him to come back to life, especially for the sake of the grandchildren and for my sister and mother, who needed his support. We pleaded earnestly and thoughtlessly, consumed in our grief.

It never occurred to me at that moment what kind of life he would have when he came back.

Within a few days, my father came out of his coma. The family proclaimed it was a miracle and a demonstration of the power of prayer. I was less enthusiastic, and beginning to have profound regrets about being in the chorus of voices inviting him back to life. I now wish we could have conveyed a less selfish message, and instead given him our blessing and consent to slip into the embrace of death if that was his wish.

In the next days it became more obvious that Dad was in constant pain, for which he was so heavily medicated that he was asleep or incoherent virtually all the time. He had an ostomy, and no hope of recovery to a normal life. He was constrained to lie in a hospital bed with no exercise, no entertainment, few conversations, and barely any recognizable contact with family and other visitors. He had no quality of life, and barely any dignity in his daily hospital routine. I had profound regrets about our entreaty to bring him back to life, given the poor quality of that life. I spent the next few days with twice daily hospital visits, hoping to catch Dad at a lucid moment and have some kind of meaningful conversation. Time was running out. Dad was comatose or in at least a drugged stupor when I announced to him that I would be leaving the next day for Calgary to resume my usual work, but I was hoping we could talk next day before I left.

The next day arrived, and I again was at his bedside, but this time he was fully lucid and making eye contact. I sensed that this would be our last conversation. Curious as always, I asked him, "Dad, you were at the door of death, and you came back. What was it like at that moment?"

He said, "Frank, it was terrible!"

"Why?" I asked, full of wonder at this window.

"Because I had no control." In that moment, I realized

that our spiritual and philosophical perspectives were radically different.

In that sudden moment, it occurred to me that I had something to offer him. I have spent the better part of a lifetime devoted to the martial arts. Socrates said "Practice dying." In the martial arts, we practice dying symbolically many times a night as we are bettered by our opponent, yet each time we rise up stronger and wiser for the experience. Like a Phoenix, we rise from the ashes of our defeat, and carry on to be more complete in our art. There is no dishonor, only a lesson to be learned and integrated in our development. So symbolically, death is rebirth into a new life, at least according to bushido, the code of the martial arts.

Of course, my father, Fred, knew nothing of this. Most of the conversations in our later adult life were around mundane topics like career, financial security, and fishing, topics that interested him, and to which I deferred. I now wish I had tried to engage him around issues of philosophy of life, and exchanged notes on what he thought. On the other hand, Dad wasn't much for talking about philosophy. He just took life as it came, and didn't spend much time reflecting on it. Still, I wonder what it would have been like to engage him more.

At any rate, those moments were long gone now, and I could tell that Dad was holding his lucidity together for our last moments together. I could tell he was starting to fade, so I told him a few short sentences to remember me by.

I said, "Hey Dad, remember when you played college football for the Western Mustangs?" He smiled and nodded. I continued, "You often told me that as a fullback, you would gain extra yards on every carry by continuing to pump your legs as hard as you could until the referee would blow the whistle to end the play. You told me that only a fool would keep pumping and pushing after the whistle blows. That would be inviting an injury on a late hit, right?" He smiled and nodded recalling our many conversations about sports, his favorite topic.

"Well, Dad, the next time you are at death's door, and you are struggling to keep in control, I want you to imagine that you are carrying the ball. When the whistle blows, I want you to stop pumping your legs, to relax and look around towards the crowd on our team bench. There you will see my smiling face as I celebrate the twelve yards you made on that play."

He said, "Thanks, son, that was one of the nicest presents you've ever given me." We smiled with our eyes slightly moist, and shared what I sensed would be our last hug, and I urged him to get some rest as I left his hospital room.

Over the following months as I heard from others that he was weak and mostly comatose, I waited for the inevitable long-distance call. When it finally came it was on a summer's evening with friends visiting. The news was final, and comforting. I just hope he was able to release into the Light in a peaceful sigh of letting go.

CHAPTER 59

BIRD-WATCHING QUESTION

LONG BEFORE MY hectic social days as a teenager and early adult, I can remember a childhood where I was quite content to spend hour after hour fascinated in the study of nature. I would get books from the library, read about birds, animals, trees, and flowers. Then I would go down and explore a ravine near where we lived, watching birds, tracking foxes, rabbits, squirrels, and raccoons, and collecting pine cones and other seeds. I could sit patiently absorbed in the subtle flow of nature for hours, waiting in a bird blind for an animal or rare bird to come by, totally unaware of my presence.

One of my favorite bird blinds was not too far from the back fence of 13-year-old Frank Woodcroft, one of our grade school's best hockey players. It was totally cool to be a star hockey player, and at my age of 10 years I knew nothing about sports and was completely awkward and intimidated by the awesome strength and stature of athletes. On the other hand, in my little world of nature, I felt peaceful and happy. One time, after watching me sit still for about a half-hour, Frank Woodcroft could bear it no longer. He called me over to the edge of his back fence, and asked me, "I don't get it. Why do you watch birds? Like, do you get a prize or something if you see the most birds of anybody for that day, or what?"

I reflected for a moment, and then said, "I don't know. I just like to watch birds."

We had an awkward moment, then he shook his head slowly and said, "Boy, are you ever weird, Young. You're crazy." He walked away. I slowly and wistfully returned to my bird-blind. I felt a little sad, but pretty soon I brightened up when I heard the whistle of a cardinal. Sure enough, it soon flew not too far away. It was such a beautiful red.

I guess this is a rather silly and simple story, but it does talk about how I began as a solitary and self-contained naturalist and child of nature. I did not seem to be too bothered at that time with being popular or "cool." I just wanted to be one with the natural world. From about age 11 onwards I shifted to the social world of athletic competition, and for a time was entirely devoted to team and later individual sports. However, the themes of middle age about striving for career excellence, relationships, marriage and raising a family became very important in my life. But perhaps more important and central was the course of my spiritual development. The chapter on Sport and Spirituality is especially relevant, as is the one on Martial Arts Metaphors, my spiritual path. The ultimate direction seems to be a sense of transcendent unity, so I end this book returning to the peace and unity of a child admiring nature. I hope you have enjoyed this journey with me. It has been my pleasure to share it with you.

FRANK D. YOUNG

PH.D., R. PSYCH.

Frank D. Young, Ph.D., is a registered psychologist in private practice in Comox, British Columbia, on Vancouver Island. He was an International Instructor, Canadian Federation of Clinical Hypnosis. Founding Editorial Advisory Board Member, Journal of Systemic Therapies. He has published articles, presented numerous workshops, and produced CDs and MP3 audiofile programs on such topics as Ericksonian approaches in hypnosis and therapy, sport psychology, meditation, imagery training, lucid dreaming, creativity and Mind State Management.

Over the past 30 years Dr. Young has practiced clinical psychology, consulting, teaching, training, mentoring, and administrating programs in hospital mental health settings and in private practice. Also, over the past 15 years he has been involved with sport psychology at provincial, national, and international levels, both with individual athletes and as consultant to several of Canada's national teams. Many of his principles of meditation and his solution-oriented approach derive from the philosophy of judo and the psychology of optimal performance.

His first book *Lessons My Clients Have Taught Me and Other Stories* is a reflection on key creative moments in a rewarding career of helping others.

The Meaning Of The
Solution Oriented Counselling Logo

This book is a compendium of stories about how people have been helped with a solution-oriented approach to dealing with life issues and dilemmas. The centerpiece of this logo is the main object of intervention, the Solution to our client's dilemma in seeking our counsel. Hopefully, the solution will incorporate both yin and yang elements of a dialogue in a gender-informed systemic way. The Solution is holistically oriented to be sustainable. These elements are offered in the open vessel of Counselling, Consultation, and Coaching.

For more of Dr. Young's publications, magazine articles, self-help programs and MP3 products for stress management, performance enhancement and lucid dreaming go to the website
www.solutionorientedcounselling.ca.